KEYS TO CARING

KEYS
TO
CARING

Assisting your gay and lesbian clients

Robert J. Kus, R.N., Ph.D., editor

BOSTON: ALYSON PUBLICATIONS, INC.

Published as a trade paperback original by
Alyson Publications, Inc., 40 Plympton St., Boston, MA 02118.
Distributed in the U.K. by GMP Publishers, P.O. Box 247, London,
N17 9QR, England.

This book has been printed on acid-free paper.

First edition, first printing: April 1990
          second printing: April 1991

Library of Congress card catalog number 89-83305

ISBN 0-932870-86-4

Contents

*To persons with AIDS
and their loved ones*

Acknowledgments

Creating a book takes the talents of many persons. This is especially true of a book of readings having several authors. This book is no exception. And although it would be impossible to list all the persons who helped in some way to make this book a reality, there are certain persons who deserve to be specifically pointed out for their contribution.

These persons are: Steve Pokorny for his super help in proofreading and editing; Barbara Gittings for her always-cheerful help in locating potential authors for the book; my primary research assistant, Steve Carlson, for his many contributions; Nancy J. Goldsmith and Laura K. Lenz of the Office for Nursing Research Development & Utilization at the College of Nursing, The University of Iowa for their secretarial help; the publisher, Sasha Alyson, for taking a chance on an unknown writer; Tom Oswalt, Rojann Alpers, R.N., Ph.D. Cand., and Margaret Q. Krach, R.N., Ph.D., for their help in proofreading; A. Lee Rogers and Craig R. Close, R.N., B.S.N. for a variety of helpful activities; and especially the individual authors who contributed to this sourcebook.

Finally, I thank the following photographers for their contributions: Steve Carlson of Iowa City; Jack Sitar of Chicago; Rink of San Francisco; and The University of Iowa Photography Service.

Foreword

It was with great pleasure that we accepted Bob Kus' invitation to write the Foreword to this book — because we know how well qualified he is to do this work, and because we know how much a book like this is needed.

In 1979, when we (Emily McNally, Dana Finnegan) enrolled in Rutgers' three-week Summer School of Alcohol Studies in New Jersey, we were alcoholism counselors living a closeted lesbian life in New Jersey's northern suburbs. At Rutgers, we met about fifteen gay and lesbian professionals. In the course of our sharing with one another and with their help and support we began the process of "coming out," both professionally and personally. At the same time, as we all shared our particular yet similar experiences and backgrounds, we began hearing about the poor treatment of many gay and lesbian alcoholics, about the lack of treatment, about common problems some gays and lesbians encountered, and about gays' and lesbians' isolation and alienation from mainstream (and quality) health care.

Partly in response to what we were learning, and partly in response to everyone's personal need to be connected with other gay and lesbian health professionals, this group started the National Association of Lesbian and Gay Alcoholism Professionals (NALGAP). The two of us became the national coordinators of NALGAP and established the national office and telephone number. Since then we have heard from gays and lesbians all over the country. Some are alcoholics struggling to recover, who want help getting good treatment or who want to tell us about the problems they have encountered in the health care system. Some are co-alcoholics who have been left out of their lovers' "family" treatment and need support. Some are alcoholism professionals who feel alone on their jobs because they must be closeted, or who have lost their jobs because their sexual orientation was revealed. Many are heterosexual health care providers who want to know how to better help their gay and lesbian clients.

Soon after we established NALGAP we joined the National Gay Health Coalition, which was the umbrella for over nineteen gay and lesbian health care groups, ranging from the Gay Nurses to the Gay Psychologists. In the Coalition meetings, we heard more about the poor or nonexistent health care available to lesbians and gay men, and about the need for more information and an organized source of such information.

Much of what we heard was disconcerting, running the gamut from casual indifference to direct hostility. Lesbians told of gynecologists who routinely asked, "Do you use birth control pills?" but did not ask about sexual orientation. Gays and lesbians reported being in hospitals and having roommates move to other rooms after complaining about having to share a room with a "homosexual."

One young man told us of going through alcoholism rehabilitation without anyone asking about his sexual orientation and without his feeling safe enough to raise the issue himself. When asked why no one asked him, he said, "It never came up." He left rehabilitation without any knowledge of where gay and lesbian meetings of A.A. were available, and he left without having his true identity acknowledged. Three weeks out of rehabilitation he relapsed, which was when he contacted us.

Other gays and lesbians reported being actively mistreated because of their sexual orientation. A gay man reported that after telling his counselor he was gay, the counselor came into his room, threw a Bible on his bed, and said, "Here, you'd better read this and change your ways." The horror stories about health "care" for gays and lesbians are many.

As we heard about these and numerous other negative experiences gays and lesbians have had with the health care system, we began to question the reasons for such mistreatment. At the heart of the matter lay *homophobia* — the irrational fear of "homosexuals" and homosexuality. It is people acting out of their homophobia who stigmatize and discriminate against gays and lesbians. The fear of having a stigmatized identity discovered, in turn, leads perhaps the majority of gays and lesbians to hide their identities "in the closet." This phenomenon of closeting creates what is, in essence, an invisible population. This invisibility is fostered and perpetuated by a conspiracy of silence. The culture rewards those who deny or hide their same-sex sexual orientation by basically leaving them alone. It encourages everyone, both gay and straight, to pretend as though gay people did not exist. The pressure to remain silent in the face of prejudice, discrimination, and mistreatment is very great. Many gay and straight people who are health care providers and health care recipients keep the silence and perpetuate both the invisibility and lack of proper treatment (or the occurrence of actual mistreatment) of gays and lesbians, which result from their invisibility.

In addition, the definitions of health in this culture, in respect to lifestyles, are very narrow and do not allow for much diversity or difference. Thus, a gay or lesbian identity is seen as unhealthy. Furthermore, most gays and lesbians are emotionally healthy, happy, stable, and consequently, invisible people, in that they have no need to come to the attention of mental health care providers. This helps to perpetuate the myth that gay and lesbian people are disturbed, unstable, unhealthy, miserable, and tragic figures. It is this kind of misinformation and ignorance that blocks health care providers from better helping their gay and lesbian clients.

We were coming to these realizations at the same time that we were presenting papers and providing workshops designed to train mainstream health professionals to work with gays and lesbians. We realized quickly the tremendous lack of information and of knowledge of resources among care providers. We also began to realize the deep concern that many health care providers felt for their gay and lesbian clients. Many of the people who attended our workshops were good counselors but were not able to do their best for their gay and lesbian clients and were severely frustrated by this weakness. Some were having difficulties because of unconscious homophobia. But more often, people were not working at their best because they lacked training, information, and practical methods. Deficient in these areas, good counselors oftentimes felt unsure of themselves and hesitated to counsel gay people. When the training experience provided them with information, informed them of resources, or taught them relevant counseling methods, they then began to operate with more confidence and were able to "be there" for their clients.

Gradually, as a part of the training events, we began to share with the participants the positive feedback we were hearing from recovering alcoholic gays and lesbians about the health professionals who *did* help them, who *did* ask them the right questions, and who *did* hold out a caring hand. In every workshop, we emphasized the importance of caring and the gratitude the gays and lesbians felt when people treated them with dignity and respect.

As we continued to do these workshops over a long period of time, we became more and more aware of the tremendous need for a written resource, designed specifically to assist those in the helping professions to become better health care providers to their gay and lesbian clients. And when we saw Dr. Kus' book, we knew that he had created just such a resource!

Keys to Caring: Assisting Your Gay & Lesbian Clients provides a forum "for gay and lesbian persons to speak for themselves, their problems, and their proposed solutions." The purpose of this book is "to meet the helping professionals' demand for a comprehensive sourcebook which will help them provide quality health care for their gay and lesbian clients."

This book provides both theory and practical approaches to helping gay and lesbian clients, and it covers a broad range of topics. Section I addresses such topics as history-taking; Section II deals with common psychosocial health problems such as coming out, alcoholism, and homophobia; Section III considers special concerns in life situations, such as the gay father and lesbian mother, and the "widowed" gay or lesbian; Section IV discusses spiritual concerns in regard to formal religious affiliations (e.g., Roman Catholic, Jewish, Protestant) and in regard to non-mainstream belief systems; Section V focuses on legal issues; and Section VI examines alternative gay and lesbian helping resources such as counseling centers, the emerging gay and lesbian hospice movement, and self-help groups.

Covering as it does this diversity of issues and concerns, this book will prove invaluable to any helping professional who really wishes to provide gays and lesbians with quality health care based on both knowledge *and* understanding. Because it is written by openly gay and lesbian professionals, this book has the distinct advantage of offering perspectives from "insiders." And because it draws on, and thereby honors, the experience of those who are gay and lesbian, this book represents a coming of age for gay and lesbian health care. Finally, as Dr. Kus has stated, "this book was designed to be a gift to helping professionals from the gay and lesbian communities." It is a richly varied gift which will help caring professionals be more capable of offering lesbians and gay men sensitive, informed, and effective care.

Dana G. Finnegan and
Emily Bush McNally
New York City

Introduction

BACKGROUND

For the last ten years or so, I have listened to gay and lesbian friends talk about the failure of the helping professions to deliver quality, sensitive care to them and their loved ones. For many, there was a perception that quality care was not given because of their sexual orientation, while others felt the deficiency was due to helping professionals' lack of knowledge about gay and lesbian persons.

Also during this time, I have had the opportunity to speak to many groups of helping professionals — nurses and nursing students, physicians and medical students, social workers, priests, and the like, on important gay and lesbian issues such as coming out and alcoholism. In all of the speaking engagements I have done in Europe and the United States, the responses to my talks have been the same: "I wish there were some book where all of this information could be in one place!" This is that book.

ASSUMPTIONS

This book is based on the assumption that the vast majority of instances of poor quality care given to gay and lesbian clients is the result of a lack of knowledge on the part of the helping professional, rather than on any deep-seated homophobia. I assume most helping professionals truly wish to be helpful and would be if they had sufficient knowledge.

I also assume that only gays can speak for the needs of gays, only lesbians can speak for lesbians. Therefore, this book is written exclusively by openly gay and lesbian persons. Complaining is not productive; offering solutions is. Therefore, this book is designed to be a labor of love, a gift from the American gay and lesbian communities to helping professionals.

Finally, this book assumes that only brief glimpses into gay and lesbian societies and cultures can be made available in a comprehensive resource book and therefore, that helping professionals will take it upon themselves to search out additional sources of information, such as other reading materials or gay and lesbian friends. This book is designed to whet, not satiate, the appetite for information.

PURPOSES

First, this book is designed to show some of the richness of gay and lesbian experiences. Contrary to some persons' ideas, gays and lesbians live a variety of lifestyles. Some are single while others are coupled. Some are in male-female marriages; more probably are not. Some have children, some do not. Some are cowboys while others are cloistered nuns. Some are deeply religious, while others meet their spiritual needs outside of religion. Many are white, and many are of color.

Second, this book is designed to show some of the common psychosocial concerns held by gay and lesbian Americans.

Third, it is created to provide suggestions for helping professionals improve their care for their gay and lesbian clients.

Finally, this book is designed to take into consideration the rural gay and lesbian clients who are quite often forgotten. To do this, several writers show helping professional in rural areas how to find needed gay or lesbian resources.

STRUCTURE

To accomplish all these purposes, a certain structure has been created: in every chapter, the writer relates and discusses problems, then offers concrete solutions for helping professionals to follow.

In Section I the reader is provided with some basic issues which are essential to consider before caring for gay and lesbian clients. Specifically, Bickelhaupt talks about how to compile an adequate health history of gay and lesbian clients. He identifies which words should be used and which should be avoided. In this same section, Irish illustrates the importance of including the client's lover — or other gay or lesbian significant others — into the plan of care.

In Section II the reader is provided with some common psychosocial concerns of many gays and lesbians. I discuss coming out, a process unique to gays and lesbians, and alcoholism, the number one health problem of gay and lesbian adult Americans. Etnyre explains gay male body image and describes potential problems, while Broadway and Krotz do the same with regard to lesbian body image. Lapierre discusses homophobia, an ever-present problem in our society, while Rofes addresses suicide and suicidal ideation, and its roots and incidence among gay and lesbian Americans. And Solomon provides us with a look at the AIDS client and the caregiver, a topic extremely important in the 1990s.

In Section III the reader is provided with glimpses into certain life situations in which gays and lesbians find themselves, is informed of the special problems they experience, and is familiarized with how helping professionals can help solve these problems. Specifically, Bozett and Goodman, respectively, discuss gay fathers and lesbian mothers, while Matteson talks about persons in mixed-orientation (male-female) marriages. Hetherington addresses the needs of the co-dependent person, while Paroski focuses on the needs of gay and lesbian teens. Other areas examined are gay couples (Silverstein) and lesbian couples (Hall and Stevens), gay and lesbian prisoners (Sable), single gays and lesbians (Moses), widowhood (Saunders), and older gay people (Berger).

In Section IV we look at gay and lesbian spirituality and how spiritual needs are met. Specifically, Hunt writes about the experiences of gays and lesbians in Roman Catholicism; Christmas writes about those experiences in Judaism; and Havey writes about those in Protestantism. Larsen shows how those persons not affiliated with organized religion can also have their spiritual needs met. Finally, the reader is shown that in between belonging to a maninstream religion on the one hand, and being unaffiliated on the other, is the possibility of being in a non-mainstream religion. Bearwoman provides this chapter by discussing Wicca.

In Section V the special legal needs of gays and lesbians are discussed by two attorneys. First, Rohovit talks about the need for power of attorney, wills, and lovers' rights. Then Rubesh discusses the legal aspects of probate, body disposition, and funeral arrangements.

Finally, in Section VI we turn to some alternative resources in the gay and lesbian communities which helping professionals may consider using. Specifically, Klein talks about the gay and lesbian counseling centers, their history, and their functions, while Catalano talks about the emerging gay and lesbian hospice movement which grew out of the AIDS epidemic. Eller and King describe self-help groups, and Ryan shows the reader how to access these gay and lesbian resources.

LIMITATIONS

No book can be all things to all people and this resource book is no exception — it has limitations.

First, the focus of this work is on psychosocial issues. Physical health problems, for the most part, are ignored. Only two diseases, AIDS and alcoholism, have chapters devoted to them; AIDS because it is so timely, and alcoholism because it is the number one health problem in the gay and lesbian communities.

Second, the focus of the book is on problems gay men experience as gays, not as men, and on problems lesbians experience as lesbians, not as women. The tremendous oppression that both American women and men experience from culture and law, while a very interesting and unquestionably important issue, is outside the scope of this book. To attempt to include all aspects of men's liberation and women's liberation would be folly.

Third, the reader is cautioned that only brief glimpses are provided on any one topic. No chapter, therefore, is meant to be comprehensive on the topic discussed.

A NOTE ABOUT WORDS

In this book, the word "gay" when used as a noun refers to men with same-sex sexual orientation, while "lesbian" refers to women with same-sex sexual orientation. "Homosexual," as a noun, is generally not used, as it is often seen as a quaint and insensitive word by gay and lesbian Americans. The term "gay people" is regularly used to refer to lesbians and gays collectively. "Homosexuality" refers to an unchosen, lifelong, irreversible state of being in which the individual is attracted sexually to one's own sex, rather than to the opposite sex.

Robert J. Kus
North Liberty and
Iowa City, Iowa, 1990

I

The Basics

Chapter 1

The health history: What to look for and how to ask

Ethan Bickelhaupt

INTRODUCTION

The health history is perhaps the most critical part of the comprehensive treatment of gay and lesbian clients. It directs the remainder of the patient's care — the physical examination, laboratory tests, ancillary procedures, and ultimately, the overall care plan. Although this suggests that the gay health history must be thorough, it need not be cumbersome. It becomes the helping professional's ally, rather than a burden. A series of systematic questions of a clear, direct, and non-judgmental nature can yield a wealth of information about the illness or concern that brings a person to the helping professional.

What follows is a guide to the specific kinds of information the health history should include, and to the manner in which this information can be most efficiently and effectively obtained from gay and lesbian clients.

THE APPROACH

When the gay client comes to you, the helping professional, with a concern, please remember that this first step may have taken considerable courage. To be respectful of this is to be non-judgmental and caring, but also frank and honest. To begin with an open-ended question, assuming the client does not spontaneously offer any information, is generally best. You might ask something quite simple, such as, "What brings you in to see me today?" or "How might I be of help?" If there is no immediate response, a quiet pause or non-verbal gesture is appropriate. For example, handing a facial tissue to a tearful client or sitting down yourself acknowledges your own openness and patience.

If these beginning questions and gestures do not lead to a clarification of the client's sexual orientation and health concerns, it may be helpful to quietly ask at an appropriate moment, "Do you generally have sexual contact with women, men, both, or neither?" Clients are usually relieved to hear by implication that their sexual orientation is of importance only to the degree to which it relates to their overall health care — and that you, as a health professional, are not interested in condemning them for who they are and what they do. If your client says he is gay or she is lesbian, the response you give in terms of facial expression and body language is at least as important as what you say. A warm smile, uncrossed arms, or leaning forward to listen better offers a clear message that you have a caring attitude and are prepared to deal with the client in an empathic manner that does not patronize.

At this juncture of the interview, it may be important to be mindful of your own prejudices, including any tendency to stereotype. If your client is a farmer or mechanic, it may seem harder to ask about sexual orientation, fearing perhaps that such questioning may be perceived as overly intrusive or even insulting. Conversely, if your client is a male interior designer or a female physical education teacher, it is not uncommon to assume that he is gay or she is lesbian. And since these prejudices have strong cultural support, they·become powerful in their own right and challenge the professionalism of health care providers in their attempt to remain fair and objective. To overcome, or at least to be aware of one's own prejudices requires disciplined soul-searching and a flexibility in attitude that is often quite foreign to one's upbringing and professional training. Because your clients grew up being instilled with similar prejudices, they will be on guard for evidence of these in you. It is critical, then, that your rapport be non-judgmental and free of conventional assumptions about gay people.

A specific area where stereotypes are often manifest is in our language, that is, in the labels we use. Even the word "homosexual" carries a negative connotation for most gay and lesbian people. It is a label with clinical coldness that may deliver a message that its user lacks both awareness and sensitivity. Therefore, it is preferable to substitute "gay" or "lesbian" for "homosexual." Similar problems with language arise when describing gay and lesbian couples. Although some couples prefer "partner" or "friend", many prefer "lover," a label that implies a special, romantic relationship between significant others, in contradistinction to its heterosexual connotation of a sexual affair outside of marriage. The use of appropriate language demonstrates a sensitivity that is the foundation upon which trust can begin to develop.

A similar degree of sensitivity needs to be developed with regard to the client's religious preference, cultural and ethnic background, socioeconomic level, and legal status in relation to significant others. Most of these issues will be covered later in greater detail, but suffice it to say here that they are critical elements in the establishment of the kind of rapport necessary for building trust between the client and the helping professional.

This sensitive approach will usually stimulate a degree of openness in clients that will allow them to share needed information honestly, especially with regard to the sexual aspects of the health history. Before launching into a more complete sexual history, which will be discussed later in this chapter, you may next wish to ask, "Do you have a special person that you would like to have involved in your health care?" If your client seems reluctant or embarrassed at this question, you might say, "Many people find that the involvement of significant others, especially a spouse or lover, is very reassuring in the sometimes frightening prospect of obtaining and receiving health care. Perhaps you know someone who could share this process with you." Most clients are reassured to hear from the health professional that it is okay for a friend or lover to be involved in such an intimate way in their treatment. Early involvement of a lover in this process often enhances gay clients' ability to be open and honest, and increases their compliance with the recommended treatment. From a purely practical standpoint, if the lover becomes alienated from this process, sabotage of the care plan, albeit often at an unconscious level, becomes a greater risk. Thus, early enlistment of the lover as an ally of the care plan, as well as a participant in formulating it, could be quite beneficial to the overall treatment process.

ASPECTS OF THE HEALTH HISTORY

To make the health history both concise and comprehensive, it must include both medical and psychosocial elements.

Traditionally important questions include allergies, childhood illnesses (especially rheumatic fever), handicaps or disabilities, trauma, surgeries (when and where), blood transfusions, hospitalizations (when and where), habits (eating pattern, smoking, alcohol and other drug use or abuse), medications (current and past, including over-the-counter types), family history (including health status of blood relatives, causes of death, and familial or hereditary illnesses such as diabetes mellitus, heart disease, kidney dysfunction, alcoholism, drug abuse, psychiatric conditions, and any inheritable disorders, such as Huntington's chorea), and social history (where the client has lived, education, military service, employment, marital status — current and past, and the presence of children — their ages, current residence, and nature of relationship to the client).

A review of systems may follow to outline any symptoms not yet covered. In a systematic fashion these include a symptom review of the head and neck, eyes, ears, nose, and throat, pulmonary, cardiovascular, gastrointestinal, genitourinary, musculoskeletal, skin, lymphatic, neurological, and psychological (including sexual and sex-related issues). The detail in which these are covered will, of course, depend on the primary focus of concern. Yet, not uncommonly, an important piece of information will surface in the systems review that might have been forgotten by the client or overlooked by the health care professional.

Three areas of concern that merit special mention with regard to the health history include alcoholism, sexual problems, and acquired immune deficiency syndrome (AIDS).

Health care professionals who treat large numbers of gay and lesbian clients generally believe that alcoholism is the number one health problem in this population. Careful screening for clues that alcohol (or other drugs) may be a problem for your client is essential. Questions regarding how much, how often, and for how long must be asked. More importantly, exploration as to how alcohol affects your clients' lives must also be carried out. It is important to know what impact alcohol has on the client's job, health, finances, relationship with a lover, family ties, spiritual life, legal status, and self-esteem. If your client is impaired in any one of these areas from alcohol use, then it is a problem that must be confronted so treatment options can be outlined.

Sexual problems commonly afflict gay and lesbian clients as much as they do their heterosexual counterparts, and it is important to explore these issues in detail. Analogous to previous discussions regarding prejudices and stereotypes, it is while taking the sex history that the prejudices and anxieties of the health care professional often emerge. Simply stated, we bring our own hang-ups to bear on what we look for regarding sexual problems and in how we ask about these problems. To recognize, understand, and work through these hang-ups is the ideal goal, but to recognize and acknowledge our limitations is an honorable compromise and demonstrates professionalism. When we face such limitations, we may need to ask another health professional for help, to research various options with the client, or to refer to another care provider.

Questions about sex relevant to gays (and, to a lesser degree, lesbians) include sexual practices (anal intercourse, rough sex, anal insertions of fingers or fists, and sex toys), sexual problems (male impotence, absent orgasm in women, premature ejaculation in men, loss of or decreased sexual desire, and painful intercourse), bisexual activities, and sexually transmitted diseases (including hepatitis, gonorrhea, nonspecific or nongonococcal urethritis, nonspecific vaginitis, Herpes genitalis, and AIDS).

In asking about sexually transmitted diseases, it is important to be very specific as to exact symptoms, course, duration, diagnostic testing, treatment, relation to sexual activity, and previous episodes. For example, if a gay male has rectal burning and discharge, in spite of a recent course of antibiotic treatment, it would be important, among other things, to determine if and when an anal culture was done, how the culture was taken, what the results were, and whether the prescribed treatment was followed. This detailed questioning is important because some clinicians and even some health clinics have the clients obtain the cultures themselves, which is fraught with methodological error.

Special mention needs to be made of AIDS. A detailed description of acquired immune deficiency syndrome is beyond the scope of this chapter, but certain health history questions need to be asked in screening for it. These include questions about prolonged tiredness, weight loss, unexplained fever, purple or dark raised blotches on the skin (especially on the legs), coughing, sore throat, or shortness of breath. If any of these are or remain present, then further evaluation is needed. Of striking importance is that many gay men and others who are symptom-free have a positive test for antibodies against the virus (HIV). These people have come to be known as the "worried well," exemplifying the unfortunate predicament of not knowing what their future holds, whether they will acquire full-blown AIDS, or develop an AIDS-related complex, or remain well. Since the outcome of a positive test for the antibodies may remain uncertain for two to eight years, those who test positive present a challenge to the health care professional. The care provider must help these clients face the possibility and deal with the fear of dying. This requires courage and compassion on the part of the health care professional.

Beyond the specifics of the health history which have been described, it is of equal importance while taking the health history to understand and outline how a specific problem is affected by the added psychosocial stressors of external homophobia, the coming out process, and being a couple in the absence of legal and economic sanctions. These psychosocial stressors are discussed in greater detail in subsequent chapters.

Maintenance of good health is the first line of defense against disease and other health problems. But when health care professionals and their gay and lesbian clients must confront health problems, the best initial resource available is the health history. It is important that the health history for gay people be thorough by including the information in the areas I have described. And it is the health care professional who knows what kind of information to ask about, and how to ask for it sensitively, who will obtain a truly comprehensive health history.

Chapter 2

Incorporating the client's support system into the plan of care

Andrew C. Irish

A FLEXIBLE CONCEPT OF FAMILY

From simple human experience, we have all come to know the value of a network of individuals to whom we can turn in time of need. Our choice of support persons depends on many factors — the nature of the need, sociocultural beliefs which we learned as we matured, and who might be available to us at a given moment. Blood relatives or spouses are often called upon, for they generally know us well, and our need to maintain appearances is usually less with such persons. If the concern is of a professional nature, co-workers understand the situation on a first-hand basis and are, therefore, good sounding boards. Close friends and peers may be helpful because of similar life experiences and points of view. The point is, we have each built up, to varying degrees, a system of supportive others with whom we share our lives and to whom we turn for help in solving some of our problems. Of these supportive others, there are those who eventually come to mean more to us than others. It is with these individuals that we share the very personal aspects of our lives. We trust them and value their opinions, and we know we can depend on them. These become our significant others.

I have avoided using the word family. This is a purposeful omission, for to many people the word has but one definition — the classic nuclear family. While such a definition can never be considered wrong, the concept of family can indeed be defined in a different manner, depending on one's point of reference. There is the family of man. Religious leaders often speak of the church family. Many companies and institutions work hard to project the idea of family as pertaining to all of the employees as a group, in hopes of increasing loyalty and job satisfaction. Close friends, too, can be thought of as family.

"The concept of family needs to be flexible and fluid, for the accelerating social changes which have an impact on it are increasing its complexity and diversification of forms and lifestyles."(5) The significant others previously referred to are, then, essentially family, for "...the family is a special kind of small group in which the members are united by blood, marriage or other bonding."(5) This "other bonding" is the main consideration of this chapter, for lesbians and gay men have little access, with the exception of adoption, to legally and socially condoned forms of bonding.

While it is true we each have a family of origin, we may or may not be close to them, either emotionally or geographically. Thus, if "the family system is organized around the support, regulation, nurturing and socialization of its members,"(5) then it can be said that for many people, blood relatives simply do not easily fall into personal definitions of family.

FRIENDS AS FAMILY

Perhaps more than any other social group, gay men and lesbians exercise the freedom to choose and construct their own family of friends. "All health practitioners should be sensitive to and considerate of the needs of their clients and significant others. The significance of other persons depends on the client's evaluation, not the practitioner's."(10) In nursing education and practice, we are constantly reminded that procedures must be tailored to the situation, and that to obtain optimal therapeutic outcomes, we must start at the level of the client and involve those with whom he shares important aspects of living. There may not be a spouse, child, parent, or sibling available to become involved in patient care and teaching. Even if such an individual is available, the client may choose not to have that person involved. Instead, there may be an apparently unrelated person with whom the client shares a common bond and from whom strength is gained who steps forth. To deprive the gay or lesbian client's significant other of information and participation would serve only to create in the patient anger and mistrust. This would be an additional burden to the feelings of loss of control and of anxiety that the client is probably experiencing — a burden the client needs to be spared.

DEFENDING THE RIGHT TO QUALITY HEALTH CARE

For most of us health care providers, an important question we want answered during the admission interview is whom to contact in the event of an emergency. Tactful questioning will elicit some explanation of the relationship between the client and the individual named as the contact person. In taking note of this relationship, we should be ready to accept friend or roommate. Very few gay men or lesbians will immediately identify this friend or roommate as a lover, and quite a few gay people choose not to use that term at all. The motive for this sort of ambiguity or prevarication is related directly to gay people's fully justified perception that homophobia still pervades the health care system. By being less than candid in explaining the true nature of their relationship with the contact person, gays and lesbians are simply defending themselves against probable homophobic reactions by their health care providers that could jeopardize the quality of care given. Certainly for those of us in nursing, "Since we know nursing techniques have psychological components that affect the delivery of care, we have to be alert to our attitudes and, if necessary, change them so that care will not be impeded."(6) No one can be expected to throw out conditioned personal values immediately, but health care professionals are expected to remember that "the patient has the right to considerate and respectful care."(1)

In the course of caring for a hospitalized client, the nurse may well be the one person on the health care team the client comes to trust most. It is to the nurse that the nature of the relationship with the contact person may be disclosed, if such information has been disguised early in the admission. Statements such as "Jane and I have been through a lot over the years" or "Bill is a lot more than just a friend, you know" might well be openings for further exploration. Believing that a façade of heterosexuality is necessary for acceptance is indeed a damaging stressor for the lesbian or gay man. Thus, an atmosphere in which the gay or lesbian client does not have to fear the consequences of disclosure should be created.(2) The interruption of one's everyday existence by a hospitalization is a serious stressor for most people, and in times of stress, we all turn to our network of support persons. "When the homosexual patient's partner visits, he or she should be afforded the same respect and courtesy as the spouse and family of the heterosexual. As with any other couple, the partners need privacy to talk and express affection.(6)

ADJUSTING TO CHANGES IN BODY IMAGE

Many illnesses and their treatment create a real or perceived change in body image. Because of our society's, and especially gay culture's, preoccupation with the desirability of a youthful and attractive appearance, successful adjustment by the patient to such changes is a difficult personal struggle to accept. It requires the support of significant others and the health care provider. For those in whom the change has, indeed, been a physical one, as in the case of a woman who has undergone a mastectomy, a man who has experienced the removal of one or both of his testicles, or a person with a newly formed ostomy or even simple scarring from surgery, there will be at first the need to adjust to a new body feel and, often, to a new appearance. Doubts about personal attractiveness and desirability are inevitable. Serious disturbances in body image and self-concept must be considered potential problems. Some preoperative preparation will help reduce the trauma of the change. Encourage the patient and the significant other(s) to express their concerns and expectations. Discussion of the meaning of a body part which will be surgically removed will help the patient regain equilibrium. In order for the significant other to be an effective part of the patient's care, he or she may also need a sympathetic ear. In order to best support our client, we must not forget those on whom he or she depends; we must be available to them, as well.

CASES IN POINT

Marie is a 41-year-old woman who has been admitted to the hospital for a breast biopsy and possible mastectomy.

She is accompanied by Jane during the admissions process, and it is her name that Marie gives when asked for a contact person. After a brief tour of the surgical floor and the nurse's own admission interview, Jane bids Marie good night, telling her she will call her in the morning before her surgery. This might be a time to gently investigate the nature of the relationship between the two women, perhaps with a simple observation such as, "Jane certainly does seem concerned. She seems pretty important to you. That's important." You may or may not get much of a reaction, but you have demonstrated an attitude of acceptance.

A good time to begin to investigate the specific fears and concerns Marie might have regarding her impending surgery is during the preoperative teaching. Here, too, the nurse might be able to approach the subject of body image, even if the conversation is cut off by Marie. Any unwillingness to discuss it will say more about her fears than words alone.

Instead of just calling in the morning, Jane comes into the hospital to wait with Marie. Make her welcome, offer a cup of coffee or tea, and make sure she knows where the surgical waiting area is located. If surgeons or anesthesiologists in your institution make a habit of speaking to those who are waiting after surgery is completed, make sure they know that Jane is there.

Marie's surgery is completed. She has required a mastectomy for carcinoma of the breast. Jane waits while she is settled back in her room, speaks to her for a moment, and tells the nurse that she will return that evening, when Marie is more awake.

During Jane's evening visit, she and Marie talk, though neither woman looks particularly relaxed when visiting hours come to an end. Jane asks the nurse how Marie is doing, and is relieved to hear that so far she is comfortable, her blood pressure and pulse are fine, and there has been no evidence of bleeding from the incision. Marie, on the other hand, is restless. She looks worried and cries occasionally. Her evening nurse, during preparations for sleep, remarks on these things.

"Well, wouldn't you be upset?" Marie cries. "It's going to be so ugly."

"Have you ever known any women who have had a breast removed?" asks the nurse.

"Yes I have — my sister, and she ended up alone!" Marie says angrily.

Marie's fear of rejection is evident. Gradually, she must be introduced to the way her body will look after the incision is healed, and to what can be done with prostheses. But at the moment, a more pressing need exists.

"Are you afraid of ending up like your sister?"

"Of course," Marie continues. "Who would want me now?"

"Who do you want to want you now?"

After an anxious silence, Marie looks at the nurse, searching her eyes for support and clues about what the nurse might be thinking, and then quietly answers with a single word.

"Jane."

Now that this is open, exploration of what Marie and Jane have discussed is in order. When dressings are changed, Marie should be encouraged, though not forced, to look at her incision. Touching is a very important way for her to reacquaint herself with her new body dimensions. She should be asked if she'd like Jane to be present for a dressing change, so that the nurses could be available for questions that Jane might have. The two should be encouraged to talk about what the change means to each of them. Literature on the order of Terese Lasser's *Reach to Recovery* could also be recommended. In private, Jane can be informed of Marie's concern about her acceptability and desirability to Jane. Involving Jane early on in the post-operative care program will do much toward reestablishing Marie's self-esteem and the equilibrium of their relationship.

Marie and Jane will need to explore together the new feelings experienced, both physically and emotionally, during lovemaking. "Lesbian couples can suffer from the same kinds of sex-related problems as nongay couples: lack of communication, miscommunication, differing or unrealistic expectations and the like."(9) But, "the exploration of sexual relationships between partners in any family system requires sensitivity and discretion on the part of the health professional, and perhaps should not be undertaken unless sexuality is an issue disturbing the system."(7) They can be encouraged to think about consulting a lesbian therapist, if they feel such assistance would be beneficial in dealing with the changes which will be necessary. I would suggest recommending a lesbian therapist over a non-lesbian therapist because the lesbian is far more likely to be aware of the ways in which lesbian lifestyles differ from those of non-lesbians.(9)

Up to now, the importance of the diagnosis of carcinoma to Marie and Jane has not been discussed. It must be expected that Marie's adjustment to her mastectomy will be made more difficult by this knowledge. A mastectomy "precipitates a period of shock and unexpected events... It leaves a change in bodily appearance... It mars the future by the prospect of shortened life and the possibility of slow, painful death."(11) The subject of Marie's cancer cannot be ignored. Both she and Jane must be given up-to-date information about further therapies, if these are to be a part of the post-operative care program. Both will need to have many questions answered. *Reach to Recovery* and the American Cancer Society are both excellent sources of answers.

Some health problems bring with them no external bodily changes. Yet, to say that no change has taken place when, for example, the patient is told she has diabetes, is absurd. The patient feels different about herself, and so a change has indeed occurred. Lifestyle changes will be necessary ... injectable or oral medication will become a part of the person's daily life. Dietary habits will have to be modified. The person will no longer be the same as she was before receiving the diagnosis. The need for support and time to adjust is quite as real as for the person whose body has been physically changed.

Bill is twenty-five, and has been admitted to the hospital for a workup. Diagnostic testing has confirmed his physician's suspicion of diabetes. The nurse begins to discuss some of the information Bill will need to know, and he quickly asks, "Does this mean I can't eat sweets? Both my roommate and I cook a lot."

"Perhaps your roommate would like to come in sometime and discuss your dietary concerns with the dietician. When will he next be in to visit?"

"Patrick will be in this evening after he finishes work. We eat out a lot, too. Can we still do that?"

"Yes, you will be able to eat out. Both of you will need to learn about the diabetic diet, though. When your roommate comes in, why don't you mention this to him, and let us know when would be a good time to sit down and begin to talk about this. You will also have things to learn about taking care of your body, and about insulin. It would be a good idea if both of you learned pretty much the same sort of thing, so that your roommate could help you if the need ever arises."

Exchange systems, foot care, insulin injections, hypo- and hyperglycemic reactions are all things that must become second nature to Bill, and familiar to Patrick, if they are to continue to live their lives in a comfortable manner. Through all of the teaching, it will be important for Bill, Patrick, and the nurses to realize and remember that the actual practice of what is learned may not be exactly what is described verbally.(9) Flexibility and creativity will be the key to per- sonalizing the care plan to fit Bill's life. When planning teaching sessions, it will be necessary to consider Patrick's schedule. Perhaps some evening or weekend sessions will be required, in which case the whole nursing team must be up-to-date on what has been taught, and on what is yet to be discussed. Time must be allowed for return demonstra- tions and further questions. After the men are on their own, they need to be checked up on to find out how they are doing emotionally with all of the adaptations they are being asked to make.

The list of examples could go on and on. Consider the gay man who has suffered a myocardial infarction and who is in the coronary care unit. Many such units restrict visitation privileges to family members only. The patient's lover or close friend could, of course, fabricate a story about being his brother, but that denies their true relationship. Disallowing visitation rights to the lover because he is not technically, or legally, a family member would only add stress at a time when the goal is to reduce stress levels on the body and mind to a minimum.(3)

Throughout this chapter, I have attempted to illustrate how woefully inadequate the traditional definition of family is. Basic to any discussion of how to incorporate the lesbian or gay client's support systems into the plan of care is the assumption that lovers and close friends do indeed comprise a family grouping for the client. To treat them otherwise is stressful to the client *and* the partner, and contrary to the goals of nursing or any helping profession. If we are to promote wellness and support the return to health and independence of our gay and lesbian clients, then we must let the client tell us to whom we can turn for teaching and counseling purposes. Let's just ask who should be contacted, and take it from there.

REFERENCES

1. American Hospital Association (1976, January). A patient's bill of rights. *Nursing Outlook, 24,* 29.

2. Brossart, J. (1979, April). The gay patient: What you should be doing. *RN Magazine, 42,* 50-52.

3. Gay Nurses' Alliance (1974). Gay people/straight health care. (Audiovisual).

4. Hartman, C.E. (1979). Elements of the teaching program. In D.R. Blevins (Ed.). *The diabetic and nursing care* (pp. 252-269). New York: McGraw-Hill.

5. Horton, T.E. (1977). Conceptual basis for nursing intervention with human systems: Families. In J.E. Hall and B.R. Weaver (Eds.). *Distributive nursing practice: A systems approach to community health* (pp. 101-115). Philadelphia: J.B. Lippincott.

6. Irish, A.C. (1983, August). Straight talk about gay patients. *American Journal of Nursing, 83,* 1169-1170.

7. Kuhn, K. and Janosik, E.H. (1980). Establishment of a family system. In J.R. Miller and E.R. Janosik (Eds.). *Family focused care* (pp. 147-165). New York: McGraw-Hill.

8. Lawrence, J.C. (1976). Homosexuality, hospitals and the nurse. *Nursing Forum, 14(3),* 304-317.

9. Moses, A.E. and Hawkins, R.O., Jr. (1982). *Counseling lesbian women and gay men: A life-issues approach.* St. Louis: C.V. Mosby.

10. Pettyjohn, R. (1976). Health care of the gay individual. *Nursing Forum, 18(4),* 367-394.

11. Quint, J.C. (1963, November). The impact of mastectomy. *American Journal of Nursing, 63(11),* 88-92.

II

*Common Psychosocial
Concerns of Gay and
Lesbian Clients*

Chapter 3

Coming out: Its nature, stages, and health concerns

Robert J. Kus

THE NATURE OF COMING OUT

Because ten percent of our clients are gay or lesbian, it is necessary for helping professionals to learn all they can about this population. And no concept is so crucial in understanding this population than the coming out process.

First, this process is unique to gays and lesbians; there is no counterpart experience in the heterosexual world.

Second, many health problems can be directly linked to this life process. Knowing which problems are related to coming out and which are not is crucial. For without this knowledge, our treatment approaches usually fail.(9)

Third, the individual stages of coming out have varying time lengths and are experienced to different degrees by each individual.(6, 7) For example, some persons never get out of Stage II or will take twenty-five years going from Stage I to Stage III, while others will go through the entire process in a year. Further, while some persons literally "go to pieces" in the first two stages of the process, others are able to handle it much more smoothly. And as both the gay liberation and the lesbian feminist movements advance and change society, and as more and more positive gay and lesbian resources become available, this process is becoming less devastating.

Fourth, the coming out process is never seen as a "ho-hum" life process. Persons experiencing it generally feel quite angry that they have to experience such a process. Later, in retrospect, they often feel grateful for the experience, or sometimes have mixed feelings toward it.

In this chapter we will examine the four stages of the coming out process, the health picture seen in each stage, and some strategies the helping professional may use to help the client. Finally, we will look at a couple of case histories of persons with health problems related to coming out, and how helping professionals were able to assist their clients in solving them.

But before turning to the specifics of coming out, a definition is in order. *Coming out is defined here as that process by which a gay or lesbian individual identifies self as gay or lesbian, changes any previously-held negative notions of gays, lesbians, or homosexuality, accepts being gay or lesbian as a positive stage of being, and acts on the assumption that being gay or lesbian is a positive state of being.(7)*

STAGE ZERO: LIFE BEFORE THE COMING OUT PROCESS

Very little is known about gay and lesbian children, and virtually nothing is known about gay and lesbian infants. Biological advances will, undoubtedly, go far in helping us understand more as we learn how gays are different biologically from other males, and how lesbians are different from other females. Researchers such as Gladue, Green, and Hellman, who have found biochemical responses differing between gay and straight men,(4) may eventually conduct studies to learn the differences in childhood and infancy.

Behavioral scientists such as myself,(6) on the other hand, have begun to uncover some basic life patterns exhibited by gay and lesbian children long before these children realize their true sexual orientations. This finding leads one to question whether sexual orientation, per se, is the critical thing making gays and lesbians different from heterosexuals, or if there are other factors operating which are yet unknown. What are these childhood patterns which the gay or lesbian child experiences before the coming out process begins? Are they the same for gays and lesbians? How do they compare with the childhood patterns of heterosexual males and females? As we shall see, the typical gay pattern is the opposite of the typical lesbian pattern. While the former mimics heterosexual female childhood, the latter mimics heterosexual male childhood.

The Gay Pattern: The typical gay pattern is what I call the Best-Little-Boy-in-the-World Syndrome, named after the classic autobiography of John Reid.(13) In this pattern, the little gay boy exhibits high achievement, heightened sensitivity to adult expectations and accompanying model performance, politeness, and non-committment to rough-and-tumble activities such as sports. Further, he realizes he is "different" from other boys, but does not know how he is different. Only when he reaches Stage I of the coming out process will he learn the source and meaning of this difference. He often finds that his enjoyment of typical childhood games such as strip poker with boys is much greater than that of his peers. Likewise, he finds he gets crushes on male heroes and fantasizes sexually about members of his own sex. Like heterosexual girls, he is likely to obey adults unquestioningly. "Don't get dirty" means exactly what it says. "Do well in school," likewise, is taken to heart. And like the heterosexual girl, he often finds enjoyment playing with girls and is interested in their leisure pursuits. However, in the early days of his teen years, as heterosexual girls find they enjoy being with boys more and heterosexual boys enjoy being with girls more, the gay teen finds he enjoys being with males more. Thus, this attraction is opposite of that of the heterosexual male. This pattern of excelling in one's pursuits would logically lead to overachievement in adulthood, and indeed it does. For unlike the heterosexual female who often buys into the "Cinderella Syndrome" in which she fails to achieve independently because of her belief that a man will take care of her, the male — gay or straight — is denied this choice of being taken care of in adulthood. Therefore, the gay boy will have to use the overachievement pattern for adult independence.

The Lesbian Pattern: Like the gay boy, the lesbian girl is also a maverick. She too realizes that she is somehow "different" from other girls. But unlike the gay boy, she often exhibits the "Rubyfruit-Jungle Syndrome," a childhood pattern named after Rita Mae Brown's book of the same title.(1) This syndrome is characterized by assertiveness, a desire to compete equally with boys, bucking traditionally "feminine" trappings of dress and behavior, and a keen interest in sports and traditional heterosexual male activities. In early childhood, she often shuns girls as playmates and enjoys being with boys more. But,in the early teen years, while her hetero-sexual sisters are now leaving girl friends for boy friends, she experiences a desire to be around females rather than males. This pattern, like the Best-Little-Boy-in-the-World pattern, should also lead to overachievement in adulthood for two reasons. First, the lesbian girl has mastered the assertiveness and determination for independence needed to be successful in the work world, and second, she knows that she will not have a man to fall back on in adulthood. And, indeed, research indicates that lesbians, like gays, often do become overachievers in adulthood.

A word of caution here: Even though these patterns have been identified and apply to many gay and lesbian children, it must be remembered that not all such children necessarily fall into these patterns. Thus, one may see gay boys very much into sports and lesbian girls very much into playing with dolls.

With this brief glimpse into life before the coming out process, we know turn to the specific stages of the process.

STAGE I: IDENTIFICATION

In the stage of identification there is a radical identity change. Even though sexual orientation is determined before the age of three,[12] if not before birth, gays and lesbians do not recognize their true identity until the teenage years or later. Gays usually reach this stage before lesbians. By age nineteen, a full eighty-four percent of the gay men know their sexual orientation, while only sixty-four percent of the les-bian women know theirs.[5]

Recognizing one's homosexual identity often takes place through identifying with gay or lesbian books, through hear-ing the word "queer" or "gay" or "dyke" and exploring what this means, through falling in love with a person of the same sex, or through identifying one's feelings with what gays or lesbians relate in the media. Further, some gays and lesbians arrive at identification only after experiencing opposite-sex sexual relations. Often, they describe these relations and their feelings as unnatural or abnormal. Such experiences may lead these gay people to conclude that they are bisexual, which is not at all the same thing as being gay. Confusing sexual orientation (a non-chosen state of being) with sexual behavior (action) is common for those persons who have not quite reached Stage I. This false labeling of self as bisexual is more common among lesbians than among gays.(5)

The Health Picture: Unlike racial and ethnic minorities, most gays and lesbians have not had the opportunity of many years in childhood to adequately learn what being a minority in America means. Also, most gay and lesbian children do not have parents and a host of gay relatives or friends as models. There is no anticipatory socialization process from them. Therefore, upon realizing their homosexual orientations, they often experience overwhelming feelings of being completely alone in their situations and isolated from everyone who cares about them. Their loneliness is born from the fear of disclosing their "deep, dark secrets."

Because gay and lesbian children have been taught many negative myths about gays and lesbians, beginning the stage of identification can cause one's self-esteem to suffer. The myths include believing that gays and lesbians are necessarily unhappy and that they lead unfulfilled lives; that gays are child molesters (an almost exclusively heterosexual phenomenon) or transvestites (an almost exclusively heterosexual male phenomenon); and that gays are highly effeminate or that lesbians are highly masculine.

Little wonder, then, that many gays and lesbians in Stage I report hating their homosexual orientation. They often fear that friends and family will reject them, that they will have future occupational difficulties, and that being gay or lesbian will not allow them to have children and families. In short, they feel that it would be so much easier if they had been created straight.

The health picture here is rather gloomy. Some of the common health problems include deep and intense guilt or shame, diminished self-esteem, stress and its physical manifestations, overwhelming loneliness, inability to focus on school or work and other life tasks, and depression. Suicidal ideation, occurring in forty percent of the gay and lesbian population,(5) is often seen here. Likewise, alcoholism begins here. Finally, there is sometimes seen a rare form of psychosis in this stage characterized by delusions of persecution and by hallucinations. This psychosis is quite temporary and is usually only seen in males. Its treatment is simple: get the person to discuss being gay and assist him with self-acceptance.(9)

To achieve maximum mental and physical health, one must move out of this stage as quickly as possible.

STAGE II: COGNITIVE CHANGES

While a radical identity change is the criterion for Stage I, the criterion of Stage II is changing one's negative notions about gays and lesbians and homosexuality. However, this stage does not entail fully accepting being gay or lesbian as a positive state of being.

Having learned a "straight reality" all through childhood, gay people in the second stage must now learn a gay or lesbian reality, a new way of seeing and explaining the world and one's place in it. Thus, this stage is similar to going to school.

Most often, gays and lesbians pass as straight while exploring what it means to be gay or lesbian. "Passing" is done out of fear — fear of rejection, fear of violence, fear of loss. And although the fear is usually much greater than the actual experience of self-disclosure of one's gay or lesbian identity, it must be remembered that this is the century which has produced such anti-gay bigots as Anita Bryant, Jerry Falwell, Adolph Hitler, Josef Stalin, and Fidel Castro, and has witnessed the effects of such anti-gay social and political forces as Nazism, Klanism, Communism, and the fundamentalist Protestant "Moral Majority."

Gays and lesbians pass as straight in a number of ways, the most common form being dating the opposite sex and entering into cosexual (male-female) marriages. But the most damaging form of passing is becoming an anti-gay crusader. In this situation, gays and lesbians may enter into right-wing political or fundamentalist religious cults or sects which seek to persecute or exterminate gays, but rarely lesbians. This is the type of person about whom Shakespeare might say, "Methinks he doth protest too much."

Also, common in this stage is a geographic movement. Gays and lesbians often move from their homes to distant cities where they can be freer to explore gay and lesbian communities and where chances of old friends and family learning of their homosexuality are negligible. Rural persons often move to cities where there are more gay and lesbian groups to join, such as yachting clubs, churches and synagogues, and gay professional associations; or they move to a university town where there is a more progressive atmosphere.

To understand and correct their preconceived negative notions about homosexuality, gays and lesbians often explore gay or lesbian communities. These persons are often very unsophisticated in the beginning and they fail to correctly discern what would be best to pursue. For example, the lesbian might accidentally get involved in a gay community center which is primarily for gays, while an apolitical gay might join a gay political group when he would be much happier in a gay bowling league.

While some folks report changing their negative notions through reading positive gay and lesbian literature, all agree that the very best way of getting through this stage is to get to know lots of gays (for men) and lesbians (for women).

The Health Picture: The health picture in this stage is similar to that seen in Stage I. First, there is a tremendous energy waste trying to live a double life behind masks.

Second, this stress of a 24-hour-a-day job of acting can lead to a multitude of physical and mental health problems associated with stress.

Third, although this is becoming less and less of a problem, the person is open to blackmail.

Fourth, there is an almost paranoid fear of being discovered — a fear permeating all aspects of life, from signing out a gay library book to being spotted at a lesbian nightclub. However, this paranoia is not to be confused with what Clark(2) calls "benign paranoia," a heightened sensitivity all gays and lesbians must possess to detect signs of homophobia which may crop up anywhere, from anyone, and at any time. For example, many gays report that if they hear a stranger using the word "homosexual" rather than "gay" to refer to a person, they are leery of that person. As a black gay man once said, "Gay is to black, as homosexual is to colored."

Fifth, all of the problems seen in Stage I continue with the possible exception of feeling alone, or isolated, and lonely. And for those men and women who have developed alcoholism, the disease progresses.

As one begins to shed the negative notions about gays and lesbians, it becomes too difficult to pass as straight. To continue passing as straight becomes an assault on one's integrity, on one's self-esteem, and on one's sensibilities. Stage II gays and lesbians begin giving clues as to their identities, such as objecting to lesbian or gay jokes, or refusing to make up fictitious accounts of dates with the opposite sex. Serious closet passing begins to fade. One moves on to Stage III.

STAGE III: ACCEPTANCE

No stage of the coming out process is more joyful than the Stage of Acceptance. Here persons begin to see their minority sexual orientation as "good news" rather than "bad news." As a result, they can move toward self-actualization as self-esteem is raised to new heights.

This stage is characterized by a type of freedom not experienced by the heterosexual person. The initial war with self is over, and a peacefulness descends. As Fisher says:

> The inner conflict is over and one is suddenly free to be himself. More important, one is no longer at war with himself. The energy which was devoted to denying one's self can now be directed toward building a happy life.(3:24)

The Health Picture: Needless to say, the health picture seen in Acceptance is much brighter than that seen in the previous stages. First, stress and its manifestations are decreased. There is a greater ability to relax.

Second, self-esteem soars as one becomes free from the guilt seen earlier. This results in a general sense of well-being.

Third, the depression and its many symptoms disappear. When their sexual orientations become "good news" rather than "bad news", and once this is internalized, gays and lesbians are ready to enter Stage IV.

STAGE IV: ACTION

Stage IV is engaging in behavior or action which results from accepting being lesbian or gay as a positive state of being. Gays or lesbians who do not accept their sexual orientations as a positive state of being, regardless of how active they may be in gay or lesbian activities or how public they are, are not in the Action stage because they do not meet the criterion of self-acceptance.

This behavior may be highly visible, such as making the irreversible public statement, "I'm gay," or very private, such as a lesbian nun making a silent prayer of thanksgiving for her new-found peacefulness.

Common types of action in this stage include intentional disclosure of one's sexual orientation, expanding one's circle of friends to include gays or lesbians, modifying, rethinking, or rejecting religious beliefs, becoming politically involved in lesbian or gay causes, volunteering for gay or lesbian hot-lines, speaking or writing about gay or lesbian issues, and even raising one's occupational sights. The person is now able to be free to discuss with friends, acquaintances, and family those aspects of life — such as lover relationships — which are important.

The Health Picture: As with the previous stage, this health picture is quite bright. The difficulties that might present themselves can usually be dealt with very effectively because of a newly achieved self-acceptance.

First, the person may be rejected by family, friends, employers, or others following the disclosure of gay or lesbian identity. This may lead to a crisis situation. But five things need to be kept in mind about this possible rejection. One, family and others who may be initially negative usually move toward acceptance in time. Also, it is extremely rare that an accepting person will become negative because of sexual orientation. Two, a crisis, however painful, may produce a period of growth and thus be a blessing in disguise. And three, when one is at peace with self, crises and rejections

– 38 –

are much easier to bear. Four, most gays and lesbians report that they experience very little actual rejection because of self-disclosure. And five, as one has built up a support system of gays or lesbians, the gay person can turn to these new friends for comfort and advice following a show of bigotry.

Second, gays and lesbians often become overachievers, which, in itself, is very good. But while it may lead to a Ph.D., it may also lead to workaholism and the perfectionism often seen in gay and lesbian adults.

Third, with the explosive burst of energy unleashed from no longer passing as straight, combined with the excitement of self-acceptance, one often becomes a "professional gay"(14) or "professional lesbian" for a period of time. One temporarily loses perspective and "being gay" or "being lesbian" is all-consuming. This phenomenon, however, is both healthy and natural and will run its course.

Having examined the stages of the coming out process very briefly, we now look at some of the things the helping professional may do to help the person go through this process more quickly and less painfully.

COMING OUT AND THE HELPING PROFESSIONAL

First, the overwhelming majority of gay and lesbian teens and adults will not seek out helping professionals to aid them in their coming out process regardless of how painful it may be emotionally, spiritually, or physically. For one thing, they may have little faith in the competence of the helping professional in this area — a belief that is usually quite justified. Also, they often feel that there is nothing specific to be done to help them get through this process as quickly and painlessly as possible.

Clients coming into contact with professionals will usually do so for other reasons, such as alcoholism, depression, inability to relax, and the like. Therefore, the professional person must always perform an adequate assessment. Is the client's problem one related to coming out or to some other factor? This is often difficult to discern, for gays and lesbians have all the life stresses, responsibilities, and problems that heterosexual clients have. The coming out process is merely an addition to these everyday stresses.

Second, remember that you are around gays and lesbians every day, whether you know it or not. Therefore, any negative comments you may make about gays and lesbians will be picked up by those persons.

Third, for the persons not accepting self in a positive way, encourage them to meet other gays or other lesbians. Places to meet include gay or lesbian support groups, rap groups, community centers, religious groups, professional groups, and gay or lesbian recreational clubs.

Fourth, encourage reading of positive gay or lesbian literature. This is especially critical for the rural person who does not have the same supportive communities found in large cities. And this is particularly useful for minors who are not able to meet others in gay or lesbian bars or other adult-only places. Today, there is an ever-increasing number of wonderful positive gay and lesbian books available.

Fifth, crisis intervention should be done with the person in crisis.(8) This may also include suicide prevention and counseling with homophobic families.

Sixth, be aware of what resources are available in the community for the gay or lesbian client. Is there a gay or lesbian counseling center? Is there a gay or lesbian crisis line? Are there gay, lesbian or gay-lesbian AA groups?

Seventh, do not ever hesitate to refer the gay client to a gay counselor, or a lesbian to a lesbian counselor, if the client requests it. Such counselors may serve not only the counseling needs per se, but also as role models for the client who may have very negative notions about gays and lesbians.

Eighth, gently yet firmly let the homophobic client know that you will not tolerate anti-gay and anti-lesbian rhetoric. Many persons in the early stages of coming out speak very disparagingly of "queers" and "perverts" and "homosexuals" and "dykes," which they desperately do not want to be. You will be doing them a great service by pointing out that "gays" and "lesbians" are just as worthy of respect and dignity as anybody else by virtue of their humanness. Let these people know that you simply will not let this homophobic rhetoric pass by unchallenged.

Ninth, you may need to dispel some of the myths held by the client in Stages I or II.

Tenth, homophobic staff coming in contact with the gay or lesbian client must be confronted and educated about their attitudes. The heightened sensitivity of gays and lesbians, which is finely tuned to pick up homophobia in the social environment, will pick up this negativity. If clients have not reached Acceptance, they will have their internalized homophobia reinforced.

Eleventh, give positive strokes and encouragement to the client who is actively working on self-acceptance by actively exploring the gay or lesbian community, by reading positive literature, or by self-disclosing.

Twelfth, strongly encourage alcohol treatment for the client who needs it, keeping in mind that self-acceptance of a gay or lesbian identity does not occur until sobriety is chosen and lived.(10, 11) For the client who does choose sobriety, encourage him or her to attend gay, lesbian, or gay-lesbian AA meetings to meet a new support group.

Thirteenth, refer the client to appropriate religious counselors if religious hang-ups seem to be the impediment to self-acceptance. Most of the mainstream churches have gay and lesbian caucuses, such as Dignity for Roman Catholics or Integrity for Protestant Episcopals. For virulently homophobic religious groups, however, this avenue is closed. The gay or lesbian person coming from totally closed religious systems will have to be supported without counseling from their religious traditions, but may be referred to a general gay and lesbian Protestant denomination, such as the Metropolitan Community Church if Protestant, or to a Reformed Jewish congregation if from an Orthodox congregation.

Finally, if as a professional you are employed by a health institution, encourage your institution to have openly gay and lesbian counselors and other helping professionals. This means also fighting for anti-discrimination policies in the institution.

CASE HISTORIES

The following cases indicate how one gay and one lesbian were helped in their coming out process by a helping professional. In the hospital setting, I have rarely observed lesbians coming for help with the coming out process, but I have seen many gays enter the hospital with coming out related problems, such as suicidal behaviors based on non-self-acceptance. Part of this may be explained by the more rigid expectations foisted on males by society from even the earliest years of life. For example, although a parent may say with pride, "Oh, she's our little tomboy," the parent never says, "Oh, he's our little sissy" with pride. Further, because the gay boy often is The-Best-Little-Boy-in-the-World and, therefore, has built his life around being good, this chink in the armor is often quite devastating to him; thus, the more troubled response.

Case #1: Paul. Paul, a 28-year-old married man and father of a three-year-old daughter, made an appointment to see his family physician, Dr. M., in his Ohio town. Paul gave complaints of intermittent chest pain (which he believed was his heart), insomnia, fatigue, and general malaise.

After listening carefully to his complaints, Dr. M., who had just finished reading about the coming out process and how it may affect health, had a hunch that perhaps this was Paul's problem. This hunch was based on his stereotypes of a gay man, i.e., Paul was good-looking, concerned about taking care of his body, friendly, and apparently sensitive.

When asked about his sexual orientation, Paul admitted that he was gay and had never told anyone. This was causing him a great deal of stress, not the least of which stemmed from the fear of losing his daughter should his sexual orientation become known.

After giving Paul a complete physical exam including several heart tests to be on the safe side, Dr. M. told Paul that he could find nothing wrong with him physically. However, he recommended that Paul see a gay counselor and get to know more gay people with whom he could share his concerns.

Paul not only followed this advice, but he was fortunate that his town had a gay fathers' support group. As he got to know more and more gay men, his self-esteem increased. His physical symptoms disappeared. He became more relaxed and had a brighter affect. He began to plan to disclose his sexual orientation to his wife.

Case #2: Donna. Donna, a 24-year-old counselor, came to a gay studies class I was teaching a few years back. When introductions were made on the first day of class she made it quite clear to the rest of the students that "I'm not lesbian, you know. But in my work I often have to deal with 'those types of people,' so I figured I should get some knowledge. I've got lots to learn."

In the beginning of the course she showed a great deal of reluctance to speak. When she did, she always referred to "those people" or, if she was feeling truly brave, she talked of gay men but never of lesbians. The rest of the students were quite patient with her, as most suspected she was lesbian. For one thing, virtually everyone taking the course was gay or lesbian, and for another, she fit the traditional stereoetype of a lesbian.

As the course developed I noticed that no matter what topic we were covering that night, all of the examples she would offer were of a religious nature. In particular, she would attempt to be the devil's advocate by showing how traditional religious beliefs were homophobic. Upon my hearty approval, she chose for her term paper topic the history of religious attitudes toward homosexuality by her particular religion, Roman Catholicism. Because I am of the same religion, I was able to give her positive gay and lesbian writings by contemporary theologians and religious historians in Roman Catholicism, reflecting more progressive and prophetic views.

As her research continued, and as she found that the winds of change had indeed begun to be felt in the Church regarding homosexuality, her classroom behavior began to change. No longer was she referring to "those people," and her insistence that "I'm not a lesbian, of course, but..." also disappeared. While she never did come out to her classmates (a very unusual event in this course), she did come out to me. "I can't tell you what a relief I feel having explored this area. All my life, that was the source of why I felt bad about myself. Now I know I can be a good Catholic and still be lesbian."

Needless to say, by the end of the course she was able to join in the usual good-natured joking with the other students and laugh at homophobic examples she saw. Further, she began confronting homophobic rhetoric in her place of employment, and her disposition became much brighter.

This particular case history, while interesting in itself, also illustrates how gay and lesbian students often choose to write about gay or lesbian topics for sociology courses and the like. This choice of topic, while usually justified because "it sounds really interesting and I don't know anybody like that," is often made as part of the person's cognitive change stage and should, therefore, be encouraged.

REFERENCES

1. Brown, R.M. (1973). *Rubyfruit jungle*. New York: Bantam.

2. Clark, D. (1977). *Loving someone gay*. Millbrae, CA: Celestial Arts.

3. Fisher, P. (1972). *The gay mystique: The myth and reality of male homosexuality*. New York: Stein and Day.

4. Gladue, B.A., Green, R., and Hellman, R.E. (1984, Sept.). Neuroendocrine response to estrogen and sexual orientation. *Science, 225,* 1496-1499.

5. Jay, K., and Young, A. (1979). *The gay report*. New York: Summit Books.

6. Kus, R.J. (1980). Gay freedom: An ethnography of coming out. *University Microfilms International* (Doctoral dissertation, Sociology, University of Montana, 1980). #8115407.

7. Kus, R.J. (1985, May). Stages of coming out: An ethnographic approach. *Western Journal of Nursing Research, 7(2),* 177-198.

8. Kus, R.J. (1985). Crisis intervention. In G.M. Bulechek and J.C. McCloskey (Eds.). *Nursing interventions: Treatments for nursing diagnoses* (pp. 277-287). Philadelphia: W.B. Saunders.

9. Kus, R.J. (1986). From grounded theory to clinical practice: Cases from gay studies research. In W.C. Chenitz and J.L. Swanson, (Eds.). *From practice to grounded theory: Qualitiative research in nursing* (pp. 227-240). Menlo Park, CA: Addison-Wesley.

10. Kus, R.J. (1987, July/August). Gay consultations in non-gay treatment settings. *Professional Counselor, 2(1),* 46-55.

11. Kus, R.J. (1988). Alcoholism and non-acceptance of gay self: The critical link. *Journal of Homosexuality, 15(1-2),* 25-41.

12. Money, J. and Ehrhardt, A. (1972). *Man and woman, boy and girl: Differentiation and dimorphism of gender identity from conception to maturity*. Baltimore: Johns Hopkins.

13. Reid, J. (1973). *The best little boy in the world*. New York: Ballantine.

14. Rochlin, M. (1979). Becoming a gay professional. In B. Berzon (Ed.). *Positively gay* (Second Printing). Los Angeles: Mediamix.

Chapter 4

Body image and gay American men

William S. Etnyre

THE BODY IN ITS OWN EYES

The focus of this chapter will be on potential body-image problems that can occur among gay American men. The information presented will provide a framework that helping professionals can use in assessing a variety of body-image difficulties and in determining how to intervene effectively. At first, I will discuss how body image develops. Later, I will present examples of specific assaults to the body that some gay men have suffered and relate the resulting impact on their body images. I will conclude with how the nurse, social worker, or counselor can help the gay man to cope with these changes.

Body image is part of our overall self-image or self-concept. It is something we all have; yet, most of us take our body images for granted and rarely think about them. It is only when disturbances occur in body image that we are forced to examine our inner picture or mental representation of our body. A review of the recent literature on body image bears this out. I found numerous articles and a few books written on what happens to body image when the body suffers traumatic change or some dysfunction; for example: severe burns, mastectomy, head and neck or ostomy surgery, amputation, congenital deformity or dysfunction, obesity and anorexia. Very little, however, is written on body image alone, or on what we might call "normal body image," as opposed to pathology in body image.(4,6) Understanding what body image is and how it develops can help the health care provider identify each patient's unique conception of his body and explain why he is responding in certain ways to an assault on his body.

DEFINITION OF BODY IMAGE

Simply stated, the body image is the mental representation or inner picture one has of his body. It is important to recognize that it is an internal or intrapsychic phenomenon. For example, I might look at a gorgeous hunk of a man and say he rates a 9.8 on a ten-point scale of handsomeness. Yet, he might see himself only as a 2.8. A 2.8 is where he is at.

Body image comprises the amalgamation of all the conscious and unconscious feelings, fantasies, attitudes, perceptions, and so on that an individual has regarding his outward appearance (2.8 or 9.8), regarding his internal sensations, and regarding the functioning of the separate parts and the whole of his body.(4, 3) It is also important to note that physical appearance is only one aspect of body image. Gay men are purported to place a great deal of emphasis on this aspect of body image. However, the functions of parts and the function of the whole body are equally significant aspects of body image. For example, if a gay man places great value on the functioning (as opposed to the appearance) of his genitals, impotence problems could alter his body image as a virile, potent, ever-ready male.

DEVELOPMENT OF BODY IMAGE

The mental picture of one's body and its functioning, which we term body image, develops over the life span, though it is fairly well established by the end of adolescence.(4) Although body image is an internal concept, it develops in a social milieu. One's inner sense of his body is greatly influenced by what others communicate verbally and non-verbally to him about his body and body functioning. How the person, in turn, perceives and integrates what he senses to be others' perceptions is equally important in the development of his body image.(3)

The newborn first experiences his world through a myriad of bodily sensations and functions. Over a period of time, these sensations and functions begin to make sense. The infant feels hungry (an unpleasant sensation that he later learns a word for) and cries. The mother offers the bottle or her breast. The infant starts learning that his body works for him; his sensations lead to a function (crying) which brings about action to satisfy his needs. These first experiences are the beginnings of body image, as well as ego development. If the parenting figures are grossly unresponsive, inconsistent, or abusive to the child, his body image will be adversely affected, in that he learns that his body sensations and functions cannot be relied upon to satisfy his needs.

As the child grows and matures toward adulthood, his body image is constantly affected by his interactions with his parents, peers, teachers, and others. What do they communicate verbally and non-verbally to him about his physical appearance and the way he uses his body? What effects do the messages of being fat, skinny, ugly, cute, good-looking, sissy, clumsy, coordinated, athletic, the last-picked-for-the-team, etc. have on him? And how does he perceive and integrate these inputs? What is his own inner sense of his body, and is this congruent with others' perceptions of his body? When his body changes in major ways, how does he incorporate these into his body image? For example, a skinny, clumsy boy may in his teen years fill out with muscles and develop athletic skills. Does his body image adjust accordingly, or does it still retain remnants of the skinny, uncoordinated kid who was always last to be picked for the team with the accompanying feelings of humiliation, pain, and loathing of his body?

DISRUPTION IN BODY IMAGE

Any experience (positive or negative) which is not consistent with the person's body image arouses anxiety. Such an experience could be a major change in, or impairment of, bodily appearance or functioning. It could also be input from others that is greatly divergent from the individual's image of his body, such as that of a man who considers himself quite unattractive, all of a sudden finding numerous men coming on to him. The degree of anxiety is dependent on the magnitude of the change, impairment, or external input; on the value the individual places on these factors; and on the value he places on the body part or function that is altered.(3)

Those of us in the health care professions are most likely to encounter problems in body image when a person is dealing with a sudden traumatic assault to the body as occurs with severe burns, amputation, or disfiguring surgery. Much has been written about the phases that a person goes through in dealing with such a crisis, variously described as 1) shock/impact, 2) denial/retreat, 3) acknowledgement, and 4) adaptation/integration.(4, 3, 6) Henker, in discussing how to help a person deal with bodily trauma, adds two additional phases. One is an initial preparation phase. In addressing this phase, he discusses how the nurse and other caregivers can help alleviate a great deal of anxiety by providing information, and by listening to how the patient feels about what is going to happen to him. He suggests that arranging for the patient to talk to someone else who has survived and thrived following a similar change to the body can be very helpful. However, preparation is not always possible. Emergency colostomy surgery that is necessitated by a knife wound, discovery of cancer, or tearing of the colon during sexual activities allows no time for preparation; whereas ileostomy surgery to ameliorate a chronic inflammatory bowel disease does allow much time to prepare the patient. Henker adds a final follow-up phase after adaptation. Positive integration of the body change into one's life and body image is something that may take many years. Regular, though not necessarily frequent, contact with the patient over the years may help ensure that his rehabilitation is successful, and that a healthy self-image and body image are restored.(3)

GAY MEN AND BODY IMAGE

Very little can be found in professional literature specifically about body image in relation to gay American men. However, much anecdotal literature about the emphasis gay men place on body appearance and functioning can be found in gay-oriented newspapers, magazines, ads, and novels. Whether gay men place more or less emphasis on body image than straights or lesbians do, it is a fact of our American culture that youth, vitality, good looks, sexiness, smelling good, and so forth, are greatly valued.

While it may be primarily a myth that gay men place greater value on physical appearance, Schwartz and Blumstein's pioneering work on couples may provide some validity to this notion. They found that men place considerably more importance on the beauty or sexy appearance of their sexual partner, spouse, or lover than do women. Straight men who are "co-habitors" placed even more emphasis on this factor than gay men.(2) However, because women don't place nearly as much importance on the good looks of their partner, straight men may not feel they have to worry so much about how they look, whereas women may feel obliged to work at their attractiveness in order to please a man. Since gay men place considerable value on the physical appearance of their partner, they know that other gay men are looking for the same. Hence, they may feel the need to work at being as physically fit or attractive as possible. The gay man's body image may undergo constant turmoil as he relentlessly strives to achieve some standard of perfection. Such striving may lead to either anorexia nervosa or bulimia. So few of us will ever look as good as those gorgeous hunks in Soloflex ads!

BODY-IMAGE PROBLEMS IN GAY MEN

Gay men may have more difficulty in developing a positive body image compared to heterosexual men. Two-thirds of the gay men in a 1973 study conducted by Saghir and Robbins described themselves as effeminate, or noted that they were called sissies or similar disparaging terms during their years growing up. Many gay men I have talked with in social and clinical situations report a similar experience. These external messages, the gay man's perception of them, and his own feelings and attitudes regarding his body become a part of his body image, as well as of his self-concept. Prytula and his collaborators further studied this issue. They found in their sample of twenty-eight gay men and twenty-eight straight men, that the gay men in general had a poorer body image in adolescence compared to the straight men. The gay men expressed greater dissatisfaction with their general physical characteristics, their feelings about their bodies, and their overall self-concept. They recalled receiving more negative comments about their bodies from peers and family members. In some of the gay men, these negative feelings persisted long into adulthood. Health care providers should be cognizant of this common gay experience when working with gay patients who are dealing with major bodily assaults, for such an experience could reawaken painful memories and feelings of poor body image which the person has worked to overcome.

Perhaps some of the fervor with which gay men pursue physical fitness and body building can be viewed as a healthy compensation in overcoming negative body image. Fortunately, many cities have organized gay sporting and recreational activities where gay men can enjoy their bodies without fear of ridicule.

While the major thrust of this chapter is on adult gay men, I would briefly like to comment on body-image problems in the adolescent boy who may or may not identify himself as gay, but who does not have the typical masculine interests. Incidentally, Bell, Weinberg, and Hammersmith in their seminal work on sexual orientation found that gender non-conformity in the early years of life, while not a cause of homosexuality, is very strongly related to a homosexual orientation in adulthood.(1) What can the school nurse, social worker, counselor, or teacher do to counteract the ridiculing that the gender non-conforming boy receives and the devastating consequences on his self-esteem and body image? Helping persons can provide a listening ear. They can arrange for special help from a caring coach or peer, if the child wishes to develop athletic skills. Perhaps class discussions or exercises to help students become more tolerant of individual differences could be helpful. Helping the youth identify positive features about his body, while not discounting his negative feelings, may be beneficial.

The following two cases illustrate how dramatic changes in the body affected the body image of the men presented. These are composite case studies based on actual experiences I have had working with and talking to many men who have had ostomy surgery or who have AIDS. Ostomy surgery is the generic term for colostomy, ileostomy, or urostomy surgery. These surgeries, which are most commonly necessitated by inflammatory bowel disease, cancer, or traumatic injury, involve removal of part or all of the colon, and sometimes part of the small intestine, in cases of colostomy and ileostomy surgery. The bladder is removed in urostomy surgery. An opening (stoma) is made through the abdominal

– 50 –

wall for the elimination of stool or urine. Usually a small, odor-proof pouch is worn to collect the waste material.

Case A: Paul is a 32-year-old man who suffered from ulcerative colitis from the age of 16. He had endured frequent hospitalizations, severe bouts of pain, and bloody diarrhea interspersed with periods of remission during which he felt healthy and was physically active. Although he had struggled to overcome earlier humiliations as an awkward and somewhat effeminate child and had become a star swimmer and runner, his chronic illness took its toll on his body image. He began to see his body as weak, a nuisance, and an impediment to him. He frequently felt angry at his body because of the severe limitations it placed on his physical activities in school and in his social life. He did manage to finish college and came out in his senior year.

Paul knew what an ostomy was, but he wasn't prepared for the shock when it became a life-or-death matter just after he turned 27. As a gay man, he was sure he would be disfigured and ugly, and that no one would ever want him for a lover. Getting a job as a freak in a circus sideshow entered his mind. He was sure he'd smell bad and have to wear a bag down to his knees. A sex life was out of the question — he'd never let anybody see that awful thing. He also knew he could never have anal sex (as a recipient) again, and this greatly upset him. He even contemplated suicide.

Fortunately, his physician and his enterostomal therapist (a nurse trained in the care of ostomies) brought in a trained visitor, John, from the local chapter of the United Ostomy Association (UOA) to talk with him. John wasn't gay, but he was a healthy, husky married man who led a very active life. He even swam and ran in ten-kilometer races. Paul couldn't believe John had an ileostomy! He didn't stink. He could eat what he wanted. He wasn't wearing overalls. He looked perfectly normal! Paul went to surgery with considerable peace of mind. He would be well for the first time in ten years, and he would stay alive.

Paul recovered physically from surgery with no major complications. He learned how to take care of the appliance and was well on the road to recovery. He rather quickly gained back the more than fifty pounds he had lost during his last most severe siege of ulcerative colitis.

His emotional and social recovery were slower. Though his friends (gay and straight) and family were very supportive, and though he had no problems with his ostomy, Paul was reluctant to venture out to the bars and gay social groups. He tended to deny having any problems; he said he was "just fine." However, in follow-up clinic, his nurse encouraged his to go to UOA meetings and to open up to her about his feelings. He did come out to her when she let his know that he could speak to her about his sexual worries, and that it didn't matter to her whether he preferred women or men. This helped.

Eight months after surgery, Paul got up the courage to have his first sexual experience. He was awkward about telling his partner, but things worked out great and his partner said that the ostomy was no big deal. Paul has encountered a few men who are turned off, but by and large, his positive and matter-of-fact attitude has helped. Three years ago Paul met Steve, and they have lived together for the past two. Steve has been very supportive and has encouraged Paul to become involved in his UOA chapter and a support network of gay and lesbian ostomates. Paul even attended a national UOA conference in Boston in 1983 where a work-shop for gay and lesbian ostomates was offered. This was great for Paul. He really knew he was not alone. He talked for hours about things he had never verbalized before.

Paul joined a gym a few years ago and now takes a shower, sauna, and jacuzzi in the common areas. Some people stare at the pouch; a few ask about it; others say, "So that's what a 'colostomy' looks like. My uncle had one." He still feels a bit self-conscious, but this is not going to stop him — besides, he likes the visual stimulation at the gym too much not to go.

Paul occasionally feels sadness, anger, and disappoint-ment about the loss of his rectum and anus, and in his ability to receive anal sex. Sometimes he thinks he can't fully satisfy Steve. He used to feel uptight about the pouch during oral sex, since it was so close to his partner's face. Now he either wears the top strap of a jock strap around his waist and tucks the pouch under it, or he wears a very small inconspicuous pouch.

By and large, Paul feels that his life is much improved since surgery. He feels better about his body too.

Discussion of Case A: Paul not only had to deal with the loss of his colon, rectum, and anus, but he also had to cope with the loss of two important bodily functions, continence and being able to receive anal sex. These losses were accompanied by feelings of shame, humiliation, embarrassment, anger, and guilt. Finding a well-fitting appliance relieved his anxieties about incontinence and odor. The loss of some sexual functioning has been particularly painful; yet, he has been able to integrate this change into his body image. He has had to get used to the pouch which is an integral part of his body image. Because he is much healthier than he had been since the onset of ulcerative colitis, his new concept of his body is that it is strong, vital, and attractive; and that it is capable of letting him pursue his occupational, social, recreational, and most sexual desires. He has been helped to regain a positive body image by the support from friends, other people with ostomies, and the matter-of-fact way sexual partners and gym mates have reacted to it.

Paul's case is typical of the thirty-three gay male ostomates who took part in a survey that I conducted in 1983. However, a few of the men did not have as positive an outcome as Paul. Twenty percent of the men have refrained from sexual contact since surgery, and some have been rendered impotent (a common problem in colostomy and urostomy surgery). Two wished they had died instead of having the life-saving surgery. As with Paul, many of the men found a great deal of support from lovers and friends. Half were in committed relationships at the time of surgery. Several found a mate subsequent to surgery.

A relatively new surgery, ileal-anal pull through, is an alternative to a standard ostomy. It can be used only in ulcerative colitis cases and involves the creation of an internal pouch which is "hooked up" to the rectum and anus. An external pouch is not required. Many surgeons are now performing this surgery. Anal sex may be possible with this surgery; however, the matter should be discussed thoroughly with one's surgeon. It should be noted that approximately a hundred thousand ostomy surgeries are performed every year in the United States, which means that many gay men and lesbians have this procedure.

Case B: Ted is a 36-year-old man who was diagnosed a year ago with Kaposi's sarcoma, one of the AIDS-related diseases. Ted had suffered some weight loss, night sweats, fevers, nausea, diarrhea, and generalized lymphadenopathy for several months prior to the appearance of hard, brownish-pink spots (lesions) on his feet.

Before his first symptoms began, Ted was the picture of health. He jogged, played volleyball with a gay team, and worked out using Nautilus and free weights. Quite simply, Ted was a good-looking hunk. He liked his body; it worked for him; it was evident that others found him very attractive.

Ted has lost about twenty pounds in the last few months. Now, occasionally, he goes to the gym when he feels well. Too much exertion or running around leave him exhausted for two or three days. He has lost most of the body tone he worked so long and hard to achieve. HIs first lesions were easily concealed. Now they are appearing on his face, arms, and legs in spite of the chemotherapy treatments. His hair has fallen out. Two months ago he had to quit a good job as a computer programmer because his energy level had dropped so much.

Ted is painfully attempting to adjust to these major assaults on his former body image. He looks in the mirror and at times feels self-loathing. He is certain that others recoil from him (which may likely be a projection of his own disgust). He is frustrated that his body just won't do what it used to do. Needless to say, it has not been easy for Ted to find a new body image, especially because his body is undergoing so many changes and fluctuations. He is also facing the ultimate and final insult to his body — death. At 36 years of age, he wasn't prepared to consider this inevitability. He also worries about becoming sicker and dependent on others to help him carry out basic tasks of living.

Ted has been immensely supported by a lover of eight

years, by a support group of people with AIDS, a Shanti counselor, and very caring physicians and nurses. In the group of other persons with AIDS, he can really let his hair down. He expresses his feelings about his body and his perceptions of others' reactions to him. He knows the others understand because he's heard their stories. The people genuinely care and demonstrate it by their interest in each other and by physical affection. The group nearly cheered the day Ted showed up in shorts and a short-sleeved shirt. He said, "The hell with what people think. I'm going to be comfortable on these hot days." Ted has found a greater dimension to his sense of humor, which is of great help to him as he confronts with dignity the challenge of making the most of the remainder of life.

Discussion of Case B: There are many variations to Ted's story among people who have AIDS. Some men have a much worse and more rapid decline in the body. Most experience frustrating periods of sickness, pain, and despair followed by remission of symptoms and hope, only to be dashed when a new or more devastating symptom appears. The body simply breaks down in people with AIDS in a frustrating, erratic, and unpredictable way. Body image is similarly affected.

These two cases illustrate how body image — a complex, multi-faceted, intrapsychic experience — is affected by, and adapts to, actual changes in physical appearance and functioning.

ROLE OF THE HELPING PROFESSIONAL
Much has been written in the professional literature about helping a person negotiate the phases of the crisis that a major bodily change precipitates. The nurse, social worker, or counselor can play an important role in facilitating a favorable outcome in terms of body image. The helping persons can provide a listening ear to understand how the person is perceiving and reacting to the body change. They can allow ventilation of intense feelings. They can help the person in returning to work, social, and recreational activities. In the case of persons with AIDS, the health care giver should keep in mind both the quality of living that is still

possible and the quality of dying as the person approaches death.

The attitude of the professionals is also important. They must convey a matter-of-fact acceptance of the person even when his condition or appearance may be quite grotesque. Are the health professionals aware of their attitudes and feelings about gay men, gay sexual practices, and AIDS? It is much better to be aware of and admit any homophobia, than to pretend you are accepting when you are not. The patient can pick up a homophobic reaction.

Helping professionals can be of great help to the gay patient, specifically by knowing the resources available to gay men. There are many self-help organizations for all kinds of problems people face. These can be of great help. The helping professional can find out if these organizations also provide specific services to gay patients. You can contact the gay counseling or community center in your area to find out what is available for the gay patient.

BODY IMAGE AND THE "AVERAGE" GAY MAN

This chapter has focused mainly on what happens to body image when a traumatic event occurs to the body. But most gay men will never have AIDS, nor will they suffer a major assault to the body of the kinds that I have discussed. What about body image in the average gay man? Based on the limited research on this topic, and on much anecdotal data derived from personal conversations, the gay media, and counseling interviews, I feel comfortable asserting that many gay men have worked very hard to overcome painful childhood feelings and memories about their bodies. Efforts to improve the body and to feel good about it can greatly help in achieving a positive body image. Yet, gay men may be their own worst enemies, if they place too much value on external packaging. Gays who don't measure up to a standard they conceive as the ideal may continue to harbor negative feelings about their bodies. I don't intend to imply a criticism of the gay men who like to work out at body building. I enjoy working out and aerobicising myself. I like the way my body looks and how it feels when I work out. It also helps get me in shape for skiing and long-distance backpacking, and generally gets me awake and going each day. But hinging one's self-image and self-esteem exclusively or primarily on one's body image is asking for psychological trouble. What happens as we age and our bulging biceps, perfect pecs, and tight tummies are no longer what they used to be? What will happen to our bodies and self-images? Will we be able to accept with grace our changing bodies? Will our body images adjust accordingly? Will we be able to love that extra roll around the middle or under the chin in ourselves and our mates, or will we relentlessly pursue an illusion of youthful attractiveness that has long passed?

Do we cheat ourselves of friendships and relationships when someone doesn't measure up to our standards of beauty, or when we fail to approach someone whom we deem more attractive because we think he wouldn't be interested in us? Very good-looking men often say no one approaches them, or feel that others discount them as a piece of fluff just because they are attractive.

I have also talked with gay men who, as a defense against painful childhood memories of phys. ed. or gym class, take the position that all sports and physical activity are of no value to them. This extreme position betrays their ongoing body-image problems, and they miss out on chances to enjoy their bodies.

The healthiest mental attitude for a gay man to have toward his body (as with other aspects of his life) is to assess his options, choose his priorities wisely, and stick with them. It is best when the person decides what *he* wants to do with his body based on his inner convictions and feelings, rather than on the external pressures he perceives, or on the "shoulds" he hears from others and himself. The important thing is for the body to be an ally to us, to help us and support us in achieving our goals and our dreams.

In this chapter we have looked at how body image develops. We have looked at problems some gay men have in developing a positive mental representation of their bodies because of actual changes or perceived deficiencies in various aspects of the body's form and function. Specific body image problems in gay men have been discussed. I hope this information will be useful to gay and non-gay helping professionals in understanding how their gay patients perceive their bodies, and how they integrate the impact of minor fluctuations in and major assaults on the body into their body images.

REFERENCES

1. Bell, A.P., Martin, M.S., and Hammersmith, S.K. (1981). *Sexual Preference*. Bloomington, IN: Indiana University Press.

2. Blumstein, P., and Schwartz, P. (1983). *American couples*. New York: William Morrow & Co.

3. Henker, F.O. (1979). Body image conflict following trauma and surgery. *Psychosomatics, 20(12)*, 812-820.

4. Norris, C.M. (1978). Body image: Its relevance to professional nursing. In C.E. Carlson and B. Blackwell (Eds.), *Behavioral concepts and nursing intervention* (2nd Edition), (pp. 5-36). Philadelphia: J.B. Lippincott.

5. Prytula, R.E., *et al.* (1979). Body self image and the homosexual. *Journal of Clinical Psychology, 35(3)*, 567-572.

6. Roberts, S.L. (1976). *Behavioral concepts and the critically ill patient*. Englewood Cliffs, NJ: Prentice-Hall.

Chapter 5

Potential lesbian body image problems

Dana L. Broadway and Tammy K. Krotz

In order to consider potential problems with lesbian body image, one must first understand the body image of lesbians in general. Since we are talking only about potential problems, it will sometimes seem that we are over-generalizing; this is not the case. We recognize the variety of body images among lesbians. However, not all of these need to be taken into consideration. Our intention is to discuss only those body images which could pose problems to the lesbian client and, thus, be of concern to the health care professional.

By far the greatest problem the health care professional encounters in understanding the typical lesbian body image is that it is so different from the typical straight woman's body image. Straight women, along with straight man, almost invariably classify people as either masculine or feminine. This practice is inappropriate when dealing with the lesbian. The lesbian's self-image is very much one of individuality. She does not categorize her traits and characteristics as male or female, but simply as unique aspects of her lesbian self. The concept of androgyny must be incorporated into one's thinking when considering lesbian body image. As Sally Gearhart so aptly states, "I am no longer a woman-in-that-I-am-not-a-man; I am a woman in that I am a woman."(1)

Noting the fact that she "no longer" identifies herself as a non-man implies that a progressive maturation has taken place. We agree that this is the case for lesbians. The lesbian you are working with may find herself in any stage of this progression, ranging from total nonacceptance to complete acceptance of self.

Many lesbians are caught up in the struggle to be either masculine or feminine, while others have gone on to realize that these are not one's only choices. It is important to accurately assess the lesbian's stage in this progression, in order to guide her toward acceptance of her individuality.

An example of the advancement toward acceptance of self can be seen in the song, "Glad To Be A Woman," written in 1975 by Betsy Rose:

So many years I was bitter
Wanting to be someone else
Nature had formed me
And the world had conformed me
Into thinking I should be less
Than the bravest and the best
Better find me a nest to take care of
And let somebody stronger take care of me

But now I'm glad to be a woman
I'm so glad to be alive
Glad for the children who take my place
Glad for the will to survive(3)

Not only is lack of acceptance of lesbian body image a problem that the health care professional may have, but it may also be a problem on the part of the lesbian client. Yet, her difficulty in dealing with this may require the assistance of the health care professional.

We have stated that assessments of a lesbian's own body image must be made by the health care professional. From here we would like to consider some specific areas of lesbian body image that will facilitate these assessments.

Dress is one of the most powerful manifestations of body image. This phenomenon is no less common in lesbians than it is in others, so observation of dress is an important method for understanding lesbian body image.

Dana relates an encounter with a therapist dealing with this very aspect of lesbian body image:

I recall getting dressed one morning, a ritual which had become a daily hassle. Faced with the difficult task of dressing as a typical college coed, I came to the conclusion that dressing in this manner did not express the image I had of myself. Tossing aside the dress pants and fancy shoes, I instead slipped into a pair of Levi's, a sweat shirt, high-topped basketball shoes, and a denim vest. Smiling and confident, I set out to face the world.

It just so happened that this was the day for my weekly visit to the therapist. Upon entering his office, my feeling of assurance was shattered. The entire visit was spent discussing my appearance and the effect it had on people's perception of me. He concluded that I was intentionally scaring off the world by trying to dress "tough." I left the office feeling even more confused than I had that morning. I didn't know whether to follow my instincts or the advice of this "professional."

Tammy and I believe that this therapist could have acted in a manner which was more beneficial to my self-acceptance. The discussion would have proved more profitable had it delved into my feelings and my reasons why I felt more comfortable with myself when dressed in this way.

Health care professionals should realize that lesbians have probably been defending the way they dress since early childhood. Many lesbians recount stories of their rejection of the typically female attire as far back as three or four years of age. It seems that many saw the dress code for the young girl as too limiting; this especially holds true in the case of the tomboy.

We found that tomboy behavior and dress is acceptable, until the lesbian reaches that magical age when she is expected to miraculously transform herself into a young lady. In most cases, this is expected to occur in the teenage years. Tammy remembers one such incident — a story with which many lesbians can probably sympathize.

One day when I was thirteen, my mother suggested to me that I begin carrying a purse, as most of the girls were doing at the time. I turned up my nose at the suggestion, but this was not enough to thwart her effort. She came home from shopping one day with a purse she wanted me to carry.

I conceded defeat, went to my room, and attempted to find objects to take up space in this so necessary purse. I finally hunted down those belongings which would be placed in my purse: my billfold (which was normally placed in one back pocket), my comb (which fit super in the other), a pen or pencil (which already had a space in my backpack), and my notebooks for school (which didn't fit anyway). I saw no real reason for disturbing my individual pattern, but decided to carry my purse to school the next day. And believe me, that's as long as it lasted! I put everything back in its proper place when I returned home, explained to my mother that it was just not me, and to this day have yet to find anything that necessitates my carrying of a purse.

The peer and parental pressure in many cases is, in itself, enough to warrant the concern of the health care professionals. They should be aware of the battles the lesbian is fighting within herself. An attempt to conform is often used by the lesbian as a means of postponing the need to defend her individuality. The health care professional needs to be in tune to this defense mechanism. Helping the lesbian to come to terms with her individuality would provide more positive results than allowing her continued avoidance of the issue.

The lesbian's choice of dress is usually a personal preference, but there is another aspect of body image relating to this, that is not quite as controllable.

We feel that the lesbian's body language is possibly the strongest indication of her body image. We see body language as consisting of several components, including carriage of body, seated posture, and gestures.

Anyone who has ever watched a high school graduation ceremony has undoubtedly seen the awkwardness of a lesbian suddenly strapped into high heels to receive her diploma. For the lesbian who walks in what is often referred to as a masculine manner, this type of occurrence is obviously an uncomfortable situation. Not all cases are going to be this obvious — far from it. Health care professionals need to be conscious of any inconsistencies, and be willing to help the lesbian work through these in a manner that is appropriate to her body image.

Seated posture is also a signal of the lesbian's body image that can be observed by the health care professional. We have noticed a tendency on the part of some lesbians to assume a more open, relaxed posture. This seems to purvey a less restricted image than that of the typical heterosexual woman.

Along these lines, we feel that many lesbians also tend to exhibit a more assertive personality through their actions and gestures. Here we are referring to the high occurrence of such things as direct eye contact and hand shakes, and hugs in the lesbian community.

The above aspects of body image, in and of themselves, usually do not present a problem. The problem may arise through a destruction of this body image by some outside source, such as mental or physical illness. We, therefore, feel it is important to point out this potential body image problem for some lesbians, so that health care professionals will know of its existence.

Another common body image we feel it is important to be aware of is the athletic or "jock" type. Some lesbians have developed a body image that revolves around their athletic ability. This could tend to give the lesbian a more masculine appearance. The health care professional should beware not to fall into the trap of assuming that a body built for competition entails all of the psychological aspects of the masculine persona, however. Holly Near sings of this apparent incongruity:

> The jock is dressed in wool tonite
> She's got a baseball glove, a cap tonite
> There's a competitive look in her eye
> In spite of her generous heart(2)

While being presumed to be ultramasculine is one of the potential problems involved with the athletic body image of the lesbian, it is not the only facet of this body image that we wish to examine. The concept of size in the lesbian body image seems to stem, in some degree, from this athletic ideal. Largeness seems to be incorporated to a greater extent into the lesbian body image than into the body image of the heterosexual female. We feel that this is related, at least in part, to the idea of athletic competence.

Lesbians seem less restricted by standards of size and weight than do heterosexual women. While physical appearance does hold some importance in lesbian culture, it does not seem to carry the same weight as it does in other sexual orientations. We mention this because it does pose some unique problems that health care professionals may encounter in their dealings with lesbians. The potential for problems again depends on the individual lesbian's point in the progression toward self-acceptance.

On the one hand, a problem may exist if the lesbian is still struggling to fulfill a set of standards which, for her, may be nearly impossible. It is not unheard of for a lesbian who is still trying to pass as straight to attempt to become thinner than is biologically possible. The physical manifestations of this attempt may be what brings the health care professional into the picture.

On the other hand, the health care professional may be faced with the other extreme, a lesbian who has totally rejected heterosexual standards. In doing so, she has allowed herself to become overweight to the point that it is unhealthy.

Another potential problem we see with the notion of size in the lesbian body image is the false sense of security that being large provides in the heterosexual world. Some lesbians see themselves as extremely capable of protecting themselves and tend to ignore the precautions taken by many hetero-sexual women. Because of this feeling, lesbians may be more inclined to endanger themselves physically.

This, in turn, leads to what we feel is one of the largest threats to the lesbian body image. While rape is devastating no matter who the victim is, there are additional ramifications for the lesbian. Many lesbians reject completely the notion of male power, and feel that male dominance is an obsolete idea. In the act of rape, the rapist forces the lesbian, at least momentarily, to assume the submissive role. The potential here for a complete destruction of the body image that the lesbian has developed exists.

The health care professional should be sure to consider this added dimension when dealing with the lesbian rape victim. We would also like to caution the health care profes-sional not to make the assumption that, because this is an unmarried woman, there are no additional problems as to lover or sexual relationships that need to be considered.

As a final reminder, we would like to re-emphasize an idea that is intertwined with everything that we have mentioned

— that is, the great likelihood that health care professionals probably do not live by the same standards as do many lesbians. For health care professionals, this is important to remember when dealing with any lesbian. But it becomes increasingly important if the lesbian is incapable of making her concerns known.

With Dana working in a care facility, we have often discussed our fears about the generic manner in which elderly women are cared for. It is possible that none of these women have body images similar to our own, but it is more likely that at least a few do. We cannot, however, identify them because they can no longer express there body images, and no one is helping them to do so. All wear dresses.

What we, as lesbians, are asking of the health care professional is a respect for our cultural differences. We have discussed, throughout this chapter, the distinctiveness of the lesbian body image. We would like to reiterate that we are in no way attempting a description of all lesbian body images. We would simply like health care professionals to become better aware of some of those images that hold the potential for problems for health care professionals and their lesbian clients.

REFERENCES

1. Gearhart, S. (1978). The spiritual dimension: Death and resurrection of a hallelujah dyke. In G. Vida (Ed.), *Our right to love: A lesbian resource book* (pp. 187-193). Englewood Cliffs, NJ: Prentice-Hall.

2. Near, H. (1983). Perfect night. *Holly Near and Ronnie Gilbert, LIFELINE*, Redwood Records.

3. Rose, B. (1982). Glad to be a woman. *Meg Christian and Chris Williamson at Carnegie Hall*, Olivia Records.

Chapter 6
Alcoholism in the gay and lesbian communities

Robert J. Kus

In this chapter, we will examine one of the greatest health problems facing adult gay and lesbian Americans: alcoholism and related forms of chemical dependencies. After a brief overview of the nature of this disease, we will look at the incidence of alcoholism in the gay and lesbian communities and consider some of the theories proposed to explain gay and lesbian alcoholism etiology. We then will look at how gay and lesbian clients, due to their vulnerability in alcoholic treatment centers because of their stigmatized sexual orientation and unpopular disease, often suffer under the treatment of those members of the staff who are homophobic, anti-alcoholic, or unknowledgeable about the gay or lesbian client. Following the discussion on problem areas often found in alcoholism treatment, hints are offered on how health professionals, such as nurses, alcoholism counselors, social workers, and physicians, can be helpful to the gay and lesbian client. Finally, we will look at a few case histories that illustrate how helping professionals have been both helpful and harmful to gay and lesbian clients.

THE NATURE OF ALCOHOLISM

Alcoholism is a chronic, progressive disease which is fatal if not treated. Further, although it is an incurable disease, it can be arrested through abstinence from alcohol. Alcoholism produces complications for its victims in all aspects of their lives.(10, 13) Besides the victims, alcoholism has grave adverse effects on realms such as the economy and public safety. It is estimated that twenty to fifty percent of all hospitalized patients in both mental and physical hospital wards are suffering from this disease, and there is great evidence that the overwhelming majority of persons suffering in this nation's prisons are there for behaviors acted out while intoxicated.

In the *Physical realm*, alcoholism creates a virtually unlimited repertoire of complications in all body systems: complications such as hepatitis, cirrhosis, esophagitis, and gastritis in the gastrointestinal system; dementia, Korsakoff's syndrome, and peripheral neuropathy in the neurological system; thrombocytopenia, anemia, leukopenia, and megaloblastic hematopoiesis in the blood system; alcoholic cardiomyopathy in the cardiac system; acute and chronic myopathy in the skeletal system; lacerations and bruises in the integumentary system; and nutritional disorders such as alcoholic pellagra, malnutrition, beriberi, and hypoglycemia. [For an excellent overview of alcoholic complications seen in the various physical and mental body systems, the reader is directed to Estes and Heinemann's *Alcoholism: Development, consequences, and interventions* (2nd edition). St. Louis: C.V. Mosby, 1982.] Further, alcoholism may produce fetal alcohol syndrome, as well as alcohol addiction, in the unborn child.

In the *psychosocial realms*, alcoholism negatively affects virtually all aspects of the victim's life. Job performance suffers in both quality and quantity as the victim's disease progresses. The financial state of the alcoholic suffers. Mentally, the victim experiences symptoms of depression and sometimes mania combined with guilt, low self-esteem, denial, rationalization, and suicidal ideation. Presentation of self begins to change; the alcoholic becomes emotionally unstable and overreacts to life's everyday problems. Problems maintaining good relationships with family, friends, and mate also appear. This often leads to estrangement of the alcoholic from significant support systems such as husband, wife, or lover. Domestic violence directed toward one's lover or children is sometimes seen. The alcoholic begins experiencing ever-increasing feelings of loneliness and of being misunderstood. Spiritually, the alcoholic may abandon hope altogether; in this case, suicide is the result.

Sexual behavior may also be affected by drinking, and this is especially dangerous today in the Age of AIDS. In recent studies exploring sexuality among gay men, for example, it was found that in their drinking days, gay American men virtually always drink before having sex.(7) This leads one to seriously consider the idea that gay men who engage in unsafe sexual practices may in fact be doing so not as a result of a "knowledge deficit" of safe sex, but rather as a result of being intoxicated.(11)

For *society at large*, alcoholism places a tremendous drain on the economy. It fills our prisons and buries thousands of victims of drunk driving.

In summary, alcoholism is like an all-pervasive poisonous vapor. Almost no one in our society escapes its distressing and often deadly touch.

INCIDENCE AND ETIOLOGY

Studies conducted in the United States indicate that between twenty and thirty-three percent of the entire gay and lesbian adult population are afflicted with alcoholism or at the very least have a drinking problem.(2, 18, 21, 22) This is a far higher percent than that found in the population at large. For example, Saghir and Robbins found that thirty-five percent of lesbians fit an "excessive drinking behavior" or "alcohol dependency" pattern compared to only five percent of heterosexual women, and thirty percent of gays compared to twenty percent of heterosexual men.(22)

Because of this high incidence of alcoholism, determining the etiology has been seen as critical. If the etiology were known, we could not only explain the incidence of gay and lesbian alcoholism, but we could take measures to prevent its development. Unfortunately, very few scientific studies have been undertaken to uncover the etiology. Rather, much of what we assume about etiology and incidence is based on untested theory.

Three major theories of etiology have been proposed: gay bar ethnotheory, multi-factor theory, and gay non-acceptance theory.

Gay bar ethnotheory is a folk explanation of etiology and of incidence of alcoholism. It holds that because gays and lesbians must resort to gay or lesbian bars to be free and to meet others of their sexual orientation, and because there is a "fraternity syndrome" atmosphere where excessive alcohol use is accepted, gay people will develop alcoholism.

The multi-factor theory holds the gay bar ethnotheory to be true, but it also attempts to explain etiology, and thus incidence, on the basis of additional factors: the internalized homophobia seen in the early stages of the coming out process, whereby the individual experiences guilt, low self-esteem, shame, and social oppression (the external homophobia manifested through discrimination against gay and lesbian Americans).

The gay non-acceptance theory(6, 15) holds that gay bars have nothing to do with alcoholism etiology in gays and lesbians. Further, it rejects the notion that social oppression per se leads one to become alcoholic. If this were so, Jews would have a very high alcoholism rate; in actuality, they have one of the lowest rates of any minority. What this theory does say is that the etiology of alcoholism is due to internalized homophobia which is seen in the stages of the coming out process which precede Acceptance. [See Chapter 3 for a description of Acceptance.] Thus, alcoholism develops in men and women who do not accept their non-chosen sexual orientation as a positive state of being. Continuing further, the theory states that if gays and lesbians could achieve Acceptance of their homosexual orientation, i.e., if they could be positive about it, then sobriety would follow.

In two recent ethnographic studies exploring these theories, all of the gay recovering alcoholic men had begun drinking alcoholically long before they experienced gay bars. In fact, most reported that they had begun drinking alcoholically from their very first drink.(10, 13, 15,) I further found that in one hundred percent of the cases, being gay was not seen as a positive aspect of self until *after* sobriety was chosen and lived for some time. Even men who thought they had accepted their orientation while drinking admitted that it was not until sobriety that they became truly thankful for being created gay. On the basis of my research findings, I rejected both gay bar ethnotheory and multi-factor theories. My findings also required that I revise the conclusion I had hypothesized. My modified conclusion is that sobriety leads to acceptance, and not the other way around. Further, the gays I interviewed all recognized that without self-acceptance of their homosexuality, sobriety would be most difficult to maintain through time and that serenity, or peacefulness, would be virtually impossible. In addition to non-acceptance of gay self, it would appear that there must be an existing genetic predisposition for alcoholism to develop.

PROBLEM AREAS IN STAFF AND TREATMENT CENTERS

Helping professionals and alcohol treatment centers are theoretically equipped with the necessary knowledge and dedication to provide all clients with top quality care. Unfortunately, this is not always true. Gay and lesbian clients often report being hindered, rather than helped, in their recovery from alcoholism by such professionals and centers. Some of these commonly experienced problems are unique to gay and lesbian clients, while others are experienced by all alcoholics. In this section, we look at some of both sorts of problems.

First, despite the fact that twenty to fifty percent of all hospitalized patients suffer from this disease, many helping professionals have little knowledge about the disease, its many complications, and its incidence. Many erroneously believe it is merely a "symptom" of some other disorder which, if treated, will make the alcoholism go away. Others, who are unaware of its incidence in society, neglect to take a careful alcohol history on their clients — a history which many times would lead to the detection of the disease. Others, oblivious to the signs and symptoms of alcoholism, misdiagnose clients. When this occurs, the treatment prescribed often not only does nothing to help the client's alcoholism, but in fact may be detrimental. For example, alcoholism leads to low self-esteem, guilt, and feelings of hopelessness. A clinician who does not recognize this alcoholic pattern may mistakenly diagnose the client as "depressed." When this occurs, anti-depressants may be prescribed. Not only does this do nothing for the client's main problem, but it may lead to polydrug abuse as the client combines the anti-depressant drug with alcohol use.

Second, many helping professionals are very anti-alcoholic. They see alcoholism not as a disease, but rather as a condition resulting from a weak character or from immature coping. Thus, clients are seen as the causative agents, rather than as the victims of the disease; alcoholism is seen as the clients' "own fault."

Third, many clinicians hold negative attitudes toward gays and lesbians. Some of these attitudes are in the *cognitive,* or belief-disbelief, realm. Examples of these attitudes would be "All lesbians are man-haters" or "Gays choose to be gay" or "Gays are incapable of establishing quality relationships." Negative attitudes in the *affective,* or like-dislike, realm are called *homophobia,* the fear or hatred of gays and lesbians. Examples would be "I'm afraid to be alone with a lesbian" or "It makes me sick to think of two men in bed together" or "I hate all queers." Finally, negative attitudes may be in the *behavioral potential* realm, the realm of "readiness to act." Examples of this type of attitude would be "I'd vote against any gay candidate" or "I don't think gays should be allowed to adopt children." Often the negativity is directed more toward one's own sex than the other sex. For example, women are often more negative toward lesbians, while men are more negative toward gays.

Fourth, the negative attitudes of staff members may be acted out against the gay or lesbian client. This acting-out behavior, called *discrimination,* is shown in many ways. Forbidding the gay client to share a room with a same-sex roommate; requiring gay clients to disclose their sexual orientation in group therapy while not requiring hetero-sexuals to do the same; treating such clients with disrespect, disdain, or pity; and using confrontation more aggressively with them than with other clients, are all examples of how this action can occur. Staff members who are highly negative toward homosexuality are also more likely to attempt to "treat" the client's homosexuality, rather than the alcoholism.

Fifth, the clinician may use language highly offensive to the gay or lesbian client. Usually this is the result of ig-norance, rather than being a deliberate act rooted in negative attitudes. For example, calling clients "homosexuals" may immediately put gay clients on the defensive, if they hate this term. And it may destroy trust, as the clients wonder, "Where in the world has this therapist been? That's like calling a black person a Negro!" The other main language offense is using the word "choice" when discussing the client's homosexual orientation. No one chooses to be gay or lesbian, and any clinician who implies that is not only insensitive but incredibly ignorant, and deserving of the contempt the client will surely feel toward him or her.

Sixth, clinicians are often unable to distinguish between gays and lesbians psychologically and socially. They erroneously believe that since they are all "homosexuals," they must be the same. This false perception is the result of a lack of knowledge about gays and lesbians. Gays' society, culture, lifestyles, and oppression as men and gays, are radically different from lesbians' society, culture, lifestyles, and oppression as women and lesbians.

Seventh, because clinicians often fail to distinguish between gay and lesbian clients, they may believe that a lesbian therapist would be good for a gay client, or a gay therapist good for a lesbian client. This is not necessarily the case. Lesbians, for example, often prefer a woman therapist regardless of her sexual orientation, while gays may prefer a therapist, regardless of sex, who is understanding and compassionate.

Eighth, clinicians are often unaware of what resources are available in the gay and lesbian communities. As a result, they often fail to inform the client about the gay, lesbian or gay-lesbian AA groups, or gay or lesbian support groups which might help the client to work on self-acceptance.

Ninth, many alcohol treatment staffs, while recognizing the extent of alcoholism in the gay and lesbian communities, still refuse to have openly gay and lesbian staff members. The idea that a gay staff member might be more helpful to the gay man, or a lesbian staff member more helpful to a lesbian client, than would be a straight male or female counselor, is met with disdain. The presence of gay and lesbian staff members is perceived by some heterosexual staff members as an admission of inadequacy, or as a challenge to competency and skill. Thus, gays and lesbians are often treated by persons who are either negative in their attitudes about gays and lesbians, or unknowledgeable about them, or both.

Finally, gay and lesbian clients' loved ones are often neglected in the plan of care. Such treatment center activities as "spouses' night" or couples' counseling or "family night" are often denied to the lovers and other support systems of gays and lesbians. After all, it is rationalized, the gay lover is "not really a spouse," and, so, does not "deserve" the same consideration and assistance that spouses in male-female marriages receive.

HOW THE HELPING PROFESSIONAL CAN HELP

First, relax! Oftentimes clinicians get so concerned with offending gay and lesbian clients that they become immobilized. The number one way you can help gay and lesbian clients is to show genuine concern and caring, to present a willingness to learn as well as to assist, and to possess a sense of humor to match that which you will most likely find in your client. This warm presentation of self will overshadow any faux pas you might make!

Second, if you are a clinician not directly concerned with alcohol treatment, expand your knowledge of this disease. Pay particular attention to the behavioral manifestations of alcoholism, manifestations such as overreacting to life situations, frequent accidents, having continual crises, calling in sick at work frequently, and symptoms mimicking depression or hypomania. Also be aware of the physical complications of the disease. I am always amazed at how often conditions resulting from alcoholism are treated without looking also at the alcoholism.

Third, expand your knowledge of gay and lesbian alcoholism issues by reading scholarly works such as Finnegan & McNally's *Dual identities: Counseling chemically dependent gay men and lesbians* (3) and Ziebold & Mongeon's *Gay and sober: Directions for counseling and therapy.*(23)

Fourth, take alcohol histories on all your clients. This is especially important in the case of adult gay and lesbian clients, due to the high incidence of alcoholism in this population. Most gays and lesbians probably will not announce their sexual orientation to you, so this is another area to explore in history-taking. Ask if the client is "coupled," instead of whether the client is married. If the answer is yes, ask questions such as "Do you live with him or her?" rather than assume the partner is of the opposite sex. And finally, when asking clients if they have sex "mostly with men, with women, or with both." This will demonstrate that you will not be blown away by any response.

Fifth, learn as much as possible about gays and lesbians. If you are in an alcohol treatment center, invite openly gay people, both recovering alcoholics and non-alcoholics, to speak with the staff. Because you are reading this book, you are already demonstrating your desire to grow in knowledge and, therefore, to grow therapeutically. Ask the speakers to recommend good books for you to read, ask them to fill you in on what resources are available in the gay and lesbian communities, and make them feel that they are valuable resources. As your knowledge increases, the chances of your using offensive vocabulary and holding myths about gays and lesbians will decrease, and you will probably feel more confident in your ability to help, rather than hinder, the gay or lesbian client's recovery.

Sixth, encourage your client to attend gay, lesbian, or gay-lesbian AA meetings. These not only allow the client to learn about Alcoholics Anonymous while sharing common concerns, but they can also help the client to deal with internalized homophobia.(9) If your treatment center does not have these meetings, and most will not, make arrangements for the client to attend one in the community, if this is possible. And do not be surprised if the client is unhappy attending such meetings at first. After all, many clients in treatment still have a great deal of internalized homophobia. But assure the client that in time, this will pass, through conscientious effort.

Seventh, share with your client some of the ways other gay and lesbian alcoholics have found help in maintaining sobriety and accepting their sexual orientation. In my studies on gay sobriety, for example, many gays reported certain things which helped them immensely: doing the Fourth Step and working through their anger and resentments, especially about being created gay; making friends with other gay recovering alcoholics; extending the concept of "powerlessness" over alcohol to include one's sexual orientation and, therefore, to expand the Serenity Prayer phrase "to accept the things I cannot change" to include sexual orientation; and to communicate with their Higher Power. Of all the above helps listed in my study, none was seen as more important than communicating with the Higher Power.(5) But don't expect miracles. Many gays and lesbians are so angry at God, the church, family, and society, that it may take a while in sobriety before the wisdom of these strategies is grasped and practiced. Even atheists can benefit from the AA approach, particularly if they interpret the AA's traditionalist religious vocabulary as metaphorically related to their own world view. Also, many recovering alcoholics find having a sponsor to be immensely helpful.(8) And they find reading positive literature to be an integral part of their recovery program.(14, 16, 17) Especially helpful is reading positive gay and lesbian alcoholism literature such as those by Michael(19, 20) and stories of gays and lesbians who are recovering from alcoholism.(4)

Eighth, if you are in a rural area that does not have the benefits of open gay and lesbian communities, encourage speakers to come from the city. Gays and lesbians are not just an urban people. At least ten percent of all your clients, whether you know it or not, are gay or lesbian. Likewise, if your community does not have a gay, lesbian, or gay-lesbian AA group, encourage one to be formed. It only takes two recovering alcoholics to have a group. If this is not possible, write and ask the national headquarters of AA to put you in contact with such a group in a nearby city, one that would extend its friendship to your rural gay or lesbian client. The client could then be considered a "loner" member of AA and benefit from contact with recovering gays or lesbians via letters, phone calls, and visits.

Ninth, examine your own negative attitudes about homosexuality. Try to rid yourself of them. The best way is to meet and interact with as many gays and lesbians as possible, as well as to read positive gay literature.

Tenth, as long as you are ridding yourself of these negative attitudes, examine yourself for signs of anti-alcoholic ideation. While this might not be problematic for the alcohol treatment specialist, it is a very common problem seen in other clinicians. Do you see alcoholism as the client's fault? Or alcoholic drinking as a failure of will power? Read about and attend lectures or workshops on the subject.

Eleventh, be the client's advocate. For example, in many treatment centers, alcoholism counselors are assigned patients on a rotating basis. Often this leads to a homophobic counselor being assigned to a gay or lesbian client, when another staff member would be much more beneficial. Fight against such rigid policies, and be ready to confront homophobic rhetoric or discrimination when observed in others.

Twelfth, remember that gays are different than lesbians. Scholars of gay studies and those of lesbian studies have both consistently shown that one's gender is far more important in understanding folks than is their sexual orientation. Do not expect lesbians to fully understand the gay male experience, any more than you should expect gays to completely relate to the lesbian experience.

Thirteenth, if you are in an alcohol treatment center, create a "set" indicating your concern for gay and lesbian clients. This can be accomplished by posting a list of gay, lesbian, and gay-lesbian AA meetings, by having gay and lesbian alcoholism literature where other literature is displayed, and by using terminology such as "lover" in groups, in addition to using the term "spouse."

Fourteenth, include the client's lover and other support systems as you would include the married person's spouse and relatives. Encourage the lover to attend Al-Anon meetings. Invite gay clients and their support systems to family night. In short, include whomever clients see as their significant others in the plan of care.

Finally, build a network of gay and lesbian therapists who are knowledgeable about alcoholism and who are willing to volunteer to visit with gay and lesbian clients. Often an outside volunteer gay therapist can work on a gay man's internalized homophobia while the regular treatment staff focuses on the alcoholism.(12) The same would hold true of a lesbian therapist working with lesbian clients. In addition, such volunteers often work with staff to help them be better therapists for their gay and lesbian clients.

CASE HISTORIES

Case #1 — Sandi: Sandi, a 53-year-old lesbian, began

having trouble with alcoholism when she was only 22 years old. Although she knew she was a lesbian and had many lesbian acquaintances, she always saw her sexual orientation as a negative aspect of self. Because she was working as an R.N. in a mental hospital when her drinking reached the crisis stage, she was taken by her colleagues to another state hospital to protect her anonymity. The physician in charge of her ward assured her that indeed, she could not possibly be an alcoholic as she was "too young." Relieved to learn this, Sandi left the hospital and lasted outside for less than a week. Six days after being discharged, she was arrested for public drunkenness, disturbing the peace, resisting arrest, and attempting suicide. The judge, following her request, sent her back to the same hospital where this time the physician agreed that perhaps she might be an alcoholic after all. For the next twenty years, Sandi attempted different strategies for dealing with her alcoholism. At times, she tried controlled drinking, always with disastrous results. At other times, she would "go on the wagon." This strategy would last until the last drunk and hangover were forgotten; then the alcoholic drinking would begin anew. And finally, Sandi attended Alcoholics Anonymous halfheartedly. Although she was able to maintain an alcohol-free existence for periods of time — she celebrated her AA first birthday at least six times — she never accepted the reality that she was indeed powerless over alcohol, nor did she accept her homosexual orientation as a positive part of herself. During this twenty-year period, Sandi was hospitalized numerous times in state mental hospitals for suicide gestures and "depression." After being unsuccessfully treated with electroconvulsive treatments (E.C.T), she was diagnosed as having "manic-depressive illness" and given the salt lithium. Also during these years of on-again, off-again drinking, she lost her R.N. license because she stole patient drugs. At age 43, she finally "surrendered," that is, she admitted that she was indeed powerless over alcohol. Through AA, she began experiencing sobriety, and in her sobriety she began to feel serenity, or a sense of peacefulness. For the first time in her life, being lesbian was seen as something good rather than evil. This sobriety, which changed virtually all aspects of her life for the better, led her to be able to cope with her losing her license. It also helped her choose another field, that of alcoholism counseling. She interpreted the state Board of Nursing's reluctance to grant her her license back as a sign from the Higher Power that a profession which does not have access to mind-altering drugs would be a better choice for her than nursing. Today, after several years of sobriety she is helping others through the sensitivity gained through suffering; she is now a "wounded healer."

This story, showing how non-acceptance of homosexual orientation may lead to alcoholism, is also important in illustrating how alcoholics are often misdiagnosed and mis-treated. In particular, they are often diagnosed as having "endogenous depression" or bipolar affective disorder ("manic-depressive illness") and treated accordingly. Inter-estingly enough, in the twenty years of hospitalizations Sandi experienced after her first brush with the psychiatrist, no one ever took an alcohol history on her, and never once in all that time did anyone do an adequate sexual history.

Case #2 — Jon: Jon, a 32-year-old L.P.N. with a bachelor's degree, began drinking at age 18 and drank alcoholically with his very first drink. When he was 28, he was admitted to a big city Texas hospital for "depression." His lesbian psychi-atrist, because she knew quite well the extent of alcoholism in the gay and lesbian communities, did a thorough alcohol history on Jon. She quickly changed his diagnosis from depression to alcoholism, a move which made Jon rather angry. However, he continued seeing this women psychiatrist for seven months, during which time he was able to remain alcohol-free. But this was not good enough for Jon, who had not accepted the idea of being "powerless" over alcohol. So he sought out a second opinion. The second physician was able to be easily convinced that Jon was not an alcoholic, but rather a "manic-depressive." Four days after learning the happy news that he was not an alcoholic after all, Jon was drinking a fifth of Scotch a day. After all, he rationalized, that was okay since he was not an alcoholic. For the next two years, Jon was able to hold down a job working on-call for a nursing agency for which he did private-duty nursing. As time went on, he began taking fewer and fewer cases, and all of his cases had to be on the eleven-to-seven overnight shift, as he was becoming more and more afraid of people. His sister, with whom he was living, watched his deterioration. He developed a terror of red cars. He would crawl down the hallway in the house and peek around the corner to see if there were anyone in the living room. If there were, he would quickly crawl back to his room, where he was remaining more and more reclusively. Finally, his sister had him committed. With alcohol treatment, plus the help of a local gay AA group, Jon finally admitted his powerlessness over alcohol, and he was able to see that the "acceptance" of being gay was not actually realized all the years he was drinking. Today he is grateful for being gay and for being alcoholic, the two things which had in the past been seen as the two things to be angry about. Today he is growing in sobriety and is especially pleased at the remarkable change in his mental and physical health.

Not only does this case show how the alcoholic can be misdiagnosed, but it also shows how staff, who are knowledgeable about gay men and their alcoholism incidence, can often pinpoint the real problem quite easily. In fact, any gay or lesbian admitted for depression or suicidal gestures should be checked out for alcoholism. Further, Jon's case also shows how alcoholic patients, by their stories, are often able to manipulate physicians and others to provide a diagnosis more "acceptable" than alcoholism. Finally, it shows how Jon used the gay AA group to help him achieve not only sobriety, but a new way of understanding what being gay is all about. Now he sees being gay as something over which he is powerless — a non-chosen state of being which is a gift from God. And, armed with that part of the Serenity Prayer which states, "God, grant me the serenity to accept the things I cannot change...," Jon is catching glimpses of a peace he has missed for so many years.

REFERENCES

1. Estes, N.J. and Heinemann, M.E. (1982). *Alcoholism: Development, consequences, and interventions* (2nd edition). St. Louis: C.V. Mosby.

2. Fifield, L. (1975). *On my way to nowhere: Alienated, isolated, drunk.*

Los Angeles: Gay Community Services Center and Department of Health Services.

3. Finnegan, D.G. and McNally, E.B. (1987). *Dual identities: Counseling chemically dependent gay men and lesbians.* Center City, MN: Hazelden.

4. Gay Council on Drinking Behavior. (1981-2). *The way back: The stories of gay and lesbian alcoholics* (2nd edition). Washington, D.C.: Whitman-Walker Clinic.

5. Kus, R.J. (1985a, September). *Gays and their Higher Power: An ethnography of gay society.* Paper presented at the first national conference of the National Association of Lesbian & Gay Alcoholism Professionals, Chicago, IL.

6. Kus, R.J. (1985b, May). Stages of coming out: An ethnographic approach. *Western Journal of Nursing Research, 7(2),* 177-198.

7. Kus, R.J. (1985c, November). *Sex and sobriety: The gay experience.* Paper presented at the National Symposium of Nursing Research, San Francisco, CA.

8. Kus, R.J. (1986). *The Alcoholics Anonymous sponsor & gay American men.* Paper presented at the 32nd International Institute on the Prevention & Treatment of Alcoholism, Budapest, Hungary.

9. Kus, R.J. (1987a). Alcoholics Anonymous and gay American men. *Journal of Homosexuality, 14(1-2),* 253-276.

10. Kus, R.J. (1987b). *Sobriety & the quality of life: Perceptions of gay American men.* Paper presented at the Seventh International Conference on Alcohol Related Problems, Liverpool, England.

11. Kus, R.J. (1987c), Sex, AIDS, and gay American men. *Holistic Nursing Practice, 1(4),* 42-51.

12. Kus, R.J. (1987d). Gay consultations in non-gay treatment settings. *Professional Counselor, 2(1),* 46-55.

13. Kus, R.J. and Stewart-Dedmon, M. (1987, June). *Heading for trouble: Early signs of relapse as identified by gay American men of A.A.* Paper presented at the 33rd International Institute on the Prevention & Treatment of Alcoholism, Lausanne, Switzerland.

14. Kus, R.J. (1988, August). Working the program: The A.A. experience and gay American men. *Holistic Nursing Practice, 2(4),* 62-74.

15. Kus, R.J. (1988). Alcoholism and nonacceptance of gay self: The critical link. *Journal of Homosexuality, 15(1-2),* 23-41.

16. Kus, R.J. (1989). Bibliotherapy and gay American men of Alcoholics Anonymous. *Journal of Gay & Lesbian Psychotherapy, 1(2),* 73-86.

17. Kus, R.J. (1988, July). *Alcoholism, gay liberation, and gay American men.* Paper presented at the 12th International Congress of Anthropological & Ethnological Sciences, Zagreb, Yugoslavia.

18. Lohrenz, L., Connelly, J., Coyne, L., and Spare, K. (1978). Alcohol problems in several midwestern communities. *Journal of Alcohol*

Studies, 39(11), 1959-1963.

19. Michael, J. (1976). *The gay drinking problem — there is a solution.* Minneapolis: CompCare.

20. Michael, J. (1977). *Sober, clean, & gay!* Minneapolis: CompCare.

21. Morales, E.S. and Graves, M.A. (1983). *Substance abuse: Patterns and barriers to treatment for gay men and lesbians in San Francisco.* San Francisco: San Francisco Prevention Resources Center.

22. Saghir, M. and Robbins, E. (1973). *Male and female homosexuality.* Baltimore: Williams & Wilkins.

23. Ziebold, T.O. and Mongeon, J.E. (Eds.) (1985). *Gay and sober: Directions for counseling and therapy.* New York: Harrington Park Press.

Chapter 7
AIDS and caregivers

Jerry Solomon

Since its appearance in the United States, Acquired Immune Deficiency Syndrome (AIDS) has reached epidemic proportions and may very well be the major health problem of the twentieth century. AIDS is characterized by the presence of a severely compromised immune system, independent from genetic causes, resulting in the occurrence of an opportunistic infection or Kaposi's sarcoma. Opportunistic infections result from the body's inability to fight off microorganisms which are omnipresent in the environment. Prior to the AIDS epidemic, Kaposi's sarcoma was a rare form of cancer usually found in elderly men of Mediterranean descent and was seldom fatal. AIDS related complex, or ARC, is characterized by many physical symptoms such as swollen glands, wounds which heal slowly, and flu-like episodes.

In the United States, the groups most afflicted with AIDS are gay and bisexual men. Other groups at high risk include drug users who share contaminated needles with each other, and hemophiliacs. However, the number of hemophiliacs contracting the AIDS virus should decline as the blood banks' screening procedures become more sophisticated.

Because the number of cases of AIDS is growing so rapidly in the United States, there is an increasing number of both gays and non-gays knowing someone who has the disease. This awareness is heightened as the media disclose well-known individuals who have been afflicted with AIDS, thus making it increasingly difficult for people to distance themselves from the devastating effects of the disease.

Unfortunately, misinformation and hysterical overreaction over AIDS have become almost daily occurrences in the United States, and this has frequently been made worse by the sensationalizing of events by the media. The numbers of people who test positive for HIV and who are concerned about getting AIDS but who remain symptomless for AIDS and ARC, the "worried well," continue to rise. This results in an increased need for accurate information and education. Unfortunately, because of the sudden onset of the disease in the United States, coupled with the almost daily increase in new knowledge about AIDS resulting from research, caregivers and other "experts" are often misinformed and become part of the problem rather than part of the solution.

Homophobia, never far under the surface in even the most liberal of communities, becomes a major factor to be dealt with since most people perceive AIDS as a gay man's disease. The image of a virus interviewing its prospective host and inquiring about the host's sexual orientation prior to "deciding" to infect the person seems laughable, yet many people advance such beliefs. Some segments of the Religious Right have used the arrival of the AIDS epidemic to fan the flames of hate and have attributed the spread of the disease to God's desire to punish the wicked and sinful or those whose interpretations of the Bible differ from their own.

It is within this climate that the caregiver faces the challenge of providing adequate care to those with AIDS and ARC, and to the worried well. While many of the issues facing gay, lesbian, and heterosexual caregivers are similar, it is important to acknowledge that issues emerge that are unique to each group. The remainder of this chapter will explore these issues and discuss some strategies which can be adopted to manage difficulties which may be encountered while providing services related to AIDS.

While it may appear obvious that the caregiver should be knowledgeable about the medical aspects of AIDS and its transmission, one must be careful not to assume that this is the case when working with either the professional or community-based caregiver. All individuals choosing to work with the AIDS issue need to commit themselves to obtaining ongoing updates as medical knowledge advances. This can be done by attending local or national conferences about AIDS, by contacting organizations which are providing services to those with AIDS, or by subscribing to established gay and lesbian publications which regularly feature articles about AIDS.(1, 2) Since new research is regularly being published in professional journals, it might be especially helpful to identify health care workers who are willing to keep current with the literature and to have them share this information with others who are working with AIDS in their community.

Because of the nature of the disease and its psychosocial implications, the person with AIDS frequently comes in contact with many different caregivers. After receiving the diagnosis of AIDS, a person may have contact with a physician, medical specialists, nurses, lab technicians, pharmacists, mental health professionals, hospital support staff, members of the spiritual and religious community, attorneys, employers, friends, and family. Each of these contacts has the potential to produce difficulties as well as support. The outcome of these encounters will be determined in part by the interaction between the degree of homophobia present and the amount of accurate information the caregiver has received about AIDS.

Homophobia within the health care establishment takes both subtle and overt forms. As with most social expressions of oppression, the more overt the manifestation the easier it is to identify and to address.

John, 36, had been hospitalized after he presented severe signs suggestive of AIDS. A physician was assigned to his case and ran an extensive battery of tests to determine diagnosis. Confidence in the diagnosis of AIDS was increased when John developed pneumocystis carinii pneumonia.

John had revealed his gayness to his physician and had expressed his concern about the possibility of having AIDS. Upon relaying diagnosis, the physician told John that his disease was a punishment from God, that his life was now in God's hands, and presented him with a Bible. On subsequent visits, the physician questioned John about his Bible readings, and would berate his when he discovered that John had not been following his Bible study recommendations.

John, distressed by his physician's actions, spoke to a friend who contacted the local AIDS caregiving group. John was advised of his right to change physicians and given the name of a physician who was more supportive of gay men. The transfer was made and John died peacefully two months later, surrounded by friends and supportive caregivers.

Although extreme, this example highlights the need for the caregiver to be willing to move into the role of patient advocate when necessary. Many clients need to be informed about their rights within the health care delivery system, and caregivers frequently find themselves in the role of overseeing and maintaining these freedoms.

The caregiver often encounters homophobia in a more direct fashion. Many people assume that AIDS caregivers are gay or lesbian and project their homophobic attitudes upon them. For the person who is comfortable being identified as gay or lesbian, these issues have probably been dealt with before. For the emerging gay or lesbian, or for those who have decided not to reveal their sexual orientation while providing services, this concern becomes more problematic. The decision to disclose oneself as gay or lesbian is complex, and no "rules" exist to assist the person in making that decision. Organizations working with people with AIDS need to be sensitive to this issue and can be most helpful by providing support, rather than criticism or dogmatic solutions and "politically correct" responses.

Equally disquieting is the homophobia directed toward heterosexual caregivers. For many heterosexuals, this is their first direct experience with homophobia and the encounter may provoke anger and activate their own unresolved homophobia. Disclaimers of their own homosexuality, such as, "I'm not gay, but..." may reveal the presence of unrecognized homophobia. Colleagues should draw this behavior to the heterosexual caregiver's attention discreetly as soon as an appropriate opportunity arises. Heterosexual caregivers can be encouraged to explore their own anxieties or fears about homosexuality through supportive dialogues or by attending groups designed to discuss this issue. The expression of anger or criticism toward those with unresolved issues is rarely helpful, unless accompanied by support, understanding, and a willingness to assist the persons in working through their concerns.

Most caregivers encounter their own irrational fears concerning AIDS while providing services. Even the most informed are not immune from anxieties and fears. A few years ago, a client I had been seeing in psychotherapy revealed that he had just been diagnosed as having AIDS and began to cry. My first instinct was to put my arm around him to provide comfort, but I was surprised by my hesitancy. Even though I "knew" that I could not become infected by casual contact, this was the first time I had come in contact with a person who actually had AIDS, and I experienced anxiety and fear concerning my own safety. I went ahead and offered physical comfort, but I also recognized a need to further examine my own fears about the disease.

Inevitably, caregivers must fact the issues of death and dying. Working with a dying person often surfaces feelings about our own mortality. In a society which is not very open to discussing the issues of death and dying, the platitudes which we have grown up with offer little comfort or direction in our search to reconcile ourselves to our own death. For many this quest for meaning is postponed until the waning years of our lives. For persons with AIDS and for those who provide them assistance, the luxury of postponement and procrastination may not be an option.

Perhaps most difficult is the relative youth of those who develop AIDS. More than seventy percent of those diagnosed with AIDS are under forty years of age. The tragedy of so many confronting death at such a young age cannot be overstated. The consequence of this reality to the caregiver can be devastating, potentially resulting in depression and early burn-out. Therefore, it becomes essential for caregivers to have a support network where they can discuss their feelings in a supportive, caring environment.

Since many persons with AIDS are relatively young, most have not done any planning regarding their property or its disposition after their death. Other legal concerns, such as burial plans and durable power of attorney, also need to be considered. The caregiver can be helpful by providing necessary referrals to gay- and lesbian-sensitive attorneys so that these matters can be addressed. The choice of who shall have decision-making power if the person with AIDS is no longer competent to advise the physician about medical treatment can be difficult and complicated, especially if blood relatives are unavailable or unaccepting of the client. Gently encouraging persons with AIDS to reach this decision can ensure a greater sense of control and peace of mind as they enter the final period of their lives. (For further information on legal issues, see the Legal Issues section of this book.)

Spiritual concerns often surface after the person has been diagnosed as having AIDS. The need for spiritual guidance may activate unresolved feelings of anger or guilt regarding a person's decision to move away from organized religion at an earlier period in life. As with most issues which the person with AIDS must address, the caregiver can best be of service by listening carefully to what is desired and by supporting the feelings as they emerge. It is important for the caregivers not to impose their own beliefs or feelings about spirituality upon the client. Likewise, at some point it might be helpful to offer a list of spiritual advisors who are sensitive to the unique issues of gays and lesbians.

One important task facing the caregiver is to identify the person's support network and to assist in dealing with the changes which will be occurring in the patient's life. For many persons with AIDS, repeated hospitalizations can be demoralizing and disruptive to the maintenance of independent living. Friends, lovers, and family can be especially helpful in minimizing the trauma of these transitions by fostering a sense of continuity in the person's life. The caregiver can be helpful by facilitating the establishment of a schedule which will allow continuity of visitation at the hospital, coordinating support when difficult diagnostic or treatment procedures are planned, and maintaining a regular flow of information about the person's life outside the hospital.

Many health care professionals believe they have never treated a gay or lesbian person and, therefore, many may not appreciate the importance of friends or lovers in lieu of traditional family relationships. Consequently, caregivers may find themselves in the role of educator, encouraging hospital personnel to re-examine rules concerning visitation and concerning communication about the health status of the person with AIDS.

The caregiver needs to recognize the impact the death of a person with AIDS has upon friends and lovers. In the absence of legal recognition and institutionalization of gay and lesbian relationships, most gay people establish lover and friendship networks in a fashion which suits their unique needs. However, the absence of formalization, as well as the newness of these alternative "family" forms, often leave the bereaved without any established rituals to assist in the mourning of loved ones. For some, the rituals of organized religions provide the necessary solace. For other bereaved persons, who may have difficulties with traditional religious services, new forms can be investigated which may better address their needs. Alternative services overseen by close friends, or local gay or lesbian leaders, may provide the needed structure to allow friends to grieve in a supportive community environment. Reading poetry or prose aloud, listening to music, or sharing remembrances of the departed are some ways in which friends and intimates can honor the memory of their friend.

Lastly, caregivers must find a place to vent their own frustrations, anger, and fears — emotions naturally evoked by their work with dying persons in an often impersonal and, seemingly, indifferent and uncaring world. Regular meetings with a supervisor familiar with their concerns, as well as ongoing support groups, allow caregivers to stay current with their feelings and emotionally available to the people they work with. Acknowledgement and appreciation are often unstated and must be inferred as the caregivers assist the persons with AIDS, friends, and family through constantly changing difficult situations. The sharing of appreciation with other caregivers provides some of the necessary support to continue working with people with AIDS.

Providing assistance to people with AIDS is a challenging and rewarding activity. Tasks continuously emerge which require ingenuity, interpersonal skill, and personal courage on the part of the caregiver. The sense of accomplishment and comradeship shared with others working in the field is enriching and sustaining. The political and personal conse-quences of AIDS will be with us well into the twenty-first century: The shape that these events take will be determined, in large measure, by those who participate now in educating the community about AIDS and in giving care to those who suffer from its effects.

REFERENCES

1. *The Advocate.* Liberation Publications, Inc., P.O. Box 4371, Los Angeles, CA 90099.

2. *New York Native.* 28 W. 25th Street, New York, NY 10010.

Chapter 8

Homophobia and its consequences for gay and lesbian clients

Ernest D. Lapierre

INTRODUCTION

When you hear the word homophobia, what comes to your mind? Perhaps you think about the definition of the word. Simply defined, homophobia is an unreasonable fear of homosexuality.(2) Perhaps a mental image comes to your mind of what a homophobic person might look like. Maybe you see this individual as large, gruesome and carrying a weapon such as a baseball bat; and you hear him muttering something about going out to do some queer-bashing. Or perhaps you think about your inner feelings, your fears, your panic feelings, your cold sweats, whenever you yourself have same-sex thoughts or whenever you think that someone might think of you as being homosexual. You might add to these feelings your thoughts about how you plan to get rid of these inner feelings that you are experiencing. They may be bothering you so much that, for you, the only way to get rid of them is to destroy yourself. This self-destruction may take many forms. For many gays and lesbians it is alcoholism; for others it is suicide. The point is that different people have different reactions to the word homophobia. The reactions can be directed inward or outward, or it may be directed both ways at the same time. It is important to note that, no matter what direction the reaction takes, it is caused by an over-whelming, unfounded fear.

In this chapter, I will look at the meaning of homophobia. Definitions of homophobia will be discussed. The question of why it is important for the helping professional to know about homophobia will be considered. Problem areas for the gay or lesbian client, as well as for the helping professional, will be addressed. Attention will be given to what the helping profes-

– 90 –

sional can do to enable gay and lesbian clients to overcome their own homophobia. Case studies will be presented as examples.

THE MEANING OF HOMOPHOBIA:
A WORKING DEFINITION

I have already stated a simple definition of homophobia. Actually, there are many definitions. Morin and Garfinkle(8) point out that homophobia has been conceptualized from an external, or cultural, perspective, and from an internal, or psychodynamic, perspective. Each perspective offers different insights into its origins, dynamics, and meaning.

As approached from a cultural perspective, homophobia defines any belief system that supports negative myths and stereotypes about gay and lesbian people. More specifically, homophobia refers to: (a) a belief system which holds that discrimination on the basis of sexual orientation is justified; (b) the use of language or slang, e.g. "queer" or "fag," that is offensive to gay people; and (c) any belief system which does not value gay and lesbian lifestyles equally with heterosexual lifestyles.(8)

Several authors have contributed to our understanding of the cultural perspective by examining the origin of the word homophobia. Churchill (1) used the word "homoerotophobia" to describe the fear of sexual contact with members of the same sex. He concluded that attempts to repress homosexuality are the direct result of socialization practices of "sex negative" cultures. Gramick(2) makes a case for Churchill's point when she compares Eastern and Western cultures. She points out that it is well known that homosexual practices were condoned and even encouraged among the ancient Greeks and Romans. The ancient Celts, Scandinavians, Egyptians, Etruscans, Cretans, Carthagenians, and Sumerians also accepted same-sex sexual behavior. Gramick goes on to point out that the Far East also tolerated homosexuality. From ancient to modern times, homosexual behavior has been accepted in China and Japan. However, same-sex sexual behavior was suppressed in Japan at the end of World War II by the American occupation forces. This last piece of information reinforces Churchill's assertion that attempts to repress same-sex sexual behavior are the direct result of socialization practices of "sex negative" cultures, such as the United States.

Other writers(3, 7) have conceptualized homophobia in terms of a "generalized cultural belief system regarding the relationship between the sexes."(8) This generalized belief system is variously termed "homosexism," "heterosexual bias," or "heterosexism" in the literature. It is important to know that all these terms have the same meaning, and that they all denote belief in the superiority of heterosexuality over homosexuality.

Homophobia may also be looked at from the personal perspective. From this perspective, homophobia refers specifically to "the irrational fear or intolerance of homosexuality,"(3) or to "an irrational and persistent fear or dread of homosexuals."(5) From the personal perspective, homophobia is a specific neurosis, rather than a generalized cultural attitude or belief.

George Weinberg(9) first described homophobia from the personal, rather than the cultural, perspective. Morin and Garfinkle(8) point out that Weinberg described the phenomenon of homophobia as "an irrational fear on the part of heterosexuals of being in close proximity to people they believe to be homosexual" (p. 32). Weinberg also made an important contribution by attempting to clarify the dynamics of homophobia among gays themselves. He postulated that the nature of this phenomenon was a self-hatred which results from the internalization of others' irrational fears. Results of studies by Lumby(4) and May (6) indicate that gay men have internalized many societal beliefs regarding homosexuality, but that they do not hold these beliefs to the extent found among heterosexual men.

WHY IT IS IMPORTANT FOR THE HELPING PROFESSIONAL TO KNOW ABOUT HOMOPHOBIA

Having provided a background on homophobia, I now look at why helping professionals need to know about it. The first reason is that clients may bring their homophobic reactions to the session. The second reason is that the helping professional may be aware of the client's homophobic reaction, but the client may not. The third is that helping professionals may experience homophobic reactions within themselves. And finally, members of society may be expressing homophobic thoughts and feelings about gays and lesbians.

If a client is suffering from internalized homophobic thoughts and feelings, or from reactions to society's homophobia, more often than not they will not be able to express their thoughts and feelings to anyone. But often the clients will exhibit symptoms of their inward hurting. These symptoms are frequently acute anxiety attacks, withdrawal, decreased self-esteem, or self-destructive thoughts. The symptoms may also include behaviors which may range from missing activities such as work or therapy sessions, to a halt in taking required medications, to alcoholism, or to actual suicide. It is important that the helping professional recognize these symptoms early on, and acknowledge that they may be a signal of internalized homophobia or of a reaction to external homophobia for the client. Quick detection and intervention by the helping professional may prevent the client from stopping therapy or even from committing suicide. More to the point, the early working through of these reactions by the client will not only more quickly increase the client's self-esteem, but it will also encourage the client's trust and promote confidence in the helping professional, thus improving and advancing the therapeutic relationship.

It is necessary for the helping professional to understand the dynamics of internalized homophobia in order to help the clients. They may not be able to connect the signs and symptoms described with their internal thoughts and feelings about their homosexuality. They may deny they are having a homophobic reaction even though the symptoms are evident to the helping professional. They may even be totally unaware they are having any kind of homophobic reaction at all. Therefore, it becomes the helping professional's responsibility to help clients connect their behavioral manifestations with their own internalized homophobia, thus establishing insight.

A third reason that it is important for helping professionals to know about homophobia is that their own homophobic thoughts and feelings may be aroused during a therapeutic encounter with a client. If this does occur, then it is the professional's responsibility to work on this matter in his or her own therapy and not in sessions with clients. If their homophobia begins to interfere with their work with gay clients, then they should reassign the clients to therapists who are not homophobic.

Sometimes it is not a homophobic reaction on the part of the helping professional or the client, but on the part of society in the form of a parent or a boss, or even an educator, that presents a problem for the gay client. Here too it is vital for the helping professional to understand homophobia. The first therapeutic intervention should aim at discouraging the member of society from any overt expression of the homophobic reaction, in order to reduce stress on the client. It also would be important to explore with such people what their concerns are about homosexuality and to find out what they believe about it. The helping professional may be able to dispel many myths early on in the relationship.

PROBLEM AREAS

One of the major destructive behaviors in the gay and lesbian communities is alcoholism. Alcohol is all too often the convenient drug of choice to deal with fears, anxieties, feelings of low self-esteem, feelings of self-hatred and worthlessness, and feelings of not being able to go on with life. Similarly, alcohol is used to block out the bad feelings generated by homophobia, so that the gay person just does not have to deal with these feelings until the alcohol wears off. Subsequent escapes take more alcohol to block out the feelings. Soon the client is progressing toward alcoholism. It is much the same picture with any chemical or substance abuse. The patterns are the same. (See the chapters on *Coming Out* and *Alcoholism* for further discussion of this major gay and lesbian health problem.)

Anxiety attacks are another problem area for gay people dealing with thoughts and feelings generated by homophobia. These attacks are sometimes devastating and crippling. Often the persons do not know why they are experiencing them. They occur without warning and seem to come out of nowhere. They may occur during work or school, while relaxing at home or enjoying a movie, or even during sleep. These attacks may cause persons to lose jobs or to drop out of school. They may disrupt family or lover relationships.

A third problem area for the gay person dealing with internalized homophobic thoughts and feelings is that of suicide. Often persons strongly believe that the only solution to getting rid of these thoughts and feelings is to destroy themselves immediately, as opposed to a more gradual self-destruction through the use of drugs or alcohol. As a gay person speaking to the gay reader, how many of us thought that we were the only gay and lesbian person in town? How many of us thought that nobody else could know what we were feeling? Those who are not lesbian or gay have not experienced these terrible thoughts and feelings of shame, guilt, and loneliness. Most of us are brought up in a culture that does not value a gay or lesbian lifestyle. From the very start, we are given messages from our parents that we must pursue a *normal* lifestyle, which above all else means hetero-sexual. And we are made to feel guilty if we do not.

Another potential area of problems with internalized and external homophobia is in the coming out process. I will not go into this process here because it was dealt with earlier in this book (Chapter 3). I would, however, like to make one point about the relationship between homophobia and the coming out process. Often gay persons think that they have purged themselves of all of their homophobic thoughts and feelings, only to have them resurface several times as they grow in the coming out process. This resurfacing may make gay clients angry or frustrated. They may think, "Oh, no, not those awful feelings again!" But it is important for the gay client to be aware that this will occur, and to know that effective therapy entails recognizing and acknowledging these feelings.

WHAT THE HELPING PROFESSIONAL CAN DO TO HELP

Today, more than ever before, helping professionals have at their disposal many resources to help them deal effectively with the gay client's reactions to internalized or external homophobia. The main goal of therapeutic intervention with such clients should be to help them to be as comfortable with their thoughts and feelings about their own homosexuality as possible. The intervention may take many forms, from sharing literature about the topic, to group work on the homophobic thoughts and feelings of the members, to intensive individual psychotherapy to get at the sources of the thoughts and feelings. There are many good sources in the literature which the helping professional can read in order to become more knowledgeable about homophobia. These sources are often good for sharing with the client. A particular source can be shared with the client and discussed in the next session. The bibliography at the end of this chapter serves as a good resource for such a therapeutic intervention.

Group therapy work allows clients to share their fears and anxieties with others. Often the homophobic feelings take the form of "But I don't want to be a homosexual, because then I will be bad, terrible, and hated by everybody." Such feelings can be addressed in the group sessions to find out how others have dealt with them. Often creative forms of resolution of these kinds of negative feelings can be discovered through the group process. Also, the feeling of safety in numbers may be the emotional condition that is needed to start a positive therapeutic process for the client.

The helping professional can suggest support groups that have been started at gay and lesbian community centers in many large cities and in smaller towns at local colleges. These support groups present a positive and realistic image of gay life. If the professional does not know of any such support groups, he can often obtain the information with local directory assistance. (For further help in locating resources, see the chapter on *Accessing Gay and Lesbian Health Resources* in this book.)

CASE STUDIES

Henry, a 25-year-old gay man, was in the process of changing jobs within state agencies. A physical was required. Henry felt comfortable with the physician doing the physical and found it easy to answer his questions. He confided that he had been hospitalized recently due to anxiety attacks related to problems in his relationship with his lover of three years. Immediately, the physician noticeably changed. He moved his chair farther away from Henry and had a look of disgust on his face. He dismissed Henry and said that he would have to discuss the case with his superior. Henry left the office visibly shaken and upset. He went to the secretary's office of the local graduate school that he was attending. Luckily, the secretary was a sympathetic listener. After hearing Henry's account of the incident and offering words of sympathy, she called the department chairperson. The chairperson listened to Henry's account. In her usual firm manner, she stated, "When are you going to learn to withhold information when it only serves to damage you?" That afternoon Henry received a telephone call telling him that he had not received the job due to mental instability. Although distraught and jobless for almost three months, Henry learned a valuable lesson and has been very careful about sharing information ever since.

Mary, a 32-year-old lesbian, was in the physician's office for a yearly company checkup. When it came time for the vaginal examination, she requested not to have it done. But the physician was very insistent that she have it done, unless she could give him a good reason for not doing it. Mary explained that she did not have sexual relations with men and, therefore, saw no need for it. The physician exclaimed, "What are you, a lesbian?" And Mary, in her immediate anger, responded, "Yes!" Mary was dismissed from her job an hour later with the excuse that she was no longer suitable for the job. Dismayed and distraught, Mary called the local gay hotline and got the number of a local gay and lesbian community center. That night, at the center, she met other lesbians and gay men who had suffered similar kinds of abuse and discrimination because of homophobic reactions from others. She joined a lesbian therapy group at the center that met once a week and worked on resolving her feelings of anger and hatred provoked by the homophobic and discriminatory behavior of others.

REFERENCES

1. Churchill, W. (1967). *Homosexuals in the male species: A cross-cultural and cross-species investigation.* New York: Hawthorn.

2. Gramick, J. (1983). Homophobia: A new challenge. *Social Work, 28(2)*, 137-141.

3. Lehne, G.K. (1976). Homophobia among men. In D. David and R. Brannon, (Eds.), *The forty-nine percent majority: The male sex role.* New York: Addison-Wesley.

4. Lumby, M.E. (1976). Homophobia: The quest for a valid scale. *Journal of Homosexuality, 2,* 39-47.

5. McDonald, A.P. (1976). Homophobia: Its roots and meanings. *Homosexual Counseling Journal, 3,* 23-33.

6. May, E.P. (1974). Counselors', psychologists', and homosexuals' philosophies of human nature and attitudes toward homosexual behavior. *Homosexual Counseling Journal, 1,* 3-25.

7. Morin, S.F. (1977). Heterosexual bias in research on lesbianism and male homosexuality. *American Psychologist, 32,* 629-637.

8. Morin, S.F. and Garfinkle, E.M. (1978). Male homophobia. *Journal of Social Issues, 34(1),* 29-47.

9. Weinberg, G. (1972). *Society and the healthy homosexual.* New York: St. Martin's Press.

Chapter 9
Notes on suicide and suicidal ideation among gays and lesbians

Eric E. Rofes

In an exhaustive 1977 survey of more than five thousand gay men and lesbians, Karla Jay and Allen Young found that forty percent of the men and thirty-nine percent of the women had seriously considered or actually attempted suicide.(2) Similar studies by Alan Bell and Martin Weinberg,(1) Marcel Saghir and Eli Robins,(3) and the Institute for the Protection of Lesbian and Gay Youth in New York City reveal an alarming relationship between suicidal ideation and the contemporary lives of gay men and lesbians in America. Despite statistics, few clinical studies and little research is available on the complex factors that contribute to making suicide prevention and intervention an important concern for professionals working with gay and lesbian clients.

Why is so little information available on suicide and suicidal ideation among gay men and lesbians? Why do entire books continue to be written about suicide in America, about teenage suicide, or about depression and suicidal ideation in women that fail to even consider issues facing the gay and lesbian population? Why do some professionals working with gays and lesbians have such limited knowledge and training in addressing suicidal feelings and gestures?

These circumstances are caused by two major factors: *Homophobia*, which inclines many researchers, prevention workers, and social scientists to either ignore or trivialize the needs of the gay population, or to consider a disposition toward suicide a basic component of the lesbian and gay personality; and *denial*, which encourages men and women active in the gay and lesbian movements to insist that among gays and lesbians suicide is an outmoded issue, perhaps a problem in the 1950s, whose residue remains as a harmful stereotype of contemporary gay people.

Meanwhile, health care providers working with the gay and lesbian population, or in suicide prevention agencies, are aware that this population is greatly at risk for suicide. What can we do to help our clients with these feelings?

It is important for care providers to be trained in issues related to suicide. They must know, for example, that many of the basic assumptions we have about suicide are nothing more than myths. While many people believe that people who talk about suicide — casually or with a counselor — rarely actually act on their feelings, the fact is that most people who commit suicide have given some kind of warning or hint. Any remarks — however casual or off-the-cuff — should be considered seriously by the provider. This does not mean that on hearing a client mutter, "I could just kill myself over this relationship, one needs to move into action to prevent an imminent suicide. It *is* appropriate for the provider to consider whether this comment might warrant some serious concern.

Talking with clients about suicide will not lead them to make an attempt. In fact, in many cases, asking clients directly about feelings of depression or suicide will remove some of their anxiety surrounding the feelings. One social worker who simply asked a client, "Have you been feeling like hurting yourself?" was amazed at her client's outpouring of feelings. "She had kept these fantasies inside herself for so long that simply having someone to talk to about her suicidal feelings relieved her tremendously. It was like removing the cap from an overheated radiator," she reported. "The steam came pouring out and the pressure eased."

SPECIAL ISSUES FACING GAY MEN AND LESBIANS

While lesbians and gay men experience suicidal ideation in a manner similar to women and men in the general population, there are particular issues to consider when dealing with the gay or lesbian client.

The trigger for a suicidal gesture for many gay people has traditionally involved scandal or public exposure. In the fifties and sixties, newspapers regularly carried accounts of men arrested on "morals" charges who killed themselves. In an article in the *Los Angeles Times* of April 18, 1953, under the headline "Skin Specialist in Morals Case Takes Own Life" we learn that Dr. Kenneth McLarand, age forty-seven, was arrested by the police, pleaded guilty to the charges, and was set free on bail, returned home, wrote a note to his wife saying, "I'm tired of it all," and took an overdose of sleeping pills.

Such suicides are not a thing of the past. In July 1981, Boston police arrested thirty-two men for "open and gross lewdness" in an early-morning raid on a bar. Two weeks later, one of the men, described by friends as "very intelligent, very sensitive, very artistically oriented," took a large dose of prescription medicine and died. Men caught up in public scandals, arrested at gay male cruising areas, bars, or baths, or simply yanked out of the closet against their will, are at tremendous risk for suicide.

Lesbians are not spared risk in this area. One lesbian schoolteacher was driven to attempt suicide by a blackmailer who forced her to pay several thousand dollars in exchange for not revealing her lesbianism to the school's administration. The blackmailer, a former roommate, continued to threaten her with exposure, even after the suicide attempt. Finally, the woman chose to leave the area, flee to New York City, and begin her life and career over.

Many people expect that, once a gay person has come to terms with his sexuality, suicide is no longer an issue. Unfortunately, coming out of the closet — personally, politically, emotionally — is not a salvation for many gay people. In fact, for some lesbians and gay men, after a few months out of the closet, a deep depression sets in. One realizes that, despite the new openness about one's homosexuality, personal problems, conflicts, and anxieties still exist. One can no longer blame all of one's trials on being in the closet. Previously eclipsed issues loom larger.

Hence, helping professionals working with lesbian and gay clients should be aware that the periods during and, often, for many months following one's coming out are often volatile, with tremendous mood swings and fears. Paying particular attention to a client's expressions of discomfort, desperation, and regrets will be helpful in supporting the client through this difficult period.

Gay and lesbian youth appear to be particularly vulnerable to suicide. The Institute for the Protection of Lesbian and Gay Youth in New York City showed that twenty percent of the young people who contacted the Institute during 1984 had seriously considered suicide. Seven percent had actually attempted suicide. Based on his work at Rescue, Inc., a counseling service for young people, Father Kenneth Murphy is quoted in *Youth and Suicide* as saying that homosexual orientation is a prime motive for suicide among gay and lesbian youth.

Despite the reports of people who work with young people and of people who work specifically with lesbian and gay youth, recent media attention focused on youth and suicide has chosen to ignore the fact that a young person who is perceived to be gay or lesbian — or a young person who is struggling with gay or lesbian feelings — is at risk for suicide. One wonders how these people hope to help young people when they ignore or gloss over the substance behind the suicidal gesture. In one case, the producer of a television documentary concerning suicidal youth meticulously edited out all references to homosexuality, despite the fact that two of the four youths who had killed themselves were gay. The viewer was left with the impression that it was a mystery why these teens had killed themselves. They appeared, after all, so wholesome and all-American. What a tragedy!

More recently, AIDS has raised the issue of suicide for many gay men. A recent annual report from the San Francisco coroner's office includes a category for AIDS-related suicides. Coroner Boyd Stephens is quoted in the San Francisco *Bay Area Reporter* (BAR) as stating that half a dozen gay men have committed suicide during the reporting year because they had been diagnosed with AIDS or because they mistakenly believed that they had the disease. The men ranged in age from their twenties to their fifties.

Issues related to AIDS and suicide fall into several distinct categories: attempts by people with AIDS to kill themselves; suicides by people who have been diagnosed either as HIV-positive or as having ARC; and suicides by men who suspect or fear they have AIDS, but who have not been diagnosed for the disease. Boyd Stephens told the BAR that a number of men who took their lives were reacting from a fear of having AIDS rather than from an actual diagnosis. "The key thing for anyone who thinks he has AIDS is to be very sure. A few people who were afraid of a mole, a bump, or a few lumps, have made very unfortunate decisions," he said.

HOW THE HELPING PROFESSIONAL CAN HELP

The best thing that helping professionals can do to help their lesbian and gay clients who are grappling with suicidal feelings is to become educated about the particular issues that relate to gay people and suicide, and to be able to respond when clients are feeling desperate. Insisting that staff members receive training in both the needs of lesbian and gay clients and the needs of depressed and suicidal people, will equip them with the knowledge and skills to work with suicidal gay and lesbian clients. Too many people — including many social service workers — ignore key comments by suicidal people because of their own discomfort with the issue or because they feel unable to respond appropriately.

If you as a care provider are unable to respond to a suicidal client in an appropriate way, it is important to refer the client to a provider who can respond appropriately. Counseling services which deal with large numbers of gay men and lesbians, suicide prevention agencies, or individual therapists, are all potential referrals. Overcoming one's feelings of embarrassment about not being able to address a particular issue should be a priority. Our key aim as health care professionals is to provide the client with the necessary support services.

Homosexuality is not the issue that forces many gay men and lesbians into a position where they consider or attempt suicide; homophobia is. Because of hostile societal reaction to homosexuality, many gay men and lesbians are forced into what they perceive as no-win situations. Keeping in mind that gay man and lesbians exist in an often hostile world, and that issues such as invisibility, lack of role models, and familial disapproval are key life issues for gay people, will allow you to better serve the gay or lesbian client struggling with issues related to suicide.

REFERENCES

1. Bell, A.P. and Weinberg, M.S. (1978). *Homosexualities.* New York: Simon & Schuster.

2. Jay, K. and Young, A. (1979). *The gay report.* New York: Summit Books.

3. Saghir, M.T. and Robbins, E. (1973). *Male and female homosexuality: A comprehensive investigation.* Baltimore: William & Wilkins.

III

**Gay and Lesbian
Life Situations:
Special Concerns**

Chapter 10

Fathers who are gay

Frederick W. Bozett

Gay men marry for many reasons, most of which are the same as for non-gays. For example, they may be in love with a woman, want faithful companionship, or may have the desire for children. Parents, siblings, or other family members may exert pressure on them to marry; they may fear loneliness or crave stability. On the other hand, some of these men may think that marriage will "cure" them. Others may use marriage as a shield behind which they can hide their homosexuality. Once married, they have several available options. They can remain married while abstaining from sex with men, or they can have clandestine, impersonal homosexual liaisons. Rarely, some men can be openly gay while married. Another option is for the couple to divorce and for the man to establish a gay lifestyle. Under this circumstance, he has the additional option of continuing to act as father to his children with or without custody, or to abrogate his parental role. Which option a gay father chooses depends upon multiple factors, such as his awareness of his homosexuality and his acceptance of it, the extent and nature of his experiences in the gay world and his perceptions of them, and his dedication to his family and father role.

The purpose of this chapter is to describe gay fathers in both the heterosexual and gay worlds, and to delineate for helping professionals areas of particular psychosocial concerns. The chapter begins with a brief historical and statistical overview, followed by a discussion of the gay father in each of the two worlds. The chapter concludes with implications for persons in the helping professions.

HISTORY AND STATISTICS

The gay rights movement became public and gained significant impetus in June of 1969 as a result of several nights of retaliation by gays to police raids on the Stonewall Inn, a gay tavern in Greenwich Village. This was at a time when the civil rights movement was highly active. Blacks, Mexican farm laborers, and Native Americans were among the minorities seeking their constitutionally guaranteed rights. Many women as well were searching for alternatives to the traditional roles of wife and mother that they frequently found unfulfilling. Consequently, women were entering the work force in numbers not seen since World War II. Concurrently, the divorce rate skyrocketed, swelling the numbers of single parents.

During this era of great unrest and change, the gay rights movement, with its concomitant publicity promoting the viability of gay lifestyles, coupled with the dramatic increase in single parenthood, led many divorced men and women to come out as gay or lesbian. These individuals chose to enter the gay world, rather than to continue to live on the fringes of both the gay and non-gay worlds, or, alternatively, once again to market themselves as eligible "heterosexuals." Hence, lesbian motherhood and gay fatherhood became more visible, resulting in increased research and writings on gay parents and their children in both professional and lay publications.

While it is impossible to determine with accuracy the number of gay fathers, it can be estimated. According to Kinsey, Pomeroy, and Martin, [19] Churchill,[11] and Kingdon,[18] approximately ten percent of the population is gay. The Bureau of the Census reported that the 1983 United States population was approximately 230 million. Hence, the gay and lesbian population is estimated to be about 23 million. Equally difficult to determine with certainty is the number of gay fathers, although crude approximations are possible. About twenty percent of gay men have been heterosexually married.[1, 17, 26] How many have married more than once is unknown. Furthermore, it is estimated that twenty-five to fifty percent of gay men who have married are natural fathers.[1, 20] Thus, it is probable that there are at least 4 million gay men who have been married at least once, with 1 or 2 million of them being natural fathers. Although accurate statistics on the number of children of gay fathers are difficult to determine, Schulenburg(25) estimates the combined number of children of gay and lesbian parents to approximate 6 million, whereas Peterson(24) believes there to be about 14 million. Thus, the incidence of gay fathers and the children of gay fathers is sufficient to warrant serious consideration by professionals in helping disciplines.

GAY FATHERS IN THE HETEROSEXUAL WORLD

It is likely that the majority of gay men who marry do not consider themselves to be gay, even though most of them are consciously aware of their sexual attraction to men. In some instances, men do not become consciously aware of their homosexuality until one or more years after marriage. Other men may consider themselves bisexual. Not uncommonly, gay men will disclose their physical attraction to men to their future wives and may even tell them that they have been sexually intimate with men. However, their disclosures seem to be couched in such a way as to indicate that these are solely past events and have no current relevance or future implications. It is the honest intent of these men to develop wholesome, satisfying, and monogamous heterosexual marital relationships. It is the rare man who is being consciously deceptive.(6) At the time of their disclosures, they are not usually aware of the significance with regard to their sexual orientations of their homoerotic feelings; however, if they are, they believe they can successfully suppress these feelings. The exception is the man who is bisexual and explains that he plans to continue bisexual activities during marriage.

After marriage, most of these men stop having gay sex. They do so because they intend to abide by the Judeo-Christian ethic of monogamy. Also, for the first year or two, heterosexual intercourse may be satisfying. Furthermore, sex with men would induce considerable guilt. However, because of the power of the sex drive, the desire for sexual relations with men increases over time. The longer the man goes without satisfying his homoerotic needs, the more intense the desire becomes. Eventually, he succumbs and begins to seek out men for sexual purposes. At first he does so only on rare occasions, but the liaisons gradually increase in frequency. The man may rationalize these sexual encounters as "therapy," or he may justify them solely on the basis of physical need rather than emotional or affectional attraction.

Gradually, more time is spent away with home in order to find sex partners and to carry out the sex act. Excuses for frequent absences from home, which often become increasingly elaborate, are concocted. Increasing feelings of guilt are induced by the non-monogamous sexual behavior, as well as by the deception that lying represents. The man may shower his wife and children with gifts in an attempt to relieve guilt.(22) Over time, the marital relationship begins to deteriorate due to intense cognitive dissonance. This dissonance is due to the feelings of desire for sexual and social relations with men, coupled with the guilt the homosexual behavior and feelings create. In addition, the man knows that his external appearance as a happily married family man is a façade, yet at the same time he may still desire the stability which a wife and family provide. He is also sincerely concerned for his wife and deeply loves his children. The result of these profound mixed feelings is increasing frustration and stress. The man is unable to fully express himself as the man he knows himself to be, yet he feels trapped by the constraints imposed by his family and his obligations to them. The frustration is usually expressed in anger, arguments, and hostility. The wife and children become scapegoats; the family agonizes. Typically, the man is closed to discussion of the situation, which only further alienates the wife and augments the stress in their relationship. It is at the height of the conflict that the man will often disclose his homosexuality (both feelings and behavior) to his wife. Individual or couples' therapy may be entered into, but is rarely successful at preserving the marriage. The wife may make attempts to keep the relationship intact by such means as reading about homosexuality in order to understand, giving the father permission to have one or more nights out for sociosexual purposes, or having a ménage à trois with her husband and another man.(4) However, these strategies are ordinarily unsuccessful, since the man remains confined by the ties of the marital relationship and is unable to actualize fully his gay identity. Separation and divorce are the usual outcomes.

The intense family disruption just described does not

always occur, however. The couple may quietly grow apart over time, with the man eventually disclosing his homosexuality. What appears to determine whether there will be sharp conflict or a gradual distancing is the history of the man's gay experiences during marriage. If he has fulfilled his homoerotic needs from the outset of marriage and his feelings of desire for men have not been pent-up, the feelings of intense anger and frustration are usually averted.

It is rare for any marriage to fail based on only one factor,(16) and so it is with marriages between gay men and heterosexual women. Many of these marriages are unsuccessful because the man cannot achieve life satisfaction constricted by society's, his own, or his family's expectations that he conform to a heterosexual lifestyle. In addition, he cannot endure the frustrations that abstinence from sex with men creates, nor can he tolerate the duplicity of his behavior generated by his perceived social need to act straight which acting on his personal need for social and sexual relations with gay men. Even so, it is difficult to separate from his family, especially because of his deep-felt love for his children.(9)

GAY FATHERS IN THE GAY WORLD

The gay husband and father separates from his wife, and the couple usually divorces. Although some gay fathers enter the gay world with child custody, most do not, though most remain committed to their parental role responsibilities. However, the man discovers that his being a father with parental obligations seldom fits in easily with many of the characteristics of the gay world. For example, the gay world is by and large a single person's world. This means that the gay man's income is his to spend at will. It means that he can readily move within and between cities without having to consider the needs of others, and that he can come and go without time restrictions. Furthermore, most gay men have no long-term commitments or obligations to another person, let alone to persons such as children. In contrast, the gay father does not experience this kind of independence, unless his children are grown or he has abrogated his parental responsibilities (which is not common). Even if his children are adults, he often maintains financial or other commitments to them, or they may even live with him. In addition, much of the gay world is youth-oriented, and since these men often enter the gay world when they are older, they may feel somewhat out of place.(5)

All of these factors make it more difficult for gay fathers to find and form gay relationships of substance. In addition, the man discovers that he may be rejected because of his father identity. Fadiman(13) refers to the need for a gay father to come out as gay to non-gays and to come out as a father to gays as a "double closet." In both instances, there is the possibility of rejection. However, because of the importance of their children to them, gay fathers rarely deny their paternal identity, in spite of the possibility of rejection. The result is that they develop close relations with gays who are accepting of both them and their children, and they distance themselves from persons who are unaccepting. It is uncommon for a gay father to develop an intimate relationship with a man who rejects his children, unless the father has given up his parental responsibilities, or his children are adults and live away with home.

Many persons who have never had children have a low tolerance for them, which makes establishing a lover relationship difficult for gay fathers, especially if they have child custody. In addition, gay fathers have experienced a committed relationship and have learned the work it takes to sustain this kind of bond. Gay men who have not had this kind of experience may not have developed the interpersonal skills necessary to nurture a long-term relationship. These men often expect to come first without having to jockey for the father's attention. Competition between the gay lover and the father's children, regardless of their age, is not uncommon, and when it occurs it usually creates serious discord.

If the father has child custody, the lover needs authority over the children, as well as physical space in the household in order to obtain needed privacy. Child discipline and the extent of the lover's authority commonly constitute major problems in gay father stepfamilies. The lover needs to learn to discipline the children, and the children need to learn to accept his authority. Likewise, they need to develop mutual respect, concern, and caring. In addition, the father needs to promote a reciprocally respectful and, hopefully, loving relationship between his lover and his children. If dissention characterizes the relationship between the lover and children, it is unlikely that the bond between the two men will be sustained, especially if the father has child custody.(7)

It is also important to note that gay fathers are aware of their children's need to have a stable home environment. Therefore, they avoid bringing into the home men whose relationship with themselves or the children is likely to be of short duration. Also, gay fathers who are coupled with another man tend to be discreet in their behavior, in order to spare their children any ridicule from their friends or others who might have learned of the parent's gayness.

COMING OUT TO CHILDREN

Coming out to children and the children's response to this disclosure is discussed separately because of its importance and difficulty.(21) Whether to disclose to children is commonly a hard decision to make, because the father fears rejection or decreased affection and respect.(3) It is important to him because his children are especially significant to him: once he has accepted himself as gay, he is no longer willing to hide a crucial aspect of his identity from them. But it is generally difficult for most parents to discuss *any* sexuality with their children: to discuss one's *own* sexuality, most particularly when it is not socially sanctioned, is a great deal more difficult. Don Clark, a gay clinical psychologist and father, believes that gay fathers should come out to their children because not to do so implies that there is cause for shame, and it is unwise to give one's children the feeling that one has cause for shame.(12)

The primary reason for gay fathers' coming out to their children is not to explain their sexual orientation, however. Rather, its purpose is to clarify the father's personal and social world. Thus, after coming out, the father can include his children in his gay world, sharing with them important aspects of his life which he would otherwise have to hide. He may also then freely clarify the reasons for the divorce, or explain his relationship with his male lover. Disclosure allows for the development of greater intimacy between the father and his children, whereas nondisclosure ensures the maintenance of an interpersonal distance. While indirect means of disclosure, such as holding hands with another man in front of the children or taking them to a gay musical event are commonly used with young children, both indirect and direct (verbal explanation) means are employed with older ones. Also noteworthy is that explanation of one's sexual orientation to children (or others) is an undertaking unique to gay or lesbian parents. Never are non-gay parents required to explain their own sexual orientation to others.

In none of the published literature, nor in the author's own research,(2, 8) is it known for children to totally reject their father after his disclosure. Quite the opposite has been found to be true. Most of the children continue to respect and love him as they did beforehand, and they admire him for having the psychological strength, personal integrity, and willingness to face potential adversity by admitting to a stigmatized identity. Even though children respect their father for his forthrightness, they are, nevertheless, sensitive to the opinions and values of their peers and of the wider society. Therefore, they are usually careful to keep their father's homosexuality hidden from most or all of their friends. They do this by such means as not telling others, by not bringing friends home if the father's gay friends or lover are there, by hiding gay artifacts such as newspapers when friends do visit, or by referring to the father's lover as an "uncle" or "housemate." Older children may refuse to participate with their father at gay events or to be seen in public places such as restaurants. They may control the father's overt expression of his homosexuality by, for example, inviting the father but not his lover to a dinner party. The extent to which the children of gay fathers are willing to be seen with their fathers and participate with them in various functions appears to be influenced by four factors.(8) First is whether the child feels a mutuality or has a bond in common with the father. An example of having a common bond is that a daughter who is overweight and has been stigmatized because of it may have a greater feeling of oneness with her father and, therefore, be more at ease with his differentness.

Second is the extent to which the child believes the father's homosexuality is obvious to others. The more overt the child believes it to be, the less willing he or she is to be seen in public with the father. Age is also a factor since older children have more control over their own behavior in relation to the father. For example, older children can refuse to go to a gay restaurant with him, whereas younger ones cannot. The last factor is living arrangements. If the children are adults and live independently, or if they are younger and live with their mother, they have more control over participation with their father than if they live with him. It is again essential to emphasize that although the children of gay fathers may be somewhat embarrassed because their father is gay, and, thus, use various strategies to keep the fact hidden, it in no way indicates diminished regard for him. The contrary seems most common. Many of these children are exceedingly proud of their father and are interpersonally close to him, their father being both a confidante and a friend. It is not unusual for the father to be the preferred parent by both daughters and sons.

Of course, not all gay fathers do disclose their homosexuality to their children. There are at least three reasons for not doing so. One is intense fear of rejection. Second is the man's own lack of acceptance of his gay identity. Few gay men reach adulthood without some degree of internalized homophobia. By virtue of a wide variety of social experiences in the gay world and by gradually coming out to significant others and receiving their approbation, most men are able to significantly reduce or eliminate entirely their cognitive dissonance, and, thus, are able to restructure their concept of their gay selves as positive.(4) However, because some gay fathers' homophobia is so deeply rooted, they never achieve wholehearted self-acceptance. In the author's research, one divorced father with four teenagers had had a lover for seven years. He admitted that he was ashamed of his homosexuality, and that it was his shame that prevented him from coming out to his children. The third reason for not disclosing is the fear that if the ex-wife were to find out from the children, she would attempt to restrict visitation, try to regain custody, inform the man's employer, or be avenging in some other way.

IMPLICATIONS FOR PRACTITIONERS

Many of the counseling needs of gay fathers are similar to those described in the chapters on coming out (Chapter 3), on persons in male-female marriage (Chapter 12), and on the coupled gay (Chapter 18). Thus, the remarks here will be limited and specific.

A major difficulty many of these men have is accepting their gay identity. During marriage, they may make every effort to refrain from engaging in gay sex. When they do engage in it, they often deny its significance by blithely explaining it as "therapy" or attributing it solely to excessive alcohol, thereby diminishing its significance.(15) In addition, the married gay father may feel overwhelmed by guilt due to his belief in monogamy or his intense homophobia. Regardless of the cause, the man needs assistance to explore his sexuality and to become more accepting of it.

Another area of concern is whether to disclose one's homosexuality to one's wife. This is a momentous decision because of its far-reaching ramifications. All of the potential implications of not disclosing (and remaining married or divorcing) and disclosing — with unpredictable consequences — need deep exploration. Frequently, what is most important to the father is his concern for his children and his future relationship with them. My research indicates that the younger the children are when told, the easier it is for them to manage the knowledge. If the children grow up knowing, then it seems natural to them. If they learn when they are older, such as in their teens, they are likely to have more difficulty accepting it, since they have had more time for homophobic beliefs to be taken in without question.(23) Concurrent with the disclosure issue is the question of whether to remain married, which also needs full exploration.

Generally, gay fathers should disclose selectively, since to do otherwise could cause undue difficulties, especially for children who might become social pariahs if their friends were to discover their fathers were gay. In addition, disclosure to one's wife may also depend on what the man might lose if she reacts negatively. For instance, if one's ex-wife were to attempt to restrict visitation, regain custody, or be vindictive in some way, it would be unwise to disclose to her or to others, including the children, who might inform her. Although this author generally believes in disclosing, there are times when it is in the best interests of the father and his children that he keep his homosexuality secret from selected persons. It is likely that one can come out later when the reasons for not doing so are no longer extant.

Another piece of good advice for gay fathers is to make public the knowledge of their homosexuality very discreetly and cautiously, so that the children do not become stigmatized. This point was made clear to the author when the fourteen-year-old son of a gay father reported that his school chums were taunting him with the epithet "homoson" because his father appeared at school wearing excessive jewelry and the boy's friends had correctly identified the father as gay. The son reported that he hated his father for it. Hence, it behooves counselors to initiate the subject of discretion, if only for a brief discussion, in order to sensitize the father to the importance of it.(10) On the other hand, it is also important to stress that the father has a role in helping the child to learn to face adversity and to hold fast to principles of individual freedom and nonconformity which are counter to societal norms. Situations may arise in which the child feels compelled to defend his father and his father's lifestyle. On these occasions, the father needs to give the child the best support and advice he can.

The last area for discussion concerns the custodial gay father who establishes a live-in lover relationship. Problems usually center on the children, such as discipline, the lover's authority, and attention of the father to the children. It is best that the two men seek couples therapy when these problems arise, since it is not a problem owned by only one of the pair. Family therapy may also be advisable, since it, too, is a family problem. In addition to couples or family therapy, gay community resources should be used. Valuable peer support and assistance can be obtained through gay father support groups located in many U.S. cities, in Canada, and in other foreign countries. The International Coalition of Gay Fathers in Washington, D.C. maintains a list of gay father support groups and contact persons willing to provide assistance.(14) Peer advice and support can be a major source of ongoing help and sustenance for the single or coupled gay father with or without custody, whether or not problems exist.

CONCLUSIONS

Many gay men do marry. Although it is likely that most of them remain married and keep their homosexuality secret, many do divorce and adopt a gay lifestyle. Their needs for counseling are often multiple and complex. To be of assistance, the professional practitioner must have an understanding of family dynamics and an appreciation for the strong feelings of attachment these men have for their children. It is also paramount that the professional be accepting of the married, or formerly married, gay male. Because it is likely that gay men will continue to marry and become fathers, it behooves professionals in various helping disciplines to develop a knowledge base sufficient to be of assistance to these individuals.

REFERENCES

1. Bell, A.P. and Weinberg, M.S. (1978). *Homosexualities: A study in diversity among men and women.* New York: Simon & Schuster.

2. Bozett, F.W. (1987). Children of gay fathers. In F.W. Bozett (Ed.), *Gay and lesbian parents* (pp. 39-57). New York: Praeger.

3. Bozett, F.W. (1980). Gay fathers: How and why they disclose their homosexuality to their children. *Family Relations, 29,* 173-179.

4. Bozett, F.W. (1981). Gay fathers: Identity conflict resolution through integrative sanctioning. *Alternative Lifestyles, 4,* 90-107.

5. Bozett, F.W. (1981). Gay fathers: Evolution of the gay-father identity. *American Journal of Orthopsychiatry, 51,* 522-559.

6. Bozett, F.W. (1982). Heterogeneous couples in heterosexual marriages: Gay men and straight women. *Journal of Marital and Family Therapy, 8,* 81-89.

7. Bozett, F.W. (1984). Parenting concerns of gay fathers. *Topics in Clinical Nursing, 6,* 60-71.

8. Bozett, F.W. (1988). Social control of identity by children of gay fathers when they know their father is a homosexual. *Western Journal of Nursing Research, 10,* 550-565.

9. Bozett, F.W. (1987). Gay fathers. In F.W. Bozett (Ed.), *Gay and lesbian parents* (pp. 3-22). New York: Praeger.

10. Bozett, F.W. (1985). Gay men as fathers. In S.M.H. Hanson and F.W. Bozett (Eds.), *Dimensions of fatherhood.* Beverly Hills, CA: Sage.

11. Churchill, W. (1971). *Homosexual behavior among males: A cross-cultural and cross-species investigation.* Englewood Cliffs, NJ: Prentice-Hall.

12. Clark, D. (1977). *Loving someone gay.* Millbrae, CA: Celestial Arts.

13. Fadiman, A. (1983, May). The double closet. *Life,* pp. 76-78 *et seq.*

14. Gay Fathers' Coalition International, P.O. Box 50360, Washington, D.C. 20004.

15. Hencken, J.D. (1984). Conceptualizations of homosexual behavior which preclude homosexual self-labeling. *Journal of Homosexuality, 9,* 53-63.

16. Hunt, M. and Hunt, B. (1977). *The divorce experience.* New York: McGraw-Hill.

17. Jay, K. and Young, A. (1979). *The gay report.* New York: Summit Books.

18. Kingdon, M.A. (1979). Lesbians. *The Counseling Psychologist, 8,* 44-45.

19. Kinsey, A., Pomeroy, W., and Martin, C. (1948). *Sexual behavior in the human male.* Philadelphia: W.B. Saunders.

20. Miller, B. (1979). Gay fathers and their children. *The Family Coordinator, 28,* 544-552.

21. Miller, B. (1987). Counseling gay husbands and fathers. In F.W. Bozett (Ed.), *Gay and lesbian parents* (pp. 175-187). New York: Praeger.

22. Miller, B. (1979). Unpromised paternity: The life-styles of gay fathers. In M.P. Levine (Ed.), *Gay men.* New York: Harper & Row.

23. Moses, A.E. and Hawkins, R.O. (1983). *Counseling lesbian women and gay men.* St. Louis: C.V. Mosby.

24. Peterson, W. (1984, April 30). Coming to terms with gay parents. *USA Today,* p. 30.

25. Schulenburg, J. (1985). *Gay parenting.* Anchor/Doubleday.

26. Spada, J. (1979). *The Spada Report.* New York: New American Library.

Chapter 11
Lesbian mothers

Bernice Goodman

Lesbian mothers (along with gay fathers) are of necessity creators and innovators of alternative lifestyles. Most lesbian mothers share loving, sexual, and caring relationships with other women. In addition, they raise children and through the family structure relate to the mainstream of society. They show others new ways of being women, of being mothers, and of being family.

Together, the lesbian mother, the lover of the lesbian mother, and their children can create a nurturing, creative environment within which family life occurs.(1) The professional working with the lesbian mother needs to appreciate and value the unique opportunity for children being raised in a lesbian household, as well as to understand the special difficulties that are possible. Regarding the lesbian mother herself, the professional needs to be aware that she is living under pressures her straight sister does not have. The lesbian mother continually confronts situations not present in the heterosexual environment, and she tries to relate to her children in ways that minimize the problems inherent in a homophobic society. These are the special situations with which the lesbian mother must regularly grapple:

1. Not only must the lesbian mother deal with existing anti-female sexist societal attitudes, but she must deal with its homophobia as well. And she must contend with the discrimination she experiences from both of these sources.

2. The lesbian mother must work hard against the homophobia invariably absorbed by her children from society, in order to create a positive and creative interaction between herself and her children.

3. The lesbian mother must help her children effectively deal with society's hostility toward her lifestyle, and deal with

the generalized hostility and violence directed at being different or nonconforming.

4. If the father is present in the children's lives, she must help the children deal with the father's values and attitudes, if they are different from her own (especially if they are homophobic).

5. The lesbian mother must help her children move beyond a defensive position regarding society's negative perceptions of her own differences and the differences in the family she is creating. Through words and actions that repeatedly celebrate those differences of hers that society views as reprehensible, the lesbian mother demonstrates that she embraces a value system that accepts individual differences and the need to develop these differences as essential to a full and complete human life.

6. The lesbian mother must come out to her children. And the younger the child, the easier the process. Coming out to one's children serves to validate the connectedness, the bonding that the mother has been nurturing all along.

External reactions and pressures that characterize a hostile society are always on the horizon, and the lesbian mother must help her children anticipate and handle them. In my professional practice, I have found that the strength of younger children to deal with and be comfortable in an unconventional family lifestyle is in direct ratio to how comfortable a lesbian mother is with her lesbianism and her lesbian lifestyle, and to how often both are discussed with her children.

Older children who have lived in a former family structure based on heterosexual values need more time to adjust to and deal with changes in their mother's lifestyle and the subsequent effect this has on their family life. I have found that the more that older children have accepted the conventional social attitudes about gays and lesbians, and the stronger they have identified with traditional gender roles, the harder time they have in this process of adjustment and acceptance. However, with older children as with younger ones (teen and preteen, respectively), the self-acceptance and openness of the mother, along with her continued demonstration of love and care for her children, were the key factors in enabling children of all ages to absorb change. Indeed, it seems that the more articulate the lesbian mother is about the advantages of her lesbian lifestyle, the higher is the comfort and acceptance level of her children.

GENERAL PROBLEMS

No matter how she attained motherhood, and regardless of the quality of her parenting, a lesbian mother is singularly different from the heterosexual counterpart. She has no legal protection against having her children taken away from her solely because of her sexual orientation.(4)

The above quote establishes the basic context within which the problems for the lesbian mother occur. The professional working with her needs to absorb the feeling of being disenfranchised and of living in a world that has the potential for being hostile each day.

Everywhere she looks, the lesbian mother sees signs and sanctions of the heterosexual family and a denial of her family. Homophobia is rampant, and she does not have institutional support for herself, her lover, her child. This lack of support is a key problem and penetrates all aspects of her life.

An additional problem to be considered in working with lesbian mothers is the individual ethnicity and class style of the particular lesbian. Her attitudes and values about child-rearing, health problems, education, and family patterns are greatly influenced by the values practiced in her family of origin. This is particularly relevant in terms of the family of origin's attitudes about lesbian lifestyles. It is necessary to evaluate and separate the individual lesbian from the stance of her family and childhood experiences.

Another significant issue, or problem, for the lesbian mother is the lack of her acceptance in certain segments of the lesbian community. The extent of this will differ in each case, but it is a common problem of which to be constantly aware. The bias against child-rearing and any connection to men is a fact within the lesbian world. Fortunately, we are speaking of a small group of lesbians, but this is an additional pressure for the lesbian mother to deal with in her life, nevertheless.

THE PROFESSIONAL HELPS

The most important help a professional can offer is a nurturing, caring environment that gives a basic comfort to the lesbian mother. This comfort will allow her to use particular professional services to the maximum. Without such a nurturing and safe environment, the lesbian mother will have great trouble using professional help when needed, and may even stop seeking it.

There are several key areas that create a high-comfort environment.

Attitudes. The professional needs to check out and correct any negative, patronizing, or judgmental attitudes of his or her own regarding gays or lesbians. One exercise that each person can use toward this end is found in *Lesbian and Gay issues: A Resource Manual for Social Workers*.(5) The following are selected from this exercise:

> This Heterosexual Questionnaire reverses the questions that are very often asked of gays and lesbians by straight people. By having to answer this type of question, the heterosexual person will get some intellectual and emotional insight into how oppressive and discriminatory the "straight" frame of reference can be to lesbians and gays.
>
> A sample of these questions follows:
>
> 4. Is it possible that your heterosexuality stems from a neurotic fear of others of the same sex?
>
> 10. A disproportionate majority of child molesters are heterosexuals. Do you consider it safe to expose your children to heterosexual teachers?
>
> 11. Even with all the societal support marriage receives, the divorce rate is spiraling. Why are there so few stable relationships among heterosexuals?(5)

Do these questions upset you? If so, perhaps you need to re-examine your feelings about gay and lesbian people.

Knowledge. The more you know about gay people, the more easily and effectively you will be able to relate to us. The knowledge of our many types of lifestyles, and of the similarities to and vast differences from some heterosexual lifestyles needs to be learned.

Through intensive study courses, through in-service training programs conducted by lesbian and gay care providers for your staff, and through direct work with lesbians and gay people, professionals can begin to re-educate themselves to become better care providers for lesbian mothers.

Office Space. The waiting room and office space should reflect the lesbian mother's life.

Can she find herself in pictures on the wall or any place in your work space?

How do you answer the following questions?

1. Does the waiting room have lesbian and gay magazines and literature?

2. Does written material describing agency services include gay and lesbian people and their needs?

3. How many staff meetings are devoted to lesbian and gay issues, as well as to alternative lifestyles?

4. How many openly gay and lesbian professionals and workers are on the staff of the agency?

5. Does the agency encourage clients to feel free to ask for a professional who is knowledgeable about lesbian or gay cultures and who has been trained to recognize homophobic attitudes, values, and practices?(2)

Service Supports. In addition to direct help from the professional person, other structures that facilitate the delivery of services to lesbian mothers are peer support groups and self-help groups. Both of these offer emotional support and problem-solving ideas that allow for a deeper commitment by lesbian mothers to the care of themselves and their families.

The content of these groups and the participants are also rich sources for educating staff, whether through utilizing participants in seminars and presentations or through other joint educational endeavors. Attending relevant conferences with lesbian mothers, asking for their participation in jointly writing or preparing papers on the subject of lesbian motherhood, and having them volunteer to help in conducting workshops on their topic may also help many mothers feel better about themselves.

The lesbian mother of today is a woman hopeful of a better future. It is a future toward which she helps to lead the way.

REFERENCES

1. Goodman, B. (1980). Some mothers are lesbians. In E. Norman and A. Mancuso (Eds.), *Women's issues and social work practice.* Itasca, IL: F.E. Peacock.

2. Goodman, B. (1985). Out of the therapeutic closet. In H. Hidalgo, T.L. Peterson, and N.J. Woodman (Eds.), *Lesbian and gay issues: A resource manual for social workers* (pp. 140-144). Silver Spring, MD: National Association of Social Workers.

3. Stallard, K., Hrenreich, E., and Sklar, H. (1983). *Poverty in the American dream: Women and children first.* New York: Institute for New Communications.

4. Steinhorn, A. (1985). Lesbian mothers. In H. Hidalgo, T.L. Peterson, and N.J. Woodman (Eds.), *Lesbian and gay issues: A resource manual for social workers* (pp. 33-37).

5. Rochlin, M. (1985). Heterosexual questionnaire. In H. Hidalgo, T.L. Peterson, and N.J. Woodman (Eds.), *Lesbian and gay issues: A resource manual for social workers* (pp. 176-177).

Chapter 12

Gays and lesbians in mixed-orientation marriages

David R. Matteson*

Imagine a married couple with whom you have been friends for years. Now assume that you have just learned that the husband in that couple is involved in a gay relationship. Most likely, regardless of whether you are gay or straight yourself, you have a variety of emotional reactions as you try to digest this news about your friend, and its meaning for his wife and family.

If you are part of the mainstream heterosexual community, this information confronts you with two taboo issues at once: the issue of sexual orientation, and the issue of extramarital sex. Most heterosexuals have a more difficult time accepting homosexuality in persons whom they identify as being like themselves. As long as a heterosexual man can think of gays as afraid of women, or effeminate, or in some other way clearly different from himself, he can keep the possibility of homosexual feelings depersonalized. But when he meets another man who is married, has children, and seems to live a lifestyle much like his own, the discovery that this man is gay threatens the safe division of the world into the neat categories of gay and straight.

The categorizing of lifestyles into "them" and "us" is not unique to heterosexuals, of course. Lesbians and gays, in

* Author's note: I want to thank the men in two Chicago support groups for married gays (Gay & Married Men, and Review) and the men and women at the 10th Men and Masculinity Conference of the National Organization for Changing Men (St. Louis, June 1985) for their suggestions and personal anecdotes. My thanks also to my wife for her help in editing and for her continuing support and love.

their struggle to affirm their own orientations, have had to reject hopes of "fitting in" to the heterosexual model of the "normal" family. Members of hidden minority groups have more to process than members of visible minorities, such as ethnic or racial groups.(16, 21) Gays and lesbians are almost without exception reared in heterosexual homes by heterosexual parents, and learn of their minority status only through their private fantasies and experiences. For most, it is a slow and often painful process of discovery. Gradually they develop or locate a community or network of their own, but it is a community rejected by and hidden from the mainstream. The division of the world into these two communities becomes a real but unfortunate part of their life experience. They are likely to view "bisexuality" as self-deceit, or at best a way station on the voyage to gay affirmation.

Thus "bisexual" lifestyles, and especially mixed-orientation marriages, are often misunderstood by both gays and straights. Unfortunately, much of the published information about these marriages is based on clinical samples, and perpetuates myths about the neurotic character of such marriages. In what follows, I will rely heavily on the seven studies of gay husbands and the one of lesbian wives listed in the bibliography, all of which used either non-clinical (more representative) samples, or were conducted in gay-affirmative settings. For reasons to be discussed later, it appears that mixed-orientation marriages in which the husband is gay and the wife is straight, are far more prevalent than those in which the wife is lesbian and the husband is straight. Since lesbian wives are rare and very little is known about their marriages, in this chapter I will refer to the gay spouse as "he" and the straight partner as "she."

After I have described the patterns of development in marriages in which the husband is actively homosexual (based largely on my own six-year longitudinal study of such couples),(14) I will comment on how the patterns may be different in marriages in which the wife is lesbian or bisexual and the husband straight. The remainder of the chapter will focus on the particular needs that mixed-orientation couples have in their dealings with professionals, and suggestions as to how you, as a professional, can be helpful.

HOW MIXED-ORIENTATION MARRIAGES DEVELOP

Developing a positive identity as an oppressed minority is especially complicated for gays and lesbians because of the lack of visible role models in their families. For the bisexual, sexual fantasies and experiences may involve both sexes, making it even more difficult to unravel how one does and does not "fit" the norms. The question "Why do gay men want to marry women?" begins with the false assumption that most of these men, at the time of the marriage, had come to terms with the gay elements within themselves.

Less than one-third of the husbands in my study thought of themselves as gay when they met their wives-to-be and committed themselves to marriage.(13) The vast majority of the husbands engaged predominantly in heterosexual behavior at the time they married. The majority presumed themselves to be heterosexuals, or believed that male-female sex behavior would make monogamous marriage possible. Eighty-three percent of the men expected to remain monogamous when they married, and most of these men were monogamous for a number of years.

More often than not, the gay husbands had had some adult homosexual experiences before they married, but also had found themselves sexually attracted to women, or at least to the particular woman they fell in love with and chose to marry. Reasons these men gave for marrying were similar to those of most men who marry: they wanted a wife and family, and they loved the particular woman they married. Most were not aware of "the male couple" as a viable alternative lifestyle.(15) Only twenty percent implied that negative attitudes toward being gay were part of their motivation for marrying.(13)

In those mixed-orientation marriages which became stable, the first five or more years of the marriage were a period of developing the primacy of the marital relationship. It seemed crucial that a high level of intimacy and trust be developed before extramarital relationships could be tolerated. However, in almost all cases, some years into the marriage the husbands' same-sex desires became compelling, and were acted upon. Usually a year or two of sporadic homosexual activity occurred before the husbands experienced a crisis in sexual identity, leading to questions about their marriages.

Some men shared their re-experienced homosexual desires with their wives early in the process. Their decisions to disclose early seemed to have been related more to open communication in the marriage, higher comfort level with their own homosexual feelings, and a perception that their wives were strong and independent enough to tolerate the disclosure.

Other men made decisions to keep their homosexual behaviors separate and secret from their wives and families. Perhaps they dropped hints, and interpreted the responses to mean that their wives were too dependent, or too rigid, to handle more complete disclosure. There is some retrospective evidence that these men were more homophobic to begin with; perhaps they chose wives who were also less comfortable with sex and sexual differences. In any case, they delayed disclosure and were left with guilt both for being "queer" and for "cheating." Frequently, the conspiracy of silence resulted in a spiral of mistrust and distance which often destroyed the emotional bond of the marriage, though the outward appearance of a conventional marriage might be maintained. (There were notable exceptions; some secretive couples appeared to share a high degree of sensitivity and respect for each other.)

At the point of disclosure or discovery of the husband's same-sex involvements, the wife had to deal with three emotionally-charged issues at once: the husband's sexual orientation, the marital infidelity, and the fact that information affecting her life was not available to her before. The degree of deceit that occurred was an important factor in whether trust and re-negotiation could occur (though sometimes the "deceit" appeared to be better described as a conspiracy of silence).

The period immediately following the disclosure or discovery was usually tumultuous. At first the husbands were so intensely involved in issues relating to their emerging, or re-emerging, gay identities that they were insensitive, or at best only reactive, to the wives' needs. In some cases the wives quickly made the decision to reject the "negative" characteristics they discovered in their husbands, and to end the marriages; less frequently the husbands moved to that decision, often on the assumption that they were gay rather than bisexual, and that the marriages could not be continued under those circumstances. However, most often both partners experienced a difficult period of ambivalence, with husbands hoping things could work out but being unwilling to surrender their newly affirmed gay life, and with wives deeply hurting and longing for support. At this stage there was a tendency for all the previous and present problems in the marriage to be blamed on this particular issue. Marriage counseling (with counselors who were not heterosexist and who were familiar with open marriages) and peer support groups seemed particularly useful at this phase (see "Resources" at end of chapter).

After a year or so, if the wives were able to acknowledge and accept the husbands' bisexuality or homosexuality, these marriages typically moved into a negotiation stage,(12) moving either toward a renegotiation of the marriage as an acknowledged mixed-orientation marriage (often with extramarital sexual experimentation on the wives' sides) or toward amicable divorce and friendship. If the couple survived two years of this negotiation phase and was still together, chances were good that it remained together.(14) It appeared to take four or more years before mutually acceptable guidelines were developed and adhered to, leading to the stabilization of the marriage and to secure intimacy.

In this process, the wives learned that they could not control their husbands' activities, but that they could state their own needs clearly and firmly, could set their limits of tolerance, and could find ways to care for themselves when their husbands were not available. The husbands gradually moved through their identity crisis issues and began to take initiative to nurture their marriages. Husbands in the couples that stayed together took more initiative than they previously had in spending time and doing things with their wives. They came to rely less on their wives to initiate or demand time together. These husbands were also more empathic toward their wives and had an appreciation of the pain their wives had experienced during the tumultuous years.(13) While the wives learned to stop trying to control their husbands' gay relationships, or to deprive them of those, the husbands learned to stop being defensive, to listen to the wives' feelings and needs, and to initiate shared activities in the interest of the marriage.

In this process the couple usually learned a responsive pattern of negotiations, compromises, and, most importantly, a deep appreciation of differences. The marriages gradually re-stabilized with each spouse understanding and respecting the other more fully, each deeply desiring to remain intimate and committed to the other, yet each developing secure areas of their own identity apart from the other.(13)

It is important to note that not all of the couples who stayed together moved through open disclosure to a re-negotiated relationship. A large portion seemed to stabilize their marriages in an ongoing "mutual conspiracy of silence." Since it would not have been ethical to contact the wives in such marriages, we have only their husbands' impressions of how much they knew about the husbands' double lives. It is clear that, as a group, the husbands in secretive marriages experienced much greater conflict about their gay activities than did the husbands in the more open or acknowledged mixed-orientation marriages. And this first group of husbands did not develop as positive gay identities as did the second group. Both husbands and wives in the acknowledged mixed-orientation marriages appeared to achieve better levels of mental health, communicativeness, and intimacy than did those in the secretive marriages, although some of those differences probably were present in the individuals even before the marriages, and were reinforced and amplified by the style of the marriage.(13)

Three further findings about mixed-orientation marriages were noteworthy. First, it was clear that marriages in which the husbands were actively gay could become stable marriages. Most of the subjects in the "acknowledged" marriages in my longitudinal study were still in the early years of re-negotiation at the time of the first interviews. When contacted two years later for follow-up interviews, two-thirds of the acknowledged mixed-orientation marriages *and* two-thirds of the secretive mixed-orientation marriages were still intact.(13) Six years after the initial interviews, I did not find a single couple, that had been together at the two-year follow-up, that had yet separated, and a number of the couples that had previously been in the "secretive" group had now become more open.(14) Clearly, once the couples had survived the crisis it was possible for those marriages to stabilize.

Second, though earlier research disputed this conclusion,(16) I later established that gay or bisexual men in male-female marriages could develop congruent sexual identities that affirmed the gay component. A positive gay identity was far more difficult to achieve in a traditional marriage in which the bisexuality or homosexuality of the husband was not acknowledged by the wife.

Third, a comparison of couples married before the emergence of gay liberation (1969) with those married afterward, showed increasingly positive attitudes toward gays for both husbands and wives in the latter group. More of those husbands accepted and disclosed their sexual orientations to their wives before marrying them.(13) For those couples it appeared that the most serious crisis in the development of the marital relationship was not in the disclosure, but in the establishment of the primacy of the marital relationship.

CHARACTERISTICS OF MARRIAGES IN WHICH THE WIFE IS LESBIAN

Large-scale studies of homosexuality suggest that a larger proportion of lesbians than of gays have been in male-female marriages. However, fewer lesbians than gays actually appear to be living in mixed-orientation marriages. There are at least two reasons for this: First, the overall incidence of homosexuality is considerably lower in women than in men;(10,11) second, lesbian mixed-orientation marriages are less likely to survive than gay mixed-orientation marriages.(3)

Only one study exists describing male-female marriages in which the wife is lesbian or bisexual.(3) Several differences emerged when that study was compared with the description in my study of gay men in such marriages. Not only did the women not think of themselves as lesbian at the time of their marriages, but the great majority of them had not had *any* homosexual experiences prior to marriage (and, in most cases, no homosexual experiences until years into the marriage). This may be explained by the fact that women are socialized to do less sexual exploration than men (especially during the late 1960s when most of these women entered their marriages).

For the majority of these women, their first awareness and exploration of a lesbian orientation occurred after they already had marriage and family commitments. The majority of lesbian wives, like that small minority of gay husbands who first explored gay sex *after* marriage, had a higher incidence of marital dissolution.(3, 13) Further, women generally seemed to have more difficulty tolerating multiple relationships than did men.(3) Perhaps partly because of internal conflicts about extramarital sex, seventy-six percent of those wives who had extramarital lesbian experiences kept those a secret from their husbands. Most of the wives who did tell their husbands were unable to negotiate with their husbands for open marriages. It appeared that the lesbian mixed-orientation marriages seldom moved to or through the negotiation state that is so important to the survival of the mixed-orientation gay marriages.

Another difference in male and female socialization that may affect the survival of mixed-orientation lesbian mothers concerns the development of intimacy skills. Men tend to develop their deepest, emotionally intimate relationships with women. Women tend to develop theirs with other women, as well as with their husbands.(5, 6) Lesbians in marriages reported stronger *emotional* attachments to their lesbian friends than their gay male counterparts reported feeling toward their gay friends.(3) The gay male scene typically accepts recreational sex, while women's socialization stresses relationship-oriented sex. The married gay was not likely to see his gay buddies as a replacement for the intimacy he had with his wife. By contrast, when a married women entered a lesbian relationship, she was likely already to have had a deeply intimate friendship with the woman, which then developed into a sexual relationship. The wives' belief in monogamy and their dissatisfaction with men's weaker training in intimacy skills led them to think of their lesbian relationships as replacements for marriage.

A final speculation concerning the earlier and more frequent dissolution of lesbian mixed-orientation marriages had to do with the fact that when couples divorced, the women were usually assured of having custody of the children. One of the reasons gay men gave for staying in their marriages was that they did not want to lose their home life and children. Women were less likely to lose the children and home life (especially if they had kept secret their lesbian identities so that it could not be used against them in the divorce proceedings). The fear of losing the children, of course, might have been a factor in the lower disclosure rates of lesbians to their husbands.

It seems clear from the above discussion that lesbian and bisexual married women are more likely than their gay counterparts to terminate their marriages because of conflicts arising from their homosexuality or bisexuality.(3) However, it must be remembered that very little is known about lesbians in male-female marriages, partly because it is so difficult to find a sample of these couples when they are still together. Part of the difficulty in locating them may have to do with the privacy of the wives, who seem less likely to discuss their lesbianism, and less likely to be in contact with other gays and lesbians, and, consequently, with the gay or lesbian counselors and researchers who study such things. It is possible, then, that there may be a hidden population of such marriages which may or may not fit the above description.

WHAT DO WE NEED FROM PROFESSIONALS?

By now it should be clear that there is no single pattern for the relationships of persons in mixed-orientation marriages. Gays and lesbians in male-female marriages live in a wide variety of lifestyles varying in at least four important aspects:

—the degree of self-affirmation regarding being lesbian or gay;

—the degree of secrecy or openness with spouse, family, friends, and the community about their gay lifestyle;

—the degree of comfort (vs. guilt) about deviation from

monogamous male-female marriage as the model for intimate relationships;

—the awareness of and sensitivity to confining gender roles.

It is crucial to recognize that the conflicts experienced by persons in these marriages are not simply conflicts about sexual orientation, but struggles with the meaning of intimacy, and with the narrow, confining standards for intimacy that our society has normalized by sanctioning only an exclusive form of love between a man and a woman. The homophobia and the sex role stereotypes that inhibit deep friendships between men, or between women, are problems for heterosexuals as well, though gay and lesbian persons may be more sensitized to these issues because of experiences of being different early in their development. The issues with which these couples struggle are merely exacerbations of the more general crisis in our culture regarding intimacy.

HOW DOES THE PROFESSIONAL LEARN OF THE CLIENT'S LIFESTYLE?

Given the invisibility of this minority group, the question arises: How would a professional become aware that he was dealing with a gay or lesbian in a mixed-orientation marriage? The first caution to be emphasized is that, in relating to *any* married client, one should avoid assuming that the client is living a traditional lifestyle. This means, among other things, being cautious in the words one uses, avoiding slang and demeaning terms, or humor that puts down any alternative lifestyle.

Suppose you have heard rumors in the community about a client's lifestyle. First, think carefully about whether the lifestyle issue has any relevance to the services you are offering the client. If it has no relevance, put aside your curiosity and avoid assuming that the rumors are either true or false. If the information *is* relevant, explain directly to the client that you have heard the rumor, that you do not want to assume anything on the basis of a rumor but that it is important for both you and the client to know the truth about the rumor, and to explore the significance of its content if the rumor is true. If your tone is matter-of-fact, rather than

– 134 –

judgmental or dramatic, most likely the client will sense the genuine importance of the inquiry and will feel fairly comfortable about discussing his lifestyle.

In one instance, the child welfare agency was called by neighbors to investigate a mixed-orientation couple. The rumor was that the gay husband was using the children to make pornographic photos. In this case the agency was obligated to investigate the rumor. To quote the husband:

> The case worker damn near fell off her chair when I told her I wasn't ashamed of my orientation and that either of them could ask any questions they wanted to regarding our relationship, or my sexual activity outside the marriage. Though they maintained a judgmental reserve, they had an opportunity to correct a number of misconceptions ... and our children were the best proof available. The older child's response, when asked about (the charges) was, "You've got to be kidding — my parents?"

The agency concluded that it was being used to harass the couple because of their lifestyle, and later used the couple as a resource for in-service training of their staff. Clearly the professional's checking out the rumor, and the openness of the couple, worked for the benefit of both.

Though some trusting and self-assured clients may disclose their mixed-orientation lifestyle in casual conversation with a professional (just as clients in traditional lifestyles may bring up family or social information), more frequently there are specific reasons why the information is relevant which lead the client to self-disclose. Examples include a medical check-up where testing for sexually transmittable diseases is desired, therapy or counseling where the lover is an important part of the client's support system, or seeking legal services where the client wants to include the lover in the will.

Because married gays and lesbians are less likely to be suspected as homosexual, they may stay closeted, and thus have little or no experience with safe disclosures. A professional has some responsibility to think through the situations in which lifestyle issues might be relevant to the professional services he offers, and to provide an atmosphere which

– 135 –

encourages such disclosures in a client who is still embarrassed, feels guilty, or has not overcome internalized homophobia.

SPECIAL NEEDS OF MIXED-ORIENTATION COUPLES

Despite the broad range of lifestyles among lesbians and gays in male-female marriages, they have at least five personal and relational concerns in common, which deserve respect from helping professionals.

1) Respect the uniqueness of each person's sexual orientation. Avoid judging gays, lesbians, and bisexuals against either heterosexual or gay or lesbian standards.

2) Respect individual attempts to meet needs for intimacy and for sexual satisfaction in those ways that are authentic for the client. Be careful not to make judgments by using monogamous assumptions about how these needs should be satisfied.

3) Respect the boundaries and contracts these individuals have worked out within their own marriages and families.

4) Respect that they are sharing confidential information and honor their assessments of the need for privacy based upon the heterosexist and homophobic society in which we live.

5) Respect their choice of the issues about which they are seeking help, and get on with the task at hand.

Discussion and examples of each of these needs follow.

1) Respect the uniqueness of each person's sexual orientation:
The professionals need to be aware that sexism and homophobia are present in almost all persons raised in our culture today, so professionals must be willing to examine their own attitudes. In face-to-face interactions with clients in mixed-orientation marriages, professionals need the willingness to engage clients as intelligent and equal partners in shared problem-solving, and to be honest about their own errors or lack of knowledge without abdicating the leadership role in providing help.(7) (Counselors and therapists are urged to read Gochros's more extensive list of "prerequisites" for working with these couples: Reference 7).

Perhaps guilt or shame is the most destructive force in the struggle to come to terms with a sexual identity that does not fit the norm — guilt or shame instilled by parents, teachers, ministers, and others in authority. It has already been noted that bisexuals have a particularly difficult struggle to find their sexual identities, due to the lack of models either in the home or in a sub-culture. On top of this, if they are in marriages, they face guilt for breaking the vows of sexual exclusivity. When gays or lesbians receive messages of guilt from professionals in authority, it serves only to delay the process of their coming to terms with their own orientations and affirming them. It is relevant at this point to dispel several myths.

First, it is clear from the histories of lesbians and gays in marriages that an active heterosexual life will not make their "weird desires" go away.

Second, the view that gay liberation is a threat to morality is based on ignorance about the history of the gay movement. The amoral view of the gay life based on aesthetics and pleasure, in vogue early in the century, is rejected by gay social activists, who seek to replace a limiting and destructive morality with a more inclusive morality.(8)

When biblical religion is used to validate prejudice and oppression against lesbians and gays, it is important to remember that those few recorded prohibitions against homosexual acts refer either to violent or coercive sex (gang rape, slave-child-prostitution) or to the rituals of rival, pagan tribes from whom the Hebrews believed they were "called apart." The prohibitions are not condemnations of a homosexual orientation per se, or of homosexual acts in a covenanted love relationship. Further, the recorded words of Jesus do not contain a single prohibition against homosexuality or against same-sex sexual behavior. (For excellent summaries of biblical scholarship on this issue see 17 and 18.)

In regard to marriage and sexual exclusivity, the Judeo-Christian scriptures were concerned that the covenanted relationship not be violated. But the covenant of marriage was not necessarily restricted to two persons (as the multiple marriages common in the early Judaic scriptures make clear).

Clergy and educators can do a great deal to reduce intolerance and injustice, if they refuse to perpetuate these myths and instead provide accurate information from both historical and literary studies of religious scriptures and from modern psychology and social science. Since professionals in small communities and the suburbs may not have friends or acquaintances who are openly gay or lesbian, the church or synagogue may be the most likely source of their own information — or misinformation.

Since married gays and lesbians are likely to continue to live with their families, rather than to migrate to the "gay ghettos" of major cities, they are likely, for example, to see local physicians or public clinics for their check-ups for sexually transmitted diseases (STDs). Instead of a staff familiar with the gay community, they will probably encounter health professionals snickering when asked for anal as well as penile and oral STD tests. One husband reported that a public health worker hostilely interrogated him with questions, such as: "Why do you do these things?" "What makes you guys like that? I just don't understand people like you." On the other hand, if a local physician is comfortable and respectful in dealing with lesbians and gays, word may get around the network of gays and lesbians in that area to patronize that particular physician.

Professionals should not only practice respect for differing lifestyles themselves, but they should help to educate their colleagues. They need to speak out against unprofessional conduct where and when it occurs. Recently, a police raid on a gay bar brought public exposure to a married man on the faculty of a private liberal arts college. The dean terminated his employment. The media carried no news of other faculty protesting the dean's unjust decision. The refusal to grant academic degrees because of a student's sexual orientation, the dramatization of homosexuality in court proceedings regarding child custody and divorce, and other public unprofessional behaviors occur regularly, but often go unchallenged by colleagues in the professions.

2) Respect the attempts of gay people to meet their needs for intimacy and sexual satisfaction in ways authentic for them:

"As we grow up we are faced with the reality that we cannot simultaneously fit in and be ourselves."(8)

This quote was written in regard to lesbians and gays. However, it applies as well to bisexuals and to straight partners in mixed-orientation marriages. The traditional marriage simply does not fit these people. If the gay or lesbian spouse finally makes the decision to stay in the marriage it is usually for reasons very similar to those of heterosexuals in marriages. Our dreams of the ideal partner and the reality of the person we discover our partner to be seldom match exactly; yet, there may be enough satisfaction and love to decide that marriage was a good decision after all, and to choose to continue the marriage.

Similarly, one can assume that a spouse who is aware of her bisexual or gay partner's activities has borne her share of pain at the loss of her idealized marriage, has erected and sought to enforce what boundaries and limits are considered necessary for her own integrity, and has focused on developing a fulfilling life of her own (rather than depending solely on her husband for a "reflected" identity). It takes strength to carry out such a decision; yet, women in these marriages sometimes report being treated as if they were to be pitied, or as if they were desperate or highly dependent.

Frequently, professionals who have not had the opportunity to know many couples with open marriages mistake the open contract as a license for promiscuity or wild permissiveness. They fail to recognize the deep level of trust, and the letting go of possessiveness and control, which can be involved in a love that is based on the needs of two unique individuals, rather than on a planned formula.

It is important that professionals examine their own values and views concerning the nature of love. Some value questions follow which may stimulate this examination: How crucial to a love relationship is honesty about oneself, or is it an act of love to protect the partner from hurtful information? Is true love possessive, or does it seek to overcome jealousy and possessiveness? Is monogamy necessarily a happier state, or is it a more intimate style of marriage? To what extent does a separate life for each individual enhance the depth of sharing within the relationship? Is love inherently limited to only one other person, or is it expansive? Does one's love for one person necessarily diminish one's love for another?

Perhaps the most important result of the examination of values is a degree of humility about the answers — and a recognition that what seems right for oneself and for one's own marriage may not be right for another person or for a different relationship.

Regardless of the particular profile the professional ends up with from a clarification of his values, professional power should not be abused by requiring or forcing compliance to rules designed to serve the traditional marriage and family. For example, a gay or bisexual person in the intensive care unit of a hospital may desire that both his spouse and his lover visit, although the visitation rules allow only immediate family to visit. The psychological intent of the rule, rather than a legalistic interpretation, should prevail.

3) Respect the boundaries we have worked out within our own marriages and families:

One of the reasons many people respond negatively to the concept of open marriage, I suspect, is their instinctive awareness of the importance of boundary issues in intimate relationships. Just as any successful couple with children must guard the primacy of the marriage from the children's demands, regardless of how much they love the children, the mixed-orientation couple, though they may embrace an ideal of unbounded love, in day-to-day life must work out times and spaces in which their couple relationship is not intruded upon by the demands of other lovers.

One manifestation of the boundary issue is the question of how much the heterosexual is told, or wishes to know. Sometimes this is worked out in careful negotiations between the two parties; in other cases, it emerges from a subtle series of nonverbal interactions leading to a conspiracy of silence. Either way, if there are "secrets," they are one of the agreements in this unique marriage and this agreement should not be violated by the professional. Consider an incident which happened several decades ago. A married gay was arrested for indecency when police "busted" a section of a public park known to be a cruising place for gay sex. The man's lawyer, notifying the wife that her husband was in jail needing bond, explained in detail the circumstances of his arrest. If the lawyer had assured the wife that her husband was physically okay and had let the husband explain the incident himself, the boundaries of both husband and wife would have been better respected. In a later meeting, the lawyer expressed pity toward the wife for putting up with the husband, which the wife experienced as both embarrassing and demeaning.

There is accommodation in all marriages. However, mixed-orientation marriages frequently involve much more individually-tailored forms of contracting and care. Once both spouses have accepted that the norms simply do not fit their personalities and needs, the freedoms and limits, the openness and the boundaries that are set are unique to each couple. The most important general rule in this regard is to avoid making any assumptions about what is open or what is secret in a particular couple's communication. It is not necessary to know all their rules; the professional simply needs to avoid acting as a message carrier between two married persons.

Many marriage counselors, myself included, believe strongly in open communication between intimates. We see secrets, in areas that affect the relationship, as potentially destructive. We also know that effective communication involves sensitive timing, not just openness; counselors should remind themselves of this when they tend to be judgmental about secrets. It is important to remember that the gay spouse has spent years trying to overcome his homophobia, and has finally come out to himself. The straight spouse may have only recently begun to deal with this issue. Appropriate timing for her may be slower than for him.

Counselors who cannot handle the complexities of knowing and respecting one partner's secrets probably should not try to do therapy with these couples. At the very least, they owe it to their clients to explain their rules regarding no secrets from the beginning, before holding any individual appointments in which the client may divulge secrets from the expectation of confidentiality.

*4) Respect that gay people are sharing confidential informa-
tion, and honor their presumption of the need for privacy as
they face a homophobic society:*

Although it is part of most professional ethics, the issue
of confidentiality has a somewhat different character in
relation to gays or lesbians facing homophobic employers,
neighbors, landlords, relatives, and work associates. Occasionally, professionals may expose information about a client
in a way that is unwarranted, if not malicious. An orthopedic
physician was treating a married man who suffered malfunc-
tion of his joints as a result of an industrial accident. When
the case went to court, the doctor, who had heard rumors of
the man's sexual orientations, raised the issue on the pretext
that syphilis was a possible cause of the medical problem.
Further medical testimony made it clear that this particular
malady could not have been caused by syphilis. The physician could have checked out his hypothesis by calling in a
consultant before making his court statement, rather than
exposing the man's private life in public court hearings — an
unprofessional invasion of privacy.

More typically, the incidents in which confidentiality is
not respected involve college professors, counselors, or clergy
who have begun to overcome their own homophobia and, in
an attempt to help others do the same, are sloppy about
confidentiality and naive about the risks of exposure for the
client. For example, a minister of a small-town church was
attending a conference and overheard a negative comment
about homosexuality. She proceeded to tell about a gay man
in her parish who was raising his children with his lover now
that his wife had abandoned her marriage and family. The
minister's intent was to stress the positive nurturing qualities
of these two men. But, by openly stating what was only
suspected in her community, she placed the men in jeopardy
of losing their jobs.

Though many of us gay people believe that the personal
and political advantages of being out of the closet in our
professions and in our communities outweigh the risks, we
also know that the risks are not simply phobic delusions;
they are real. And the power to make decisions as to when
and where to take these risks belongs to the lesbian or gay

person along with the lover or spouse, and not to the professional.

5) *Respect the gay person's choice of the issues needing professional help, and get on with the task at hand:*
The most frequently stated criticism concerning professionals' work with mixed-orientation couples is that they get fixated on the uniqueness of the lifestyle and lose sight of the issues for which services are being sought. It appears common for counselors or ministers to assume that the lifestyle is the basic problem, regardless of the stated reasons the client gives for seeking professional help. One woman, married to a gay man, described three months of therapy with a counselor, during which time the woman tried to resolve an issue with her daughter. After a resolution was achieved, the counselor expressed surprise at the mother's level of relief. "You really *were* that upset over your daughter!" the counselor exclaimed. "That really *was* the problem, not your husband?" The counselor had not believed that the husband-wife relationship could be stable, and had assumed it was the cause of the problem. At least, in this case, the counselor was able to admit her own mistake.

Both gay and bisexual people and their straight partners have reported therapeutic relationships which the client finally terminated because the counselor seemed unable to shift from focusing on the mixed-orientation marriage as the problem. The issues of communication, problem-solving skills, too much criticism, failure to give positive strokes to each other — issues common in marriage counseling — may be overlooked when the counselor is distracted by the uniqueness of the alternative lifestyle.

Counselors and ministers are not the only professionals who make the error of focusing too long on the mixed-orientation marriage to the neglect of the issues for which the client seeks help. Incidents related by persons in these marriages include a physician who, at each check-up, asked the gay husband, "Are you still endangering your health by your gay life?" though the physician failed to address the patient's heavy cigarette smoking; a well-intentioned minister whose first topic of conversation whenever he met the parishioner

– 143 –

was some news item regarding gays; and a teacher who, at each parent-teacher conference with the straight wife, brought up the issue of "the effect of your marriage" on the child. As one gay husband wrote me, there are many issues within our lives that need to be addressed which are not dealt with when "professionals see the mixed-orientation marriage itself as the sole issue."

CONCLUSIONS

Most of the special issues that concern lesbians, bisexuals, and gays in mixed-orientation marriages have to do with the fact that (like other gays, bisexuals, and lesbians) they can choose to hide their lifestyles in an effort to avoid discrimination. Every lesbian and gay faces the question of how hidden to be (with the resulting fears of exposure, the sense of being dishonest, and the difficulty in integrating the different parts of one's life), or how open (with the threats of limiting job opportunities, losing friends, and risking rejection from family). For bisexuals, gays, and lesbians in heterosexual marriages, this decision is complicated by their desires to continue to live with their spouses and families, and to be part of their straight communities.

Most of the illustrations I have cited of the relationships between lesbians, gays, or bisexuals in mixed-orientation marriages and their professional helpers have focused on problems, and may, thus, have given too negative an impression of these relationships. Sometimes our history of oppression leads us gay and bisexual people to expect rejection where none is present. Sometimes professionals are wonderfully human and compassionate, and the barriers of prejudice and feelings of rejection melt away. An older gay husband who has never dared come out to his wife felt the isolation with particular intensity during two agonizing years when his lover was dying of AIDS. Several weeks after the lover died, the husband developed a bad skin rash and went to the family physician. The physician suspected the rash might be a symptom of second-stage syphilis, and asked the husband directly, "Are you by any chance gay?" The husband, having been closeted for years, quickly and routinely denied it. Once the patient left the doctor's office, he began to wonder why the doctor had asked, and convinced himself that the doctor suspected he had AIDS. By the next week, when he returned to the doctor's office for test results, he was panicked, and blurted out, "I lied to you last week. I want you to know that I am gay. But my wife doesn't know it." The physician responded by calmly putting his arm around the patient, and assuring him that this was information shared in professional confidence and that there was no reason the physician would need to tell her. The patient was tremendously relieved, not just that the physician respected his boundaries, but that his manner communicated no judgment or rejection, but rather empathy toward the man's panic.

Respect is an interpersonal phenomenon. Some of us, with years of being open, and with sensitive and supportive wives, families, friends, and colleagues, can approach homophobic professionals without letting their prejudices affect us personally. But others, with less experience in coming out, and who are less secure in self-acceptance and self-respect, are more vulnerable. My hunch is that professionals like yourself, who are reading this book, are making the effort to become sensitized to others' vulnerabilities, not just because you are professional, but because you care. For that, I respect you.

RESOURCES
Some organizations that may provide support to persons in mixed-orientation marriages

One of the most helpful resources for partners in mixed-orientation marriages who feel alone and overwhelmed is a peer support group that includes others struggling with the same issues. Most large cities now have support groups for gay married men. The quickest way to locate them is to call the local Gay Hotline or Gay Switchboard. Many of the organizations also have a rap group for the wives. To the best of my knowledge, at present there are no groups solely for lesbian wives.

Since gay and bisexual people in mixed-orientation marriages often feel their marital situations are not understood in either the gay or straight community, groups which consciously attempt to foster dialogue between gays and straights are often supportive. For women, consciousness-raising groups of chapters of NOW may be helpful. For men, local affiliates of NOCM are usually supportive. To obtain local addresses contact:

National Organization For Women, 1401 New York Ave., N.W. Washington, D.C. 20005

National Organization For Changing Men, 794 Pennsylvania Ave. Pittsburgh, PA 15221

REFERENCES

1. Bozett, F.W. (1982). Heterogeneous couples in heterosexual marriages: Gay men and straight women. *Journal of Marital and Family Therapy, 8,* 81-89.

2. Coleman, E. (1981/1982). Bisexual and gay men in heterosexual marriage: Conflicts and resolution in therapy. *Journal of Homosexuality, 7(2/3),* 93-103.

3. Coleman, E. (1985, Spring). Bisexual women in marriages. *Journal of Homosexuality, 11,* 87-99.

4. Coleman, E. (1983, Fall). Personal discussion. Chicago.

5. Douvan, E. and Adelson, J. (1966). *The adolescent experience.* New York: John Wiley & Sons.

6. Garbarino, J. (1985). *Adolescent development: An ecological perspective.* Columbus, Ohio: Charles E. Merrill Co.

7. Gochros, J.B. (1989). *When husbands come out of the closet.* New York: Haworth Press.

8. Harrison, J. (1985, Spring). Salmagundi review: Distorting the gay vision. *Changing men, 14,* 20-21, 42-43.

9. Humphreys, L. (1969). *Tearoom trade: Impersonal sex in public places.* Chicago: Aldine.

10. Kinsey, A.C., Pomeroy, W.B., and Martin, C.E. (1948). *Sexual behavior in the human male.* Philadelphia: Saunders.

11. Kinsey, A.C., Pomeroy, W.B., Martin, C.E., and Gebhard, P.H. (1953). *Sexual behavior in the human female.* Philadelphia: Saunders.

12. Latham, J.D. and White, G.D. (1978). Coping with homosexual expression within heterosexual marriages: Five case studies. *Journal of Sex and Marital Therapy, 3,* 198-212.

13. Matteson, D.R. (1985, Spring). Bisexual men in marriage: Is a positive homosexual identity and stable marriage possible? *Journal of Homosexuality, 11,* 149-171.

14. Matteson, D.R. Mixed-orientation marriages: A six-year study. In process.

15. McWhirter, D.P. and Mattison, A.M. (1984). *The male couple: How*

relationships develop. Englewood Cliffs, NJ: Prentice-Hall.

16. Miller, B. (1978). Adult sexual resocialization: Adjustments toward a stigmatized identity. *Alternative Lifestyles, 1,* 207-234.

17. Nelson, J.B. (1978). *Embodiment: An approach to sexuality and Christian theology.* Minneapolis: Augsburg.

18. Olson, Mark. (No date). Untangling the web: A look at what scripture does and does not say about homosexual behavior. Philadelphia: The Other Side.

19. Ross, H.L. (1971). Modes of adjustment of married homosexuals. *Social Problems, 18,* 385-393.

20. Ross, M.W. (1983). *The married homosexual man: A psychological study.* Boston: Routledge & Kegan Paul.

21. Weinberg, T.S. (1978). On "doing" and "being" gay. *Journal of Homosexuality, 4,* 143-156.

22. Wolf, T.J. (1985, Spring). Psychological and sociological aspects of male homosexual behavior in marriage. *Journal of Homosexuality, 11.*

Chapter 13
The co-dependent client

Cheryl Hetherington

Co-dependency is an emerging health concern for many helping professionals. In the past, it has been associated with chemically abusive families. Although co-dependency often does develop in chemically abusive family environments, it is born out of the rules of the family, and not as a result of chemical abuse. In essence, co-dependency involves accepting oppressive rules within the family which support compulsive-obsessive behavior patterns, such as overeating, overworking, perfectionism, and chemical abuse. When the behavior is related to alcohol, some refer to the co-dependent person as a co-alcoholic, but for purposes of maintaining a broader perspective, in this chapter the syndrome will be referred to as co-dependency.

Co-dependency is defined specifically as:

> an emotional, psychological, and behavioral condition that develops as a result of an individual's prolonged exposure to the practice of a set of oppressive rules — rules which prevent the open expression of feeling, as well as the direct discussion of personal and interpersonal problems.(7)

When these rules are integrated into day-to-day life, co-dependents consider their feelings secondary to the feelings of others or, in some cases, they may be unaware of their own feelings. As a consequence, painful and confusing patterns are developed by people whose beliefs, feelings, and behaviors center on individuals and things outside of themselves.

Gay and lesbian co-dependents are often the lover, friend, drinking buddy, relative, or co-worker of a chemically dependent person. The co-dependents will take care of the chemically dependent persons by picking up the pieces that they are no longer able to handle. They may clean up the messes, call in sick, cook the meals, and make excuses to friends about inappropriate behavior of the abusive partners. Thus, the co-dependents may rescue and, eventually, assume greater responsibility for life decisions, come to depend on being needed by the chemically dependent partners, and actually become addicted to the abusers just as the abusers are addicted to a substance. When this pattern is in place, both the chemically dependent persons and the co-dependents function in a system of denial, low self-esteem, depression, social isolation, and high stress.(10) This is compounded when gay men or lesbians exist "in the closet" or without community support.

DEVELOPMENT FROM FAMILY RULES

Smalley(6) suggests that co-dependency patterns begin when a critical caregiver is insensitive to the physical and psychological boundaries of a child. The invasion of these boundaries can include lots of criticism, name-calling, negative comparisons to others, or blaming. For example, a mother might say, "You are just like your stupid father; you don't appreciate anything I do." If a child internalizes such messages, he or she learns inappropriate responsibility and low self-esteem.

Adult children of chemically dependent parents grow up with a set of rules which encourage further painful and confusing patterns. These rules are called the "don't talk, don't trust, don't feel" rules.(1) They are described as follows:(8)

a. *It is not okay to talk about problems.* This is the "no talk" rule, where communication is poor, and where outward expressions of emotions are discouraged. Children learn to ignore or hide their feelings; thus, personal identity and needs come second. They feel as if they are "walking on eggshells."

b. *Feelings should not be expressed openly.* This rule is learned by hearing things like "I don't know what you are so happy about" or "I'll give you something to cry about." According to this family rule, children learn that it is more acceptable to deny feelings than to express them. As a result of being cut off from their emotions, people often develop tension headaches, ulcers, rashes, loss of sleep, and depression.

c. *Communication should be indirect.* With the family functioning under this restriction, often one family member will act as a messenger between the other two (triangulation). Here, the child becomes a mediator for the mother and father, trying to patch up arguments. The child is used by the mother or father, or both, to avoid talking face to face. Messages get mixed or confused. The development of co-dependency happens as the child learns not to communicate openly and to feel responsible for others' personal problems.

d. *Be strong, be good, be right, be perfect, make us proud.* With this rule, the parent conveys unrealistic expectations to the child. There is often only one right way to do things in the home, and the child begins to learn that "enough is never enough." Co-dependents create an ideal in their heads about what is good or right or best, and the ideal is so far removed from what is possible that they end up feeling punished because they do not meet their expectations.

e. *Do not be selfish.* Under this rule, children learn to view themselves as wrong for placing their own needs before the needs of others. Co-dependents try to feel good about themselves by taking care of others, and eventually their self-esteem becomes dependent on their success in caring for others. Without someone to take care of, the co-dependent is left without purpose or worth. For co-dependents who grow up in this system, where this rule is rigidly applied to every situation, one feeling emerges with certainty: guilt.

f. *Do as I say, not as I do.* This rule teaches a child not to trust. Co-dependents believe that their parents are not honest because they see behavior that is inconsistent with the spoken rules. They begin to protect themselves from the pain of this inconsistency by not trusting at all.

g. *It is not okay to play.* Children in a family with oppressive rules are deprived of the carefree play of childhood: their time is spent taking care of ... or being a mediator. Co-dependents expect themselves to work twice as hard as everyone else just to feel okay. It becomes increasingly important to their feelings of adequacy that they have something to do *all* of the time. Ultimately, they deny their need to play. The more that they begin to suffer, the more they see playing in spontaneous or silly ways as too frightening. Play is viewed as being a selfish, irresponsible, and useless activity.

h. *Do not rock the boat.* This rule seeks to maintain an unhealthy balance in the family. Diversity is not accepted. The orders are "We don't talk about our problems. We don't show our feelings." The family does not allow any healthy change because it is too frightening. This rule — don't rock the boat — oversees and directs all the other rules in the family.

Gay and lesbian co-dependents have also learned the rules of "don't rock the boat" and "don't talk" concerning their sexual orientation. Their employers, friends, and families typically do not want to hear about their lifestyle. Thus, the reinforcement of the co-dependency rules creates even greater fear, confusion, and self-doubt.

The ability to be self-disclosing is especially important to the mental health of gays and lesbians who have been subjected to long-standing societal directives that say: Be silent, be invisible. The repressive family rules that lead to co-dependency and the oppressive societal rules regarding the lifestyles of gays and lesbians go hand in hand in creating a powerful developmental block. The repressive effect on the ability of gay people to make themselves known to others is detrimental to the successful establishment of relationships with other people. Overcoming this repression and acquiring the ability to self-disclose is not only critical to social development, it is essential to the growth of intimacy in close, loving relationships.(2)

Co-dependents are generally the loyal, responsible, good kids that help out in times of need. They do not necessarily come from homes where one of the parents is chemically dependent, but in many cases, co-dependency is developed in such families. The roles that are taught and developed within chemically dependent families, and that assist individuals in functioning within that family, are self-destructive in the outside world. One of these roles is that of the family hero. A child in this role is a compulsive achiever, and is often the pivotal figure around whom the family stakes its claim to being a normal healthy family.

The family hero has usually played a large part in rescuing and protecting the chemically dependent parent by softening the blows of the effects of the parent's behavior. The hero may clean up after the parent, take the parent to the hospital after an injury, or call the boss to report illness. Requests for help become chronic by the abuser. The family heroes, who see themselves as responsible, covet this family role of "responsibility" and often become co-dependents. A family hero who is also gay or lesbian may be particularly frightened of losing this role and the love of the family if sexual orientation is revealed.

RECOGNIZING CO-DEPENDENT CLIENTS

There are some common characteristics of adult co-dependents. They appear to be "strong" and in control of their lives. Yet, beneath the public images of strength and security often lie the opposite feelings of insecurity, self-doubt, and confusion. Many co-dependents say, "Everyone thinks I am so strong. All my friends come to me with their problems. If they really knew what I am like, they would be very surprised and probably wouldn't even be my friends." There is a large gap between the public image and the private image. By continually doing what seems to be the appropriate thing to do, co-dependents gradually ignore and deny their feelings and have a self-identity associated with a public image. Again, this is consistent with societal messages regarding the gay and lesbian lifestyle. The straight world tends to ignore, deny, or respond with hostility to gay and lesbian individuals. The gaps between the public and private self are reinforced for this homophobic norm.

Additional behaviors can signal co-dependency. Co-dependents may be addicted in areas such as compulsive spending, compulsive working, compulsive sexual activity, excessive drinking, or obsession with food (anorexia, bulimia, or constant eating). Often there are stress-related physical problems, such as headaches, backaches, or gastrointestinal distresses.

There are some clues that often indicate that a person is co-dependent.(9) These include:

a. Super responsibility: "If I don't take care of things, they just won't get done."

b. Pseudo-fragility: "I don't know how much more of this I can take!"

c. Hypochondria: "I hardly get over one cold when I catch another."

d. Powerlessness: "I've tried everything to get him (or her) to stop."

e. Self-blame: "I should have planned for that."

All of these are defensive postures by which co-dependents avoid looking honestly at their position and doing something about it. Their focus is on another person or activity.

Some particular groups learn to be other-focused. Women have been socialized to be good care-givers; to be warm, forgiving, nurturing, and supportive. Men have been taught that they must never rely on others, but rather provide for their wives, children, households, and car repairs. Helping professionals are expected and trained to be warm and flexible sponges, absorbing others' troubles. It is no wonder that those in helping professions (including counselors, nurses, and clergy) are at high risk for co-dependency. They are especially encouraged and conditioned to ease the load for others, to be helpful, or to take care of others' needs. Co-dependents tend to be more focused on caring for others than for themselves, tend to work or live in high-stress environments, are often self-neglectful, hostile, and outwardly defiant but not good to themselves. It has been said that co-dependents are "so busy helping everyone else, it gets lonely."(6)

Typically, co-dependents are intensity junkies and get addicted to things outside of themselves. This may be a job, a political cause, or a lover. Often this extreme devotion is rewarded in society, but it is also similar to a moth around a light bulb. If the light is turned off, i.e. if the lover leaves or gets sober, the co-dependent will find another addictive agent. In many gay and lesbian communities, couples will quickly fall in love, move in together, and spend most of their time together. For co-dependents this intensity is a delight, until the lover begins to withdraw from the closeness. The co-dependent may go to great lengths to maintain the relationship. If the lover is chemically dependent, the co-dependent will encourage the dependency cycle by taking care of the needs of the abuser. Intensity is maintained outside of the self.

In relationships, co-dependents will "work on" the relationship at the expense of not being themselves and without regard for their own needs. Co-dependents are well-meaning and go to great lengths to make a lover happy. Co-dependents have difficulty in determining boundaries for themselves and tend to over-extend themselves. They surround themselves with a protective shell that can be a result of long exposure to the unpredictable reactions of the chemically dependent parent or lover.

Other signs of co-dependency, when associated with a chemically dependent lover, are:

a. Making excuses for what the abuser says or doesn't say; making excuses for what the abuser does or does not do.

b. Worrying about the lover's abuse or neglect of care of self.

c. Tolerating the lover's abusive behavior and taking care of her or him.

d. Feeling like the cause of the chemical abuse or feeling responsible for its consequences or costs.

e. Threatening to leave, but not carrying this out.

f. Cutting out activities for fear that people may find out how things really are.

g. Being embarrassed by a lover's chemical abuse.

h. Being worried for or afraid of the chemically dependent person.

i. Calling work to give an excuse for a lover who cannot go to work because of a hangover or drug-related illness.

j. Feeling angry that the relationship is in jeopardy because so much money is being spent on alcohol or drugs.

k. Calling bars, neighbors, or friends, looking for the abuser.(5)

Co-dependents make adjustments in their lives as the abuser becomes more dependent. "A natural law exists in all relationships: If one partner makes a change, the other partner must accommodate to that change with changes of his [or her] own to balance the relationship, else it ceases to exist."(4) For example, if a gay or lesbian client begins to drink excessively, the co-dependent lover will accommodate to ease the immediate pain and to take care of the needs of the drinker. As alcoholism advances, the co-dependent will assume more and more responsibility for accepting the consequences of crises that the alcoholic creates by drinking.

By focusing on the drinking the co-dependent becomes more self-neglectful and isolated. The co-dependent develops what is called the "over-extended stance" — over-drive, over-close, over-do, over-use.(6) This leads to compulsive behavior that is addictive and often leads to difficulties in emotional and physical health.

At some point, co-dependents may have tolerance breaks. These may include crying, yelling, and hitting, and can be violent and frightening experiences. It may be very difficult for them to integrate these breaks and the violence because it is so different from the controlled, kind, and loving public image. Co-dependents who have been dishonest about their tolerance in the past will find these breaks shameful. However, this is consistent with their private self-image of "never being enough" or of not being okay. For those who rarely show their vulnerability, this can be a humbling, even humiliating, experience.

HOW TO HELP

Co-dependents are very difficult to bring into treatment, particularly since they are typically self-neglectful and afraid of change. Helping professionals may need to go to some lengths to secure assistance for co-dependent clients. Such clients should be referred to professionals (counselors, nurses, social workers, clergy, and physicians) who are trained in the areas of co-dependency or substance abuse.

Gay and lesbian co-dependents need gentle, non-evasive

treatment with a professional who can help them define their own boundaries of space and of emotional closeness. In order to trust the helping professional, co-dependents must perceive none of the surprises and unpredictability they encountered with their families or partners. The goals are to help co-dependent clients get comfortable within themselves and within their relationships.

Deprogramming is a long and arduous process. In their formative years, gays and lesbians are all exposed to the same anti-gay jokes and the same stereotypes of lesbians and gay men as are their non-gay counterparts, and to the same misinformation as peers. Gays and lesbians swallow this psychosocially toxic material, and it works against them from the inside; while society's homophobes (persons who fear homosexuality and have an antagonistic and punitive attitude toward gay people) work against them from the outside.(2)

The helping professional can assist by believing whatever the client says and by respecting the boundaries of the client. This is a start in helping the co-dependent develop greater identity and self-respect. Encouraging clients to keep a personal journal that is private and written to themselves in the future (five years from now) is another method of nurturing the internal focus. Often co-dependents have been good "impression managers"(6) — that is, they have a public image of which they are always conscious. By writing in a private journal, co-dependents can collect data about themselves and observe themselves without worrying about the "unseen audience."

Co-dependent clients need encouragement to be playful and spontaneous. They are generally good spectators, controlled and unwilling to participate in parallel play with others. A loosening of this rigidity can encourage inner awareness and expression. A sense of humor can be encouraged through modeling by the professional.

Once an internal focus has begun, the histories of relationships can be explored with clients. Although there may have been a habitual pattern of recurring relationships with addictive lovers, co-dependents can begin to make other choices as they become more aware of their own unfulfilled internal needs.

The most commonly available treatment for co-dependents is as part of an alcoholism recovery center, which generally includes treatment of all chemical dependencies. Treatment centers often use the family model. It has been said that, in treating a chemically dependent system, the treatment of only the abuser is like a garage that changes only the right front tires of the car.(3) However, "what precisely constitutes the 'family group' for a gay male [or lesbian] abuser, and what unique aspects of gay [and lesbian] relationships should treatment personnel be aware of when attempting to facilitate recovery from [chemical dependency]?"(10)

Treatment centers may have their own biases, and they may not accept or include co-dependents, particularly if they are gay men or lesbians. Individuals who are homophobic focus on the "pervasive, socially conditioned negative treatment of gays and lesbians."(11) Staff may center on sexual orientation as a problem, rather than on the co-dependent behavior pattern.

Since gay or lesbian partners and gay friends may not be naturally invited into the treatment process, they will need a great deal of support, patience, and encouragement from helping professionals to prompt their participation in chemical dependency treatment with dependent partners or friends. Helping professionals can be supportive and can serve as advocates with treatment center staff.

Alcoholics Anonymous (AA), Al-Anon, and Alateen are non-professional organizations which help alcoholics and their lovers, families, and friends. AA is primarily for alcoholics, but many meetings are open to anyone interested or involved with chemical dependency.(4) Since it is more likely that there are gay and lesbian AA groups than gay and lesbian Al-Anon organizations, these open AA meetings may be important for clients.

Al-Anon is for the adult lover, family member, or friend, whether the abuser is presently using or not. These meetings are free. Gay and lesbian Al-Anon meetings are powerful self-help groups that are very effective in helping members gain an understanding of themselves. Al-Anon can help the previously mentioned "law of relationships" work for, instead of against, its participants. When co-dependents make constructive changes in their own behavior, the dependent user is pressured to make similar changes in return. These changes are often constructive. Co-dependents will feel comforted for not contributing to the progress of the disease, and will find more self-esteem and productivity by focusing on their own healthy actions.

The purpose of these groups is to help co-dependents live their lives in a more meaningful manner, to change attitudes, old patterns, and habits, and to find serenity. With such support, co-dependents can learn to be good to themselves, to detach with love, and to feel, accept, and express their feelings. Ultimately, they can learn to build self-esteem and can regain their own emotional health.

Helping professionals need to be aware of the gay and lesbian Al-Anon meetings and Adult Children of Alcoholics support groups in their communities. If these groups are not available, it is the responsibility of the helping professional to assist in the development of such groups.

There are a number of treatment programs for co-dependency around the country. Given that co-dependency is an emerging issue, more will be initiated each year. Special treatment centers for gay men and lesbians will undoubtedly open more slowly, if at all. It is the responsibility of the helping professional to know the location and philosophy of each center, so that appropriate referrals can be made.

REFERENCES

1. Black, C. (1981). *It will never happen to me!* Denver: M.A.C.

2. Berzon, B. (Ed.), (1979). *Positively gay.* Los Angeles, CA: Mediamix.

3. Greenleaf, J. (1984). Co-alcoholic/para-alcoholic: Who's who and what's the difference. In *Co-dependency: An emerging issue.* Hollywood, FL: Health Communications.

4. Maxwell, R. (1976). *The booze battle.* New York: Ballantine.

5. O'Donnell, M. (1979). Alcoholism and co-alcoholism: There is a solution. In *Lesbian Health Matters.* Santa Cruz, CA: Santa Cruz Women's Health Collective.

6. Smalley, S. (1984, November). Treatment of co-dependency. Presentation sponsored by the Mid-Eastern Council on Chemical Abuse and Iowa Department of Substance Abuse, Iowa City, IA.

7. Subby, R. (1984). Inside the chemically dependent marriage: Denial and manipulation. In *Co-dependency: An emerging issue.* Hollywood,

FL: Health Communications.

8. Subby, R. and Friel, J. (1984). Co-dependency: A paradoxical dependency. In *Co-dependency: An emerging issue.* Hollywood, FL: Health Communications.

9. Wegscheider-Cruse, S. (1984). Co-dependency: The therapeutic void. In *Co-dependency: An emerging issue.* Hollywood, FL: Health Communications.

10. Whitney, S. (1982). The ties that bind: Strategies for counseling the gay male co-alcoholic. *Journal of Homosexuality, 7(4)*, 37-41.

11. Woodman, N.J. and Lenna, H.R. (1980). *Counseling with gay men and women.* San Francisco: Josey-Bass.

Chapter 14
Gay and lesbian teens

Paul A. Paroski, Jr.

INTRODUCTION

According to Kinsey's studies of the American public, approximately 13% of the male population and 8% of the female population are exclusively or predominantly homosexual.(6) This population has unique concerns and considerations when receiving health care.(13, 10) These include psychological problems peculiar to being closeted and to coming out, and the significantly higher incidence of sexually-transmitted diseases among the gay male portion of this population than is experienced among the male portion of the heterosexual population.(4, 8, 9) Furthermore, we know that there is a great deal of reluctance on the part of gay and lesbian patients to be open with their health care providers concerning their sexual orientations and sexual practices.(1)

Saghir reports that homosexual characteristics appear to be established before adolescence, even though these individuals at that early age may not be participating in same-sex activities. However, the matter of sexual orientations is complex, as indicated by several investigators who have described similarities between the childhood behaviors of heterosexual and homosexual children.(3) Of little consolation to them at the time of this discovery would be their knowledge of the fact that all adolescents have numerous concerns about and problems with their sexuality.(12) If the adolescent shares these concerns or problems with anyone at all, it is presumed to be with a health care provider, such as his pediatrician.

Recently, the Committee on Adolescence of the American Academy of Pediatrics made the recommendation(5) that it is the responsibility of the pediatrician to provide appropriate health care and guidance for young people who are struggling with issues of sexual expression. Furthermore, it acknowledged the special concerns and needs that gay and lesbian adolescents may have. Unfortunately, little has been written defining their special needs and concerns.

METHODS

One hundred and twenty-one individuals — eighty-nine males and thirty-two females between the ages of fourteen and seventeen — completed questionnaires upon presenting themselves for health care at a New York City clinic which is known to be operated by and for the gay and lesbian communities. These individuals responded to the questionnaire in consecutive order over a period of eighteen months, ending in July 1981. Forty-one (twenty-four males and seventeen females) of these individuals were followed over a period of eighteen months, and they completed sections of the questionnaire on multiple occasions. These individuals were also interviewed on each subsequent visit to the clinic. All the participating individuals were self-identified as lesbian or gay, and came to the clinic for various medical concerns.

The questionnaire and interview were designed to assess numerous areas of the adolescents' lives. These included: 1) the adolescents' concepts of gay and lesbian stereotypes; 2) the process that adolescents go through when accepting their own sexual identity; 3) how adolescents learn about the gay and lesbian lifestyles; 4) how adolescents learn to hide their sexual orientation from themselves and society; 5) coping mechanisms used by the adolescents when dealing with peer groups, school, and family; and 6) specific concerns and recommendations of the adolescents.

RESULTS

In our society where there is a paucity of appropriate information available to adolescents concerning homosexuality and the gay or lesbian lifestyle, it was noted that adolescents turned to various sources to learn about both (Table 1). The vast majority (95%) of male adolescents in this study stated that they used sexual encounters to learn more about the gay lifestyle. This method of discovery was not significantly explored by the adolescent females. In contrast, the majority (87%) of the female adolescents relied on

TABLE 1

HOW A GAY OR LESBIAN ADOLESCENT FINDS OUT ABOUT GAY AND LESBIAN LIFESTYLES

METHOD	Male N=89	Female N=32	Signifi- cance
Through sexual encounters	85 (95%)	5 (16%)	0.001
Via television and other media	81 (91%)	28 (87%)	N.S.
Through word of mouth	77 (86%)	26 (81%)	N.S.
By frequenting locations known or thought to be gay or lesbian	72 (81%)	10 (31%)	0.001
By looking up the word gay or lesbian in the telephone directory	38 (43%)	9 (28%)	N.S.
By associating with a person thought or known to be gay or lesbian	37 (42%)	16 (50%)	N.S.
At health care facilities or from practitioners	18 (20%)	4 (12%)	N.S.

N.S. = Not significant

television and other media to fulfill this need. It was found that both female and male adolescents relied heavily on word of mouth for information. However, there was a significant difference between the males and females when it came to frequenting locations thought or known to be gay or lesbian. Of the males, 81% reported frequenting these locations as a way of discovering information, whereas only 31% of the females frequented these locations. Regarding using the telephone directory to get information about being gay, 43% of males as opposed to 28% of the females used telephone information sources. The least frequently reported source of information was health care providers or health facilities. Only 20% of the males and 12% of the females reported using this source.

Numerous questions were asked in an attempt to ascertain the images that the adolescents had concerning gays and lesbians. The results demonstrated that gay adolescents have

TABLE 2
CONCEPTIONS THAT A GAY OR LESBIAN ADOLESCENT HAS ABOUT GAY AND LESBIAN PEOPLE

CONCEPT	Male N=89	Female N=32	Significance
Gay men are always effeminate	71 (80%)	25 (78%)	0.1
Lesbians are always masculine	70 (79%)	27 (84%)	0.05
All gays and lesbians are unhappy	52 (58%)	13 (41%)	N.S.
All gay men dislike women	33 (37%)	18 (56%)	N.S.
All lesbians dislike men	46 (52%)	7 (22%)	N.S.
Through a satisfying sexual encounter with a woman, a gay man can become heterosexual	26 (29%)	13 (41%)	N.S.
Through a satisfying sexual encounter with a man, a lesbian can become heterosexual	37 (42%)	6 (19%)	0.05

N.S. = Not significant

accepted the societal stereotypes as true representations of lesbian and gay individuals (Table 2). Of the males 80% and of the females 78% believed that gay men were always effeminate. Of the males 79% and of the females 84% felt that lesbians were always masculine. Furthermore, conceptions such as all gays and lesbians are unhappy (58% of males and 41% of females); all gay men dislike women (held by 37% of males and 56% of females) were reported. The idea that a satisfying heterosexual encounter would sway the person to a heterosexual life was present in a significant percentage of the respondents. Interestingly, at least 40% of both the male and female respondents believed that a person of the opposite sex could change his or her sexual orientation from gay to straight by having a satisfying heterosexual encounter, while a hefty majority of both the male and female respondents did not believe this change was possible for gay people of their own sex.

TABLE 3
THE PROCESS THROUGH WHICH AN ADOLESCENT ACCEPTS HIS OR HER OWN HOMOSEXUALITY

1. The realization of one's desire to have same-sex relationships and encounters.

2. The development of guilt and shame about, and fear of discovery of one's homosexuality, and a sense of engaging in abnormal behavior if homosexual sex is engaged in.

3. An attempt to change to heterosexuality through behavior and fantasy.

4. Failure to change sexual orientation, and development of poor self-esteem.

5. Investigation of the homosexual lifestyle through many methods.

6. Acceptance and development of a positive gay or lesbian identity. Possible for about half of gay adolescents.

The vast majority of the forty-one adolescents followed over the eighteen-month period generally described the process by which they accepted their homosexuality as shown in Table 3. Initially, there was a realization of their desire to engage in same-sex activities and relationships. This was closely followed by a period of guilt, shame, fear of discovery, and feeling that homosexual sex is abnormal. Subsequently, of the forty-one, 78% reported an attempt to change to being heterosexual by engaging in heterosexual activity and relationships. Upon failure to develop a fulfilling heterosexual relationship, all thirty-two of these individuals began to investigate the gay or lesbian lifestyle through the previously described methods. Twenty-one of the forty-one (51%) stated that they eventually accepted a gay or lesbian lifestyle, and that they had developed a positive gay or lesbian identity.

Of these same forty-one individuals, twenty-seven (66% — nineteen males and eight females) reported their family responses. Without exception, the initial family response was perceived by the adolescents as anger or rejection. Twenty-five of the twenty-seven reporting adolescents (eighteen males and seven females) reported that their families made

TABLE 4
RATIONALE FOR THE CHOICE OF
HEALTH CARE PRACTITIONER
BY GAY AND LESBIAN ADOLESCENTS

CONCERN	Male N=89	Female N=32	Significance
SPECIFIC CONCERNS OF GAY AND LESBIAN ADOLESCENTS ABOUT GOING TO "JUST ANY" HEALTH CARE PROVIDER			
Fear of identification of homosexuality and humiliation	77 (86%)	9 (28%)	0.001
Concern about provider's gentleness when dealing with the adolescent's body	11 (12%)	30 (94%)	0.001
Lack of knowledge concerning specific gay or lesbian health care problems	46 (52%)	20 (62%)	N.S.
Fear that the adolescent would not receive non-judgmental care	77 (86%)	22 (69%)	0.05
THE ADOLESCENT'S BASIS FOR CHOICE OF HEALTH CARE PRACTITIONER			
Based solely on sexual orientation — Gay or lesbian provider	84 (94%)	7 (22%)	0.001
Based solely on gender of practitioner	5 (6%)	25 (78%)	0.001

N.S. = Not significant

attempts to change their sexual orientations through various methods, including psychotherapy, forcing the adolescents to have heterosexual activities, and religious intervention. All twenty-seven responded that it was their impression that their parents were ashamed of them and that they felt some degree of guilt in "causing" the homosexuality of their child.

The adolescents attending our facility had specific concerns surrounding the selection of a health care practitioner

(Table 4). There were significant differences between males and females in this area. The males (87%) were deeply concerned about being identified as a gay and, subsequently, being humiliated, and equally concerned about receiving non-judgmental care. On the other hand, the females (94%) were primarily concerned with the practitioners' gentleness when dealing with their bodies. Majorities of both males (52%) and females (62%) expressed concern over practitioners' knowledge of the specific gay and lesbian health care problems.

Of the males, 94% reported that the primary selection criterion was that the health practitioner be gay or lesbian. In contrast, 78% of the females used the sex of the practitioner as the primary selection criterion, preferring females.

The adolescents made several suggestions on what would make obtaining health care easier for gay and lesbian adolescents. Their suggestions included: 1) that persons should not make the assumption that all adolescents are heterosexual; 2) that peer support groups be available; 3) that there be openly gay role models in various professions and careers; 4) that resource materials and persons that could provide answers to their questions be available; and 5) that someone supportive be available to talk with concerning their feelings and fears about school, home, and family.

IMPLICATIONS AND DISCUSSION

In a society which is homophobic and which has a lack of public positive gay and lesbian role models, gay and lesbian adolescents are placed in an extremely difficult situation. The peer group, which is a strong force for any adolescent, may not be available for these young persons, since gay peer groups are rare. Lacking positive role models and even the opportunity to support and learn from and with each other, at least adolescent gay males will most often resort to the method for finding out about homosexuality that is least condoned by society — sexual encounters.

It is clear that many of our attitudes, assumptions, and expectations are learned in early life through exposure to family, peers, media, and society at large. There is no reason to believe that the socialization process of gay and lesbian adolescents and its content are different from what they are for straight adolescents. The negative presentation of gay and lesbian lifestyles by society, and the adolescents' perception of these negative images and messages clearly color the adolescents' view of homosexuality and gay people.

We see that numerous myths concerning homosexuality are incorporated by and reinforced in these gay adolescents. These include the concepts of the effeminate gay male and the masculine lesbian, and the stereotypic perceptions that all gays and lesbians are unhappy and that they dislike members of the opposite sex. We find that gay and lesbian adolescents do develop a gay identity. But, for the reasons I have just discussed, this identity is unhealthy. It is, unfortunately, based on information and assumptions that have little and often no relationship to the realities of the lives and personalities of the vast majority of actual gay people.

We can assume that gay and lesbian adolescents are probably, on the whole, at greater distance from their parents than are their heterosexual peers. For the adolescents who choose not to tell their families, one clearly sees the establishment of a significant barrier. For those who do choose to tell them, the responses of the families are usually not supportive (certainly this seems initially to be the case). Negative and unsupportive reactions also result in placing considerable distance between the gay teen and the family. In such a no-win situation, and without defined support groups, it is very understandable that the gay or lesbian adolescent should feel alone and isolated.

There are other implications apparent in a consideration of the data. Our health care system usually does not meet the needs of gay and lesbian adolescents. We see that these adolescents are uncomfortable with going to "just any" provider, and most communities have no identified gay or lesbian health care facilities. Again, we see alienated adolescents, who perceive themselves as alone. Moreover, the use of sexual activity as a method of exploration places the teenage gay male at a very high risk for sexually-transmitted diseases (STDs). This compounds the problems a teenage gay male is likely to be experiencing, since adolescents are already underserved in the area of STDs. To rectify this situation, we must provide appropriate screening for STDs in our gay male adolescents.

Heterosexual activity in adolescents does not mean the adolescents are heterosexual. Adolescents may use heterosexual activity to hide their homosexuality from society, or as a method of denial. We must become sensitive to this fact, making no assumptions when eliciting a sexual history. Likewise, the pregnant adolescent should not be presumed to be heterosexual in orientation. It is quite possible that she is a lesbian whose pregnancy is an attempt to "pass as straight."

We see that the gay male teen is concerned with the fear of identification and humiliation, whereas the lesbian teen is concerned with the gentleness of the provider. In order to develop a health care system responsive to the needs of our gay and lesbian adolescents, medical practitioners and health care providers obviously need to be gentle and non-judgmental in dealing with all teenagers, but especially with those whom we find out are gay or lesbian. Presenting a personal image that is non-threatening and accepting is crucial.

The gay teen has a preference to visit a provider of his own sexual orientation, whereas the lesbian teen makes the choice on the basis of gender. To provide the availability of this type of selection in a facility may be difficult and, in most places, impossible. But again, one can assure that these adolescents receive non-judgmental and supportive care.

We, as pediatricians and other health care professionals. must begin to lay the groundwork to provide the necessary support for both these adolescents and their families. We can begin by not making the assumption that all persons are heterosexual. We need to realize the sense of isolation, the process of learning to hide one's homosexuality, and the conflicts of our lesbian and gay teens. In order to provide a supportive therapeutic environment, open and non-judgmental communication needs to be established early in the patient-health care provider relationship. Furthermore, we must become knowledgeable about the specific and unique medical and psychosocial concerns of gay and lesbian adolescents. Finally, a supportive referral network should be established along with community resources, such as peer support groups (Gay and Lesbian Youth and family support groups (Parents of Lesbians and Gays).

REFERENCES

1. Darkick, L. and Grady, K.E. (1980). Openness between gay persons and health professionals. *Annals of Internal Medicine, 93,* 115-119.

2. Grellert, E.A. (1982). Childhood play behavior of homosexual and heterosexual men. *Psychological Reports, 51,* 607-610.

3. Grellert, E.A., Newcomb, M.D., and Bentler, P.M. (1982). Childhood play activities of male and female homosexuals and heterosexuals. *Archives of Sex Behavior, 11,* 451-478.

4. Judson, F.N., Penley, K.A., Robinson, M.E., and Smith, J.K. (1980). Comparative prevalence rates of sexually transmitted diseases in heterosexual and homosexual men. *American Journal of Epidemiology, 112,* 836-843.

5. Homosexuality and adolescence. (1983), *Pediatrics, 72,* 249-250.

6. Kinsey, C., Pomeroy, W., and Martin, C.E. (1948). *Sexual behavior in the human male.* Philadelphia: W.B. Saunders.

7. Martin, A.D. (1982). Learning to hide: The socialization of the gay adolescent. *Adolescent Psychiatry, 10,* 52-62.

8. Owen, W.L. and Hill, J.L. (1972). Rectal and pharyngeal gonorrhea in homosexual men. *Journal of the American Medical Association, 220,* 1315-1318.

9. Owen, W.F. (1980). Sexually transmitted diseases and traumatic problems in homosexual men. *Annals of Internal Medicine, 92,* 805-808.

10. Paroski, P.A., Jr. (1982). The unique considerations and concerns of the homosexual patient receiving care for sexually transmitted diseases. *Sexually Transmitted Diseases, 9,* 51-52.

11. Saghir, M.T. and Robins, E. (1973). *Male and female homosexuality: A comprehensive investigation.* Baltimore: Williams & Wilkins.

12. Sondheimer, A. (1982). Anticipation and experimentation: The sexual concerns of midadolescence. *Adolescent Psychiatry, 10,* 208-227.

13. Whyte, J. and Capaldini, L. (1980). Treating the lesbian or gay patient. *Delaware Medical Journal, 52,* 271-280.

Chapter 15
Older gays and lesbians

Raymond M. Berger

Do gay men and lesbians self-destruct at the age of forty?

In the late 1970s, when I first decided to work with older gays and lesbians, I was asking myself this question. The social and political organizations in which I had been involved had few older persons, and the professional literature on aging gave one the impression that homosexuality did not exist among the elderly. But my knowledge of the Kinsey data, which showed that gays existed in substantial numbers across the age span(7, 8) and my personal impressions gained from conversations with older gays suggested otherwise.

If we assume that eight percent of the adult population is same-sex oriented,(3) then gays and lesbians sixty-five or older number over 1.75 million persons in the United States alone. Older gays and lesbians have been the *Silent Pioneers* of the twentieth-century sexual revolution, as illustrated by the recently released film of that name. They have been ignored by both gerontological researchers and by service providers. Their special needs have nearly always gone un-identified and unmet, and they have withstood the effects of societal hate and discrimination to an extent at which many younger gays and lesbians might marvel. This is all changing.

In this chapter I will review recent research which has debunked much of the mythology of gay and lesbian aging, and I will highlight some ways in which being gay or lesbian actually makes it easier to grow old. Although most psychosocial needs of older gay people are the same as those of other older people, several special needs will be reviewed, and I will mention some ways in which professionals can be helpful to this group.

FICTION AND FACT

No gay person can ignore the extreme stereotypes of gay

aging which are popular in our culture. Plays, novels, and even (until recently) scholarly presentations have painted a bleak future for young gays and lesbians. The older gay man is said to become increasingly isolated and effeminate as he ages. Lacking both family and friends, he is desperately lonely. He must settle for no sex life at all, or he must prey upon young boys to satisfy his lust.

The older lesbian, where she is said to exist at all, is purported to be a cruel witch. Cold, unemotional, and heartless, she despises men. Devoted solely to masculine interests and career pursuits, she has no friends and is repeatedly frustrated by the rejections of younger women whose attention she solicits.

My guess is that these stereotypes have had a devastating effect on all gays and lesbians, young and old. They have been used to discourage gay people from accepting themselves, and they have wrought havoc on their self-concepts. Many sociologists feel that our self-concepts are determined by our beliefs regarding others' evaluations of us.(11) Negative stereotypes, then, are the most important weapon in the arsenal of low self-esteem messages that society wields against unpopular groups. And they have helped to ensure that gays and lesbians remain the most unpopular of unpopular groups.

But the beauty of these stereotypes is that they are so far out of line with reality that only a little research was needed to open them to serious question. Today we have enough research evidence (less so for women, unfortunately) to say with confidence that only a very small minority of older gays and lesbians fit the stereotypes.

For example, in a questionnaire study of 1,117 gay men of all ages, Weinberg and Williams(11) found the older respondents to be as well adjusted as the younger ones, and in some ways more so. Older gay men worried less about disclosure or discovery of their homosexuality, were less likely to desire psychiatric treatment, and had more stable self-concepts. Minnigerode(9) found that gay men do not perceive themselves as aging sooner than heterosexual men.

Other questionnaire and interview studies by Kelly(6) and by me(4) also debunked the old myths about older gay men.

Almost none of the respondents could be described as loners, and most preferred to socialize with age peers rather than with younger men. The great majority had had a lover or a spouse for a significant period during their lifetimes, and were integrated into supportive social networks. This was true despite the fact that both Kelly's study and my own included respondents who did not participate in public aspects of the gay community, such as bars and social clubs.

Most older gay men remained sexually active and were generally satisfied with their sex lives. Compared with younger gay men, older ones scored favorably on measures of depression and psychosomatic symptoms. When compared with the general population, they reported similar or higher levels of life satisfaction.

Although older lesbians are a less studied group, the available findings also debunk the myths about this group. Wolf(12) suggested that older lesbians use "fictive kin"; that is, they use friends as substitutes for the family relationships that are more prevalent among straight women. This idea was confirmed by Raphael and Robinson(10) on the basis of twenty interviews with lesbians who were fifty or older. All except one (a woman who relied solely on her lover) had friendship networks, and none of the respondents fit the stereotype of the desperately lonely lesbian. Middle-aged and older lesbians preferred other older women as intimate partners, and were often able to find them.

Almvig's(1) questionnaire study of 74 lesbians, fifty and older, depicted similar patterns. Almost three-quarters described their mental health as good or excellent and said their lesbianism had been a source of great joy and satisfaction to them. A few over half had a current lover and only half lived alone. Bell and Weinberg(2) found that older lesbians were less sexually active than younger lesbians, but that the majority were still sexually active, and that most of their partners were age peers.

These research findings paint a new picture. Most older gays and lesbians are reasonably well adjusted. They are generally well integrated into social networks and relate primarily with age peers.

LESSONS TO BE LEARNED

It is often the case that majority groups, which tend to dismiss the contributions of minority groups, come to learn a few lessons from the very people they have despised. This may prove to be the case with heterosexuals regarding older gays and lesbians. Those of us who have been studying older gays and lesbians are beginning to find ways in which the unique adaptations of this group provide healthy pathways for a good adjustment to aging. In some ways, being gay is an advantage for the aging person.

How can that be? Francher and Henkin(5) were the first to suggest that early life experiences of older gay men led them to develop skills and attitudes that helped them adapt to growing older. For example, one of the tragedies of growing older in our culture is that old people are stigmatized: they are treated as useless and incompetent. (This was beautifully illustrated by Henry Fonda in the film, *On Golden Pond*, in which the elderly father struggled against loss of control and ridicule by others.)

The advantage for gays and lesbians is that they have learned how to cope with a stigmatized identity very early in life. Most gays and lesbians are able to insulate themselves from the worst effects of societal stigmas by developing self-affirming attitudes and by seeking support from others. Can it be that these skills and attitudes are also useful in adapting to the stigmatized status of being an older person? They probably are.

A closely related idea is that gay people also experience a "crisis of independence" in early adulthood. As their heterosexual age peers make the comfortable transition from family of origin to family of procreation, gay people cannot take family and other social supports for granted. They learn self-reliance skills that become crucial in old age as friends and lovers die, and as social roles become constricted. One of these skills is role flexibility. The sex-role divisions which are the norm in heterosexual relationships are much less common among same-sex couples, in which both partners learn to do "male" *and* "female" tasks, both of which are necessary for survival.

I like to tell the story of my elderly father's experience when my mother was hospitalized for two weeks. We discovered that he did not know how to turn on the washing machine. He was helpless. This sort of occurrence is quite unlikely among gay and lesbian couples, for both partners know that they must be able to prepare meals as well as get the car fixed. Although loss of a partner is traumatic regardless of sexual orientation, the older gay man or lesbian is better able to manage the day-to-day requirements of getting on with life.

There is another factor related to sex roles that may play an important part in the older gay and lesbian's adjustment to aging. One of the most difficult parts of growing older for all of us is learning to accept the physical changes of aging. They are usually not welcomed. From the point of view of traditional heterosexual sex roles, the changes that come with age make the man less masculine and the woman less feminine. For instance, many men have trouble adjusting to diminished physical capacities; they feel outdone by younger, more virile men. And women are perceived to be less feminine, and hence, less desirable, when their skin wrinkles and their hair turns gray.

Again, earlier life experiences serve older gay men and lesbians well. They are likely to have less personal investment in following traditional notions of virility and masculinity, or sexiness and femininity, respectively. The physical changes that accompany old age, then, may not seem like insurmountable hurdles. In simple terms, younger men who are comfortable with any of their feminine attributes, and younger women who are comfortable with any of their masculine attributes will find it easiest to adapt to the physical changes of aging. It seems to be that this is particularly likely for older lesbians, especially those who have taken a feminist stance, because feminism provides a healthy perspective on the meaning of femininity. This factor is also likely to be operative for older gay men. But the relatively recent cult of machismo among younger gay men may change all that, as these men, who have invested heavily in their macho image, begin to grow older; and the same may be true concerning the revival of femininity among younger lesbians.

WHEN THINGS GO WRONG

Not all is rosy for older gay men and lesbians. The fact is that being old is not easy in a society which treats its elders badly, and yet keeps them alive longer than ever before in history. In my conversations with countless older lesbians and gay men, I was struck by a simple fact: the problems they faced were, for the most part, the problems faced by all older people. The two most important concerns were: "Will I have good health?" and "Will I have enough money to support myself comfortably?"

Of course, layered on top of these concerns are a number of issues unique to older gays and lesbians. Social service agencies and helping professionals often fail to recognize the needs of their older gay and lesbian clients. The reluctance of most gays and lesbians (older and younger) to reveal their sexual orientations perpetuates the problem, but their reluctance did not create it. When seeking services, gay men and lesbians are not likely to come out because they have assessed, often accurately, that this will cause difficulty or will result in poor service.

In some situations, the sexual orientation of the older person will not be relevant. Thus, it may not be necessary for social security or health care personnel to know that the applicant, or patient, is a gay person, if a minor medical procedure is involved and all goes well. But what if a same-sex partner dies? How many social agencies are able to provide sensitive and well-informed bereavement counseling for a gay surviving partner? Where will a sexually dysfunctional same-sex couple turn to for help? Will an older gay man have to hide his lifestyle from the homemaker or home health aide upon whom he depends so heavily? And what about the older lesbian who just needs a bit of support in handling life's difficulties: can she really open up to a counselor who may not accept her homosexuality?

Traditionally, mainstream social service agencies have addressed homosexuality within a limited context: only when it appeared in a non-elderly person, and only when the intervention was designed to uncover the cause of the homosexuality and to eliminate it. Under any circumstances, a professional fixation on causation and conversion is counter-

– 175 –

productive, but it seems particularly silly when providing services to the aging.

It is hard to get more than anecdotal data about the treatment of older gays and lesbians by helping professionals. There have been comments in the literature about the lack of responsiveness of mainstream social service agencies to the needs of the gay and lesbian communities, and about the ways in which helping professionals have added to oppression by misdiagnosing, stigmatizing, and "treating" such clients. So I suspect these problems are even more severe for elderly gay people, although no hard data exists to support this suspicion.

When the elderly come to the attention of a helping professional, they are likely to be dependent and vulnerable. I am thinking, for example, of the nursing home resident or the frail older person who requires in-home services to survive. That these people might be gay is something that is never considered. Since most helping professionals in the Aging Services Network believe that all elderly are heterosexual, they are uniquely unequipped to provide fully adequate service to their gay and lesbian clientele.

A social worker recently brought to my attention a survey of human service agencies which was conducted in 1984 in a medium-sized midwestern city.* Every human service agency in the community was asked if it provided any resources specific to gays and lesbians, if it did outreach to them, if it had any philosophy about such services, and if it had any staff with particular expertise or sensitivity in this area. The survey was most notable for the consistency with which most agencies answered "No" to all these questions.

Of all the agencies in this city, there were thirteen which provided services specifically to the elderly. Included were all medical centers, since the elderly are heavy consumers of health care. None of the thirteen agencies provided any outreach, nor did they have a specialized resource or staff person. Five of the agencies stated that their philosophy

---

* I would like to thank Mr. Jeffrey J. Gerhardstein, M.S.W. for making these data available to me.

included non-discrimination, but the remaining agencies made no comment about services to gays and lesbians, or were hostile.

Of the six nursing homes in the community, only two completed the questionnaire, and both of these said they were unaware of how homosexuality related to their services. One response was that a philosophy about services to this group was "not needed." The response of another home, which refused to complete the questionnaire, was all too typical: "As a skilled nursing facility providing medical care to the elderly, we feel this questionnaire is inappropriate/irrelevant to our services." Consider that a nursing home with a census of 200 residents is likely to have sixteen to twenty elderly gays and lesbians. And consider what sort of treatment they would be likely to receive in such a home if their sexual orientations were to become known.

Institutional policies present some of the most difficult problems for older gays and lesbians because of the dependence of patients on staff. If the homosexuality of a patient becomes known, it may result in neglect or poor treatment by staff, and ostracism or abuse by other patients. Because institutions are largely hidden from public view, it is not known how much of this goes on. And even in cases of clear abuse, the patient may not want to call attention to the situation because of the stigma attached to homosexuality and the patient's continued dependence on the institution. Few nursing homes allow for conjugal visits, or sexual expression, of their heterosexual residents. They are even less likely to allow an older lesbian or gay man to have an intimate visit with a lover.

Formal policies may also create problems for the older gay or lesbian. Most intensive care units allow visits by blood relatives and spouses only, excluding lifelong same-sex partners. When the older person is incompetent or otherwise unable to make decisions, the patient's lover must often stand by helplessly, as relatives (who may be distant, or hostile to the patient's homosexuality) make life-and-death decisions.

The legal system can also create severe problems for the older gay or lesbian. Most often these are problems of omission rather than commission; that is, the problem is not created by laws which prohibit sexual conduct, but rather by the fact that gays and lesbians are not afforded benefits or protections which apply to heterosexuals. For example, an older gay man or lesbian may experience discrimination in rental, home purchase, employment, public accommodations, and insurance. In most areas, such discrimination is legal.

Many legal problems arise because same-sex couples are not recognized by law. For example, it is not uncommon for a same-sex couple to put their business and home in one person's name — this may be done to protect the couple's anonymity. If that partner dies, the surviving partner may be forced to watch in horror as disapproving relatives inherit the entire estate, despite the survivor's lifelong contributions. Even where there is a will, the influence of blood ties is so well recognized in law, that relatives can contest the deceased's desire to leave the estate to a lover on the basis of "undue influence." Same-sex partner rights are limited in other ways as well. Unlike a heterosexual spouse, a same-sex partner cannot make a claim to inherit the property of a deceased partner's relative or sue a third party for wrongful death of the lover.

Finally, same-sex partners are not able to share job-related benefits, such as health insurance, which are routinely made available to heterosexual partners. Until recently this was true everywhere. Within the past year, two communities — Berkeley and West Hollywood, California — have passed "domestic partner" legislation, which makes these benefits available to both opposite-sex and same-sex unmarried partners. (For a more detailed look at legal issues affecting gays and lesbians, see the chapters by Rohovit and Rubesh in this book.)

NEW ROLES FOR PROFESSIONAL HELPERS
As we live increasingly longer lives, as medical technology creates a class of older persons whose survival depends on intensive-care services, and as personal incomes continue to be insufficient to meet the needs of the elderly, the likelihood increases that each of us will need professional help in our

later years. This makes it particularly important that helping professionals be knowledgeable about, and sensitive to, the needs of *all* the elderly. What can helping professionals do to be responsive to the needs of gay and lesbian elderly?

Not surprisingly, the first step is knowledge. The most important knowledge is the kind which cannot be adequately gained by reading books like this one. It is acquired only through personal contact with older gays and lesbians, and it requires that professionals set aside judgmental attitudes and learn to feel comfortable with this group. Professionals who feel threatened by older gays and lesbians need to examine and challenge their homophobic feelings before they can be helpful.

In many areas, the Aging Services Network is characterized by homophobia, or, just as bad, by the belief that gays and lesbians do not exist among older persons. This was certainly the case in the community survey presented earlier. An appropriate role for helping professionals is to speak out within their agencies against anti-gay policies and homophobic comments of co-workers. Professionals should advocate for an agency non-discrimination policy which includes sexual orientation. They should stock their shelves with positive literature on homosexuality to foster a climate of open discussion. Where speakers or films are available, professionals can bring these into their agencies.

The professional should also be familiar with gay and lesbian lifestyles and with local resources, such as support groups, information and referral services, and social clubs. Unfortunately, most communities do not have resources designed specifically to meet the needs of gay and lesbian elders, but even in these communities, the professional should be aware of which resources are useful to older gays and lesbians, and which are not. For example, gay and lesbian churches and synagogues, such as the Metropolitan Community Church, which has many branches all across the country, have provided support to older gays and lesbians, while some bars and social clubs have excluded them.

An important new role for helping professionals has been the creation of gay-sponsored social service agencies for the elderly. Seniors Active in a Gay Environment (SAGE), in New

York City, is the most comprehensive such agency and serves as a model for what can be done elsewhere. With a budget of $127,000 raised through individual donations, special events, and municipal and private grants, SAGE provides a range of services to hundreds of gay and lesbian seniors. SAGE offers friendly visiting, escort services, telephone contact, bereavement support, information and referral, monthly socials, and support groups. They conduct workshops for financial planning, for public speaking, for acting, and for writing the recollections of seniors. Best of all, through a professionally coordinated volunteer program, they have brought younger and older gays and lesbians together. Professionals play a variety of roles ranging from grantsmanship, to assessment of the social service needs of homebound elderly, who are then served through the volunteer program.

In the last few years, similar but less comprehensive services for gay and lesbian elderly have been started in Minneapolis, Los Angeles, Washington, D.C., and Chicago. These specialized services and others like them afford an opportunity for helping professionals to learn about, and to meet, the needs of older gays and lesbians.

SUMMARY

Gay men and lesbians do not self-destruct when they grow old. This will become apparent as more and more older gays and lesbians choose to come out. For the most part, gay and lesbian seniors are unremarkable people who lead well-adjusted lives. They are not doomed to a lonely old age. In some ways they are even better able than their heterosexual counterparts to adjust well to aging. While the Aging Services Network has not been responsive to the needs of older gays and lesbians, that situation may change as specialized services sponsored by the gay and lesbian communities themselves raise public visibility and conquer stereotypes of gay and lesbian aging.

REFERENCES

1. Almvig, C. (1984). *The invisible minority: Aging and lesbianism.* Unpublished master's thesis, New School for Social Research, New York, New York.

2. Bell, A.P. and Weinberg, M.S. (1978). *Homosexualities: A study of diversity among men and women.* New York: Simon & Schuster.

3. Berger, R.M. (1982, May). The unseen minority: Older gays and lesbians. *Social Work, 27,* 236-242.

4. Berger, R.M. (1984). *Gay and gray: The older homosexual man.* Boston: Alyson.

5. Francher, J.S. and Henkin, J. (1973). The menopausal queen: Adjustment to aging and the male homosexual. *American Journal of Orthopsychiatry, 43(4),* 670-674.

6. Kelly, J.J. (1977). The aging male homosexual: Myth and reality. *Gerontologist, 17(4),* 328-332.

7. Kinsey, A.C., Pomeroy, W.B., and Martin, C.E. (1948). *Sexual behavior in the human male.* Philadelphia: W.B. Saunders.

8. Kinsey, A.C. and Gebhard, P.H. (1953). *Sexual behavior in the human female.* Philadelphia: W.B. Saunders.

9. Minnigerode, F.A. (1976). Age-status labeling in homosexual men. *Journal of Homosexuality, 1(3),* 273-275.

10. Raphael, S.M. and Robinson, M.K. (1980). The older lesbian: Love relationships and friendship patterns. *Alternative Lifestyles, 3(2),* 207-229.

11. Weinberg, M.S. and Williams, C.J. (1975). *Male homosexuals: Their problems and adaptations.* New York: Penguin.

12. Wolf, D.G. (1980). *Life cycle change of older lesbians and gay men.* Paper presented at the Annual Meeting of the Gerontological Society, San Diego, California.

Chapter 16
Gay and lesbian prisoners

Ronald Sable

INTRODUCTION

This chapter on gay and lesbian prisoners will include a relevant background on the criminal justice system, generalizations about gay men and lesbians within the system, special problem areas including AIDS in prison, several cases of the experiences of real people to illustrate the problems discussed, and some suggestions about what you as a care provider can do to help gay and lesbian prisoners.

BACKGROUND

During 1984 there were 450,000 people in federal and state prisons and 200,000 in local jails. Between three and five times that number are processed through the system from police lockup to jail to prison and, finally, to halfway houses or work release and probation. Currently, there are estimated to be ten million people living in the U.S. who have had contact with the criminal justice system. It is often pointed out that the rate of incarceration in the U.S. is third in the world behind the Soviet Union and South Africa. It is important to note that among the 200,000 held in local jails, approximately two-thirds or more are detainees. They have not been convicted of any crime but are too poor to afford bail.

The prison population is relatively young — the average age is thirty-five, and the ratio of men to women is ten to one. The racial composition varies from state to state, but racial and ethnic minorities are vastly overrepresented in comparison to their number in the larger population. There are many stereotypes about what people in prison are like, but in many cases people in prisons are not that different from you and me. The vast majority — over ninety percent for many prisons — have not been convicted of a crime involving violence against a person.

There are a number of excellent books which give insight into what the criminal justice system is all about. Two of the most thorough and helpful are discussed in the references — *Kind and Usual Punishment* by Jessica Mitford and *Struggle for Justice* by the American Friends Service Committee. One can argue about the various functions of and justifications for prisons — to punish, to rehabilitate, to protect the larger community — but there is little question that they have failed by many measures and are costly in the extreme. Whatever one's view of the solutions to the problem of crime, few who have experienced prison would disagree that they are controlling, oppressive, and violent places that often contribute to the degradation and dehumanization of the people confined there. Importantly and sadly, prisons and jails are largely hidden from public view. Since the uprising at Attica in 1971, American prisons have been opened up to a small extent to outside scrutiny but most remain closed and secretive. The most effective thing that could happen for reform of the criminal justice system would be for every "law-abiding" American to spend a week in a county jail and to translate that experience into action for change of the system.

GAYS AND LESBIANS IN PRISON

There are a number of reasons to believe that the density of gay men and lesbians in prisons and local jails is greater than in the general population. First, recall that engaging in same-sex sexual acts is still criminal in twenty-three states and in the District of Columbia. While there are no accurate statistics regarding how many people have been prosecuted and convicted under these laws, there are certainly scores of men and women who are in jail simply for living their gay lives.

A great many gay men are prosecuted for sex with minors — which may actually mean a young man of sixteen or seventeen. In addition, there are a number of factors which tend to lengthen the time spent in incarceration after sentencing: being involved in violence — often unwillingly — results in punishment for violation of institutional rules and loss of good time; being kept in protective custody means losing opportunities for work and being denied access to the law library — an important avenue of "self defense." Most gay inmates describe being subject to discrimination at the hands of the parole board, especially if they are not repentant or apologetic about their sexual orientation or are resistant to "treatment."

While some of the following issues are also ones that apply to heterosexually identified inmates, they are issues of particular concern to gay men and lesbians. Safety is of paramount importance, and a pervasive fear of assault is a common feeling for incarcerated gay men. Validation of one's sexual identity, while not always possible even on the outside, is virtually impossible in prison. Intimate relationships with someone of the same sex are largely forbidden or punished, and whatever sense of community an individual might have previously enjoyed is denied. The support and nurturance that every person needs is rarely obtainable.

Attitudes of staff, both correctional and civilian, will vary from one institution to another but will largely reflect the attitudes of the generally rural community from which the institution draws its work force. One would expect to and does find the same sort of bigotry and intolerance that gay people experience on the street. It seems that this intolerance is increased within the context of the control functions of the institution and the atmosphere of brutality that the system fosters. Many wardens will say that there are few "truly gay" people in their prisons, but that there is a great deal of homosexual activity. Those who are interpreted to be gay are those who fit the most narrow cultural stereotypes — very effeminate men and male transsexuals, as well as very tough or masculine women.

Institutional rules also vary with regard to self-identified gay people. Any sexual act is a violation of the rules, though in reality a great deal of sexual activity may be tolerated. Self-identified gay men may be put in protective custody, ostensibly for their own protection, but such classification severely limits their opportunities for education, vocation, and recreation.

Inmate codes of behavior are important and, as a rule, are brutally homophobic. Self-identified gay men are targets for sexual exploitation and sexual assault. Violent or exploitative sex is okay. The insertive or dominant male in the relationship is not stigmatized as being gay, while the receptive partner — regardless of his self-identification — is the "woman" or the "punk." Rigid role definitions, based on our society's conventional sex-role models, are the rule.

In spite of the fact that the American Psychiatric Association no longer considers homosexuality to be a disease, it is not unusual to find gay men and lesbians in prison settings involved in some sort of forced, or coerced, psychiatric care because of their homosexual orientation.

PROBLEM AREAS

At the onset, a gay man or lesbian faces the decision about whether or not to be out in prison. If he or she is stereotypically effeminate or butch, there may not be a choice. But if there is a choice, most opt for staying in the closet. The stakes for openness are simply too high. With this choice of staying in the closet comes the constant fear of exposure, the consequences of which are always more severe than on the streets.

Problems that all incarcerated people who are identified as gay experience, whether they are gay and lesbian youths or adult gay men and lesbians, are ostracism, isolation, and discrimination in assignments for housing, jobs, and educational programs within the institution. They experience forced separation from lovers within the institution if such relationships are discovered, as well as lack of support, and an almost constant fear of violence from other inmates and from officers. Attitudes toward gay people are an exception to the rule that most inmates will support one another against the officers or the institution. It is clear that, at times, inmates and the institution are simultaneously involved in the exploitation and brutality directed against gay inmates.

If a gay man chooses protective custody, or if it is chosen for him, to secure his safety and his freedom from sexual assault, then he will have less access to educational programs, no job assignment, and little access to the law library and recreational program. These deprivations further negatively affect his opportunities for parole and work release. Protective custody ends up being solitary confinement but, ostensibly, not assigned as a punishment. The gay man is in this custodial management because the institution cannot insure his safety in any other way. Finally, the negative effects on mental health of such isolation and deprivation may be very long-lasting.

For lesbians, the loss of custody of their children is a virtual certainty when they are incarcerated. They are more likely to be the subject of assault by male guards and often will be segregated from other women inmates to "protect" the latter from these "aggressors." Any friendly relationship with another woman is suspect, and efforts will be made, as with men, to separate women who seem to be forming "particular relationships."

For gay youth, incarceration comes at a time of development of the individual's sexual identity. But the climate of fear that pervades correctional institutions, and the homophobia that is rife there are not conducive to healthy sexual development.

For gay men, the fear of assault is an overwhelming part of prison experience. They have few choices. If they are capable of staying in the closet, they must constantly be on guard to project a tough image and fight back if attacked or challenged. If they are identified or labeled as gay, either by choice or by the authorities or by rumors within the population, they must either choose protective custody, fight back, find a "protector" and hook up — thereby yielding to sexual exploitation in return for protection from a more violent assault — or accept the position of being used at will by other, stronger inmates.

While sexual victimization is not limited to gay-identified men in a prison population, such men are preferential targets of such violence and exploitation and they are overrepresented in the numbers of those who are so abused. The institution may intentionally house a gay man with an inmate who has a long sentence or a history of institutional violence in the belief that this will reduce escape attempts and violence against officers. More importantly, the pervasive homophobia in society — like racism — is manipulated in many ways by the institution to reinforce hierarchies and increase divisions between groups of inmates. Whatever violence and disruption results from such divisions is preferable to a situation of inmates banding together to confront the institution. To say that gay inmates want to be free from fear of sexual violence is not to imply that they would not welcome opportunities for non-coerced sexual expression. The institution makes no such distinctions and uses rules about sexual behavior to manipulate and divide.

The situation of gays in prison could not be adequately dealt with today without some consideration of the impact of AIDS. To date, there have probably been between 100 and 150 recognized cases of AIDS in the federal and state prison systems — mostly localized to those states and regions with the largest number of cases in the general population. The impact will vary according to the size of the institution, its location, the level of security, the number of open gays, and the local incidence of AIDS. In general, the problems inside mirror those AIDS-related problems on the street, but are more extreme.

Because AIDS is incorrectly perceived as a gay disease, gays have been even more isolated, feared, and discriminated against. They are held responsible for the existence and spread of the disease.

Misconceptions about the contagiousness of AIDS have led to the most irrational demands by staff for "space suits" and elaborate precautions when handling or transporting people with AIDS or ill gay people suspected of having it. Inmate groups have demanded exclusion of gays from handling food — a demand which has no rational basis.

Accurate information about those at risk, about symptoms of AIDS, and about how to protect oneself have not been widely distributed by institutions — certainly not before the first case, or suspected case, created panic. At the same time, even accurate information from the authorities is suspect to an inmate population that sees the administration as simply trying to calm fears, but not necessarily committed to telling the whole truth.

In some institutions, the poor quality of the medical system, the ignorance about key symptoms among inmates, and the lack of specificity of those symptoms all contribute to problems of recognition, at least until the disease is far advanced.

AIDS highlights the irrational institutional attitudes about sexuality. Any sex is against institutional rules, and no distinction is made between coerced and consensual sexual activity. This means that on the one hand most coerced and violent sexual exploitation goes unrecognized and unpunished, and on the other that the institution is enjoined from distributing information about safer sex or making condoms available — both measures which experts believe would substantially reduce the risk of AIDS transmission if adopted or used properly.

CASE HISTORIES

Bill is a young gay man who was detained for several weeks in an urban county jail. Because he acknowledged at intake that he was gay, he was placed on the gay tier by the classification officer. He felt that the officers considered him a troublemaker and later transferred him to a tier in the general population, though he was still required to wear the identification bracelet that marked him as having been housed on the gay tier. A week after the transfer he was raped by three other inmates while the night officer looked on. He did not report the rape until the next morning, but was not taken for a medical evaluation until three days later. Though it has been over two years since the assault and Bill is now out of jail, the rape has created a serious barrier in his relationship with a new lover.

Vicky is a lesbian who was convicted of bank robbery and has spent several years in various federal and state prisons. The robbery was committed in league with a group that held a distinctly critical view of society and was in the context of liberating money to finance radical political causes. At her trial, Vicky was unrepentant about her leftist political views and her lesbianism. She received a sentence several years longer than that received by her comrades for similar charges. She is a physically strong and masculine-appearing woman who regularly lifts weights, and because of her appearance and lesbianism, she has been subjected to prying inquiries and invasive examinations to determine whether or not she is "really" a woman.

Mark is a slender, young gay man who spent several years

in various federal prisons for a weapons charge that he feels was a setup against him in retaliation for his political work among drug abusers. Because he was open about his gayness, he was forced to spend many months in protective custody and was, therefore, restricted from programs that would otherwise have been open to him. His lover was stabbed to death one evening by another inmate who felt he "owned" Mark and was angry at him for rejecting his advances. Since his release, Mark's problems with substance abuse have made his transition to civilian life a difficult one, though he has been responsible for starting a support project for gay and lesbian prisoners in the city to which he was paroled.

WHAT YOU CAN DO

If you work in a correctional institution, some of what has been presented in this chapter is probably not new to you, though you may not have thought previously about how being gay or lesbian especially affects an individual in prison. You are in a particularly good position to help out gay and lesbian inmates. You can encourage discussion of these special problems during training and orientation sessions for correctional officers and other staff. Any accurate information given — especially by credible members of the local gay community — can also be helpful and you may be able to help establish or support such a liaison.

Any measures you can take to establish the distinction between coerced and consensual sexual contacts — and that the latter should not be punished — would be an important contribution. Understand the pervasive fear that gay male inmates, in particular, live with, and do what you can to insure that they have the same access to programs and the same opportunities that other inmates enjoy. Any openness and expression of acceptance of gay men and lesbians helps reinforce those feelings in staff members who might not share the bigotry, but who lack the courage to speak up themselves. The sense of isolation that gay people in prison feel can be alleviated to some extent by access to gay books and periodicals. Institutions have been largely closed to such materials until recently, when pressure from legal groups have opened the system to some extent. Such openness should be encouraged by you.

If your work is outside a correctional institution, remember to think about incarceration in the course of gathering whatever information about an individual is pertinent to your area of work. Understand that for a gay man or lesbian such an experience may, and often will, have been physically and psychologically maiming, and that reintegration of the sexual dimension with the rest of the personality may be particularly difficult. Specifically, ask about sexual harassment or sexual assault. If the individual has been assaulted, some treatment or referral for rape trauma syndrome is appropriate. Understand that alcohol and other substance abuse may be a particular and related problem.

Join a citizens' watchdog group if one exists in your area, or join the local chapter of the ACLU, which frequently does prison advocacy work. Within these groups raise the issues of gay and lesbian prisoners and find out how the group is specifically addressing these problems.

If your community has some sort of gay counseling service or support services network, contact that organization about what, if any, services they offer to gay and lesbian prisoners or ex-offenders. Approach the local Metropolitan Community Church if one exists in your area about doing pastoral outreach within the local prison or jail.

RESOURCES

1. *Struggle for Justice — A Report on Crime and Punishment in America,* prepared for the American Friends Service Committee. NY: Hill and Wang, 1971. This is a critical analysis of the criminal justice system including the perspectives of those who have experienced it. It is strongly critical of the concept of rehabilitation which combines treatment with punishment. It examines the class and racial biases and the repressive functions of the system and suggests areas for reform and action.

2. *Kind and Usual Punishment,* by Jessica Mitford. NY: Vintage/Random House, 1974. The single most important book for understanding the corrections system in the U.S. today. The author reviews the history of prison reform, notions of "criminal type," and what "counts as crime" in the U.S. She discusses the phenomenon and impact of indeterminate sentencing, treatment strategies, medical experimentation, prison industries, and prisoner protests. She ends with a chapter entitled "Reform or Abolition?"

3. *Gay Community News*, 62 Berkeley St., Boston, MA, 02116. Nationally circulated gay and lesbian newspaper with a strong commitment to gays behind bars and regular features about prison conditions. Its "prisoner project" communicates regularly with those who receive the paper and offers self-help packets on various issues for those wanting to organize for change.

4. *No More Cages*, P.O. Box 90, Brooklyn, NY, 11215. Nationally distributed magazine produced by the Women Free Women in Prison Collective. It focuses on the situation of women in prison and is very sympathetic to the special needs of lesbians.

5. *Men Behind Bars — Sexual Exploitation in Prison*, by Wayne S. Wooden and Jay Parker. NY: Plenum Press, 1982. A study of sexuality in a medium-security men's prison in California. This book offers a true inside view and the authors discuss both the exploitation of heterosexual men and the abuse of gay men. They consider the limitations on true consensual sexual activity and make suggestions for institutional reform. The book describes very well the complex reality of prison sexuality for men.

6. *Victims of Sexual Aggression*, by Irving Stuart and JoAnn Greer. NY: Van Nostrand Reinhold, 1984. This book includes a chapter on prevention of and intervention in sexual assault within prisons, by A. Nicholas Groth and Donald Cotton. The chapter explores the scope of the problem and how it goes unrecognized and unaddressed. It discusses the dynamics of inmate sexual assault and its consequences for the individual. It offers suggestions for prevention and a model protocol for intervention and treatment.

Chapter 17
Single gays and lesbians

A. Elfin Moses

Single gays and lesbians face many of the same problems as their heterosexual counterparts, but there are some concerns unique to, or complicated by, a gay or lesbian lifestyle. This chapter will address five issues or problems that are particularly relevant to gays and lesbians without partners.

Three of the issues identified are most likely to apply to gays and lesbians who have never had a same-gender love relationship. These are constructing a gay or lesbian identity, learning about same-sex relationships, and developing a "family of friends" (Note 1). The two problems discussed that are relevant to all single gays and lesbians are those connected with membership in the gay or lesbian community as a single person and making social contacts.

CONSTRUCTING A GAY OR LESBIAN IDENTITY

The time when being single is likely to be most complex and problematic is during the period between identifying oneself as gay or lesbian and forming a committed partnership with someone of the same gender. During this time, single lesbians and gay men are often working to form a conception of themselves as individual women and men who are lesbian or gay; that is, they may be said to be developing a gay or lesbian identity.

The culmination of this process is, ideally, to develop a concept of self in which being lesbian or gay is a positively valued characteristic. Three factors seem to be of particular importance in achieving this outcome: commitment to gayness or lesbianism as a valued lifestyle, contact with an affirming gay or lesbian community, and self-disclosure to heterosexuals.(3, 6, 7, 13) The first two of these are the ones most likely to be relevant to single gays and lesbians. Helping professionals can provide valuable assistance in each of these areas by affirming the importance and centrality of these issues in the lives of these individuals and by helping them build healthy belief systems about homosexuality and gay people.

COMMITMENT TO A GAY OR LESBIAN LIFESTYLE

Commitment to a gay or lesbian lifestyle is often connected with a positive self-concept.(5, 8) One of the first phases of commitment, and a very important one, is the change from the perception of homosexuality as pathological, immoral or, at least, primarily problematic, to the perception of a gay or lesbian lifestyle as desirable, perhaps even preferable, to a heterosexual lifestyle. During this period, many gays and lesbians associate exclusively with other gays or lesbians, avoid social contact with heterosexuals completely, and begin to develop a sense of "gay pride" or "lesbian pride."(3, 13)

This represents two positive transitional steps for gay and lesbian individuals. First, it indicates a move from a negative to a positive conception of homosexuality and, by extension, to a positive conception of one's self. Second, according to some researchers, it signifies a differentiation between self-definition on the basis solely of sexual attraction or activity (self as "homosexual") and self-definition as a member of a cultural or social group (self as gay or lesbian). During this phase, sexual orientation may be the primary factor in an individual's definition of self, rather than simply one facet or aspect of that definition.

Heterosexuals are often offended by, threatened by, or even contemptuous of this kind of stance on the part of lesbians and gay men. They may see it as immaturity or as personal rejection, since lesbians and gays may be actively hostile toward heterosexuals and heterosexual values, traditions, and beliefs during this phase. Helping professionals can handle this positively and productively by realizing that it is important for gays and lesbians to take this kind of position as a step toward an integrated sense of self in which sexual orientation and activity are only parts of a more complex self-image. Single gay men and lesbian women who are struggling with these issues are in need of the support such identification provides and can be encouraged to amplify, rather than diminish, their ties with the gay and lesbian communities.

It is also appropriate at this time to encourage gay and lesbian clients to focus on differences, as well as similarities, between themselves and heterosexuals and to accentuate the positive aspects of being gay or lesbian. It is only through doing this that they will be able to cognitively restructure the homophobic messages of the larger society. As is true of other oppressed groups, when gays and lesbians can learn to value in themselves the things devalued by heterosexual society, they can then move toward meaningful, healthy relationships with the members of that society.

CONTACT WITH AN AFFIRMING GAY OR LESBIAN COMMUNITY

Most gays and lesbians want and need contact with a supportive community, but this need is particularly acute for those who are single and involved in the process of self-definition. Gays and lesbians often begin this process in childhood by noticing a sense of "differentness."(9, 6, 12, 13) This may develop further into an awareness of the ways one *is not* like heterosexuals long before it develops into a conception of what one *is*.

The definition of what one is as a "homosexual" is primarily a social definition and is taken originally from the larger society. As a consequence, the self-definition of gays and lesbians usually starts out as negative. It is often only through contact with the gay or lesbian community that gays and lesbians can begin to define themselves positively.

COMMUNITY RESOURCES

Gays and lesbians who are just coming out are usually unaware of gay or lesbian community resources. This is particularly likely to be a problem in non-urban areas where the gay and lesbian communities have low visibility. It is, therefore, desirable for helping professionals to be aware of community support systems for such clients.

First, there are those local support groups, organizations, gathering places, and resource persons to whom a gay or lesbian can be referred. These include local or regional organizations such as the Metropolitan Community Church (M.C.C.) or other supportive religious groups, hotlines, bars, and restaurants, lesbian or gay-identified health and helping professionals, and local or regional chapters of organizations such as Parents and Friends of Lesbians and Gays (P-FLAG).

It is also important to be aware of the existence of professional and political organizations which are either traditionally, or in principle, supportive of alternative lifestyles, such as the American Civil Liberties Union (A.C.L.U.), the National Organization for Women (N.O.W.), and the National Women's Political Caucus (N.W.P.C.). Many professional groups, including the National Association of Social Workers, the American Nurses' Association, the American Library Association, the American Teachers Union, the American Medical Association, and the American Lawyers' Guild have either a task force or a caucus, or both, representing gays and lesbians within that profession. Even if an individual does not belong to or wish to join one of these professional groups, knowing that they exist can be a source of support and encouragement.

Along with knowledge about these kinds of resources, it is a good idea for helping professionals to be aware of resources especially for lesbians and gays, including: publications; organizations, such as the National Gay and Lesbian Task Force (N.G.L.T.F.) and P-FLAG; book clubs; literature; and music. For lesbians and gay men who are feeling isolated from the gay or lesbian community, such resources can provide a vital link with the wider national and international lesbian and gay communities and can help provide a sense of belonging. Such resources are positive and affirming and are useful in counteracting the negative messages of the wider society.

LEARNING ABOUT GAY AND LESBIAN RELATIONSHIPS

The first exploration of the gay or lesbian community is usually linked with the beginning of self-acceptance and is often what is meant by the term "coming out."(6, 8) This phase "provides the opportunity to interact with other homosexuals, legitmates the homosexual experience and thereby enables the individual to develop an acceptance of a gay or lesbian identity."(8)

For men, at least, the formation of a love relationship often seems to follow acceptance of a gay identity.(7, 13) Such relationships may also increase the sense of commitment to a gay lifestyle for both women and men.(4, 13) As noted above, self-acceptance is also a function of contact with others within the gay or lesbian community. Thus, it is important that single lesbians and gays begin to learn about and develop social and love relationships with gay people.

In order to become socialized into the gay or lesbian community, gays and lesbians need to learn appropriate social skills. They need to learn how to recognize and interact with other gays and lesbians, and how to make both sexual and social contacts. Just as important is the need to learn the "rules" of being gay or lesbian within a homophobic society. Standards of attractiveness, sexual styles and sexual conduct, and many other issues are different depending on the community in which one finds oneself (i.e., gay, lesbian, or heterosexual).

Single lesbians and gay men who have never had same-gender partners may not know how or where to meet people, how to initiate or respond to sexual contacts, or how to act as gays or lesbians. In rural areas, for example, it is not uncommon for those who are not exposed to gay or lesbian role models to believe in outdated stereotypes. One client, for example, believed he would have to wear "drag," would be able to meet gay men only at gay bars, and would be instantly recognizable as a gay person once he actually came out.(11) Many gays and lesbians have not developed, at this point, the basic kinds of relationship skills necessary for beginning, developing, and maintaining love relationships.(12, 10)

DEVELOPING APPROPRIATE RELATIONSHIP SKILLS

Most adolescent gays and lesbians do not date or, more likely, they date someone of the opposite gender. While they learn some relationship skills in the process, many of these are different from the ones they will need in same-gender relationships. Furthermore, it is difficult to take these relationships seriously when one's attention is elsewhere. This means that more gay men and lesbian women enter adult-hood without having had an open, meaningful relationship with someone of the same gender.(4, 10, 12) Those in-dividuals who marry may be in their thirties, forties, fifties, even sixties before they get a chance to practice same-gender relationship skills.

For the most part, the experiences with heterosexual relationships that gays and lesbians have before they come out do not help them learn how to form and maintain long-term, same-gender relationships. While heterosexuals are using male-female dating to learn how to form opposite-gender relationships, young lesbians and gays are learning how to "pass." Adult gays and lesbians often remember clearly their discomfort when they were dating during adoles-cence or early adulthood. Some were aware of deliberately attempting to "pass" to fool parents, peers, or themselves, while others recognized only later that this is what they unconsciously were doing.(12)

Clinicians who are familiar only with heterosexual ex-perience may label gay and lesbian clients as "immature" or perceive them as suffering from "arrested development." This is, undoubtedly, in part because they are seeing people who have spent years learning how to live and to pass in a hostile environment, and because the people they see have not had the opportunities that heterosexuals have had of experiment-ing during adolescence with the formation of meaningful partnerships.(4, 10)

LEARNING THE MEANING OF SAME-GENDER PARTNERSHIPS

Gays and lesbians who have not been in committed rela-tionships which they identified as gay or lesbian may find the thought of forming such relationships emotionally loaded. Some individuals may fear the forming of partnerships be-cause of what it means to them as a statement about their sexual orientation. Others may want to rush into partnerships in order to gain entry into the gay or lesbian community.

FEAR OF FORMING A PARTNERSHIP

Forming a partnership is, for most gays and lesbians, the

closest approximation they have to the formalizing of their sexual orientation. For such persons, it is also an important step in developing an identity which includes their sexual orientation as only one facet of their personalities. Because of this, forming a committed partnership may seem risky to persons who are unsure about what it means to be gay or lesbian, or who are unsure about whether they want to accept their sexual orientation as part of their self-definition.

Some individuals may believe that forming such a partnership commits them irrevocably to either a gay or lesbian lifestyle. The reality, of course, is that it does not, any more than being married commits one to a heterosexual lifestyle. People have same-gender partnerships and then change their minds, just as persons in male-female marriages may decide that they are gay or lesbian and make lifestyle changes.

Because forming a love relationship with someone of the same gender can be perceived as representing commitment to gayness or lesbianism, the anticipation of forming such a relationship may also be accompanied by a sense of impending loss. Commitment to a gay or lesbian lifestyle almost inevitably means giving up a traditional lifestyle, and usually means giving up a relationship with one's family and friends in which one is perceived as heterosexual.

It means giving up the possibility of publicly expressing affection for one's lover without the threat of social reprobation, giving up an openness about one's life that heterosexuals take for granted. It may mean both real and imagined loss of respect, love, friendship, and closeness with heterosexual friends and family members. It often means giving up the possibility of having children and, for some, it means losing custody of children one already has.

These kinds of losses are far from trivial, and helping professionals can expect gay and lesbian clients to show the same kinds of grief responses toward these losses that are typical toward other kinds of losses. There is little chance for most lesbians or gays to express their fears or to examine these grief responses. The gay and lesbian communities often do not recognize these losses in any formal way, and many helping professionals never realize they exist.

Often, the response of others to the sense of loss is to try to convince such individuals that they really are not losing anything or that the loss can somehow be replaced. Helping professionals can aid lesbian and gay clients immensely in this process of experiencing loss by being willing to accept and validate the sense of loss and the fear and grief that accompany it.

PARTNERSHIP AS MEMBERSHIP

Establishing a love relationship may be especially important to individuals who want the security of belonging to the gay or lesbian community. Such a partnership may be perceived as signifying the individual's entrance into this community, a way of establishing one as a bona fide member, a step that will earn the individual acceptance into a coveted social group.

Many gays and lesbians experience both anxiety about establishing a relationship and the desire to form such a relationship in order to have a sense of belonging. Indeed, these issues are related. Forming a partnership is a step that usually and, perhaps, ideally follows the beginning of acceptance of oneself as a gay or lesbian person and of comprehension of what that means in this culture. Such acceptance is facilitated by contacts with other lesbians or gays, and it is through such contacts that partnerships often develop.

FINDING A "FAMILY OF FRIENDS"

A third task faced by unpartnered lesbians and gays has to do with establishing a place in the gay or lesbian community, with creating a "family of friends." Lesbians and gays who have just come out and who have just entered the gay or lesbian community often feel isolated and lonely. If they are newly self-identified, they need the support of others who share their orientation. Particularly in non-urban areas, they are likely to be unaware of any local or national cultural groups and support systems for gays and lesbians. For them in particular, it is easy to confuse the loneliness they feel because of cultural or social isolation with the need for a partner, and many gays and lesbians do so.

DIFFERENCES BETWEEN FAMILY OF ORIGIN AND FAMILY OF FRIENDS

Heterosexuals often clearly distinguish between family of origin and peer social groups as sources of support. The expectation (if frequently not the reality) is that the family of origin provides a number of crucial supports different from those provided by a peer group: a sense of continuity with the past, affirmation of one's sexual and emotional support, and understanding. For the most part, gays and lesbians cannot expect to find these kinds of support from their families of origin.

Family gatherings are events which support and confirm the values of a heterosexual lifestyle. There is little or no place in these gatherings for a gay or lesbian family member to fit in comfortably *as* gay or lesbian. Most families of origin do not recognize and cannot incorporate gay or lesbian traditions, celebrations, community, or history as part of their cultural or group history.

This means that lesbians and gays need both their family of origin and a "family of friends" because it is nearly always the family of friends that is aware and supportive of gayness or lesbianism as good and acceptable. Partnered lesbians and gays can create such family structures for themselves. But this sense of family may be of even greater importance, and even more difficult to achieve, for these unpartnered individuals, who do not fit clearly into any traditional, recognized family system.

PROBLEMS FACING ALL UNPARTNERED GAYS AND LESBIANS

Membership in the Gay or Lesbian Community: A major problem for unpartnered gays and lesbians has to do with membership in the gay or lesbian community as a single person. As is true of heterosexual social groups, adult gay and lesbian groups are frequently composed of identified couples. In heterosexual groups, an unpartnered individual may be perceived as a potential competitor for half of the individuals in the group. In a gay or lesbian social group, an unpartnered newcomer is a potential competitor for all members.

Because of this, there may be more pressure within the gay and lesbian communities for an unpartnered individual to establish a committed relationship, thereby taking him or her out of the field of competition. There may also be a reluctance to include an unpartnered individual in a group of couples. This means that unpartnered gays and lesbians are likely to feel isolated.

Coping with Isolation: While isolation and loneliness can certainly be problems for single heterosexuals, the degree and type of isolation and loneliness are different for gay people. Single gays and lesbians, particularly those who have just come out or who are new to a community, face an absence of both social support in general and social support for their lifestyle. Unless they live in progressive or urban areas, or unless they are familiar with gay or lesbian community resources, gays and lesbians will probably find it difficult to make social contacts.

The most frequently identified source of social contacts is through gay and lesbian friendship networking. Single gays and lesbians who have just come out probably do not have such a network and must be reassured that such networks take time to develop. Those who are single because of the dissolution of a previous relationship may find that their friends are also divided by separate loyalties, and one or both partners may end up experiencing isolation. This is a time when individuals often need to refresh their social skills and to receive support while they develop new friends.

Gay, Lesbian, or Gay and Lesbian bars: Another source for contacts is the gay, lesbian, or gay and lesbian bar. These are more likely to be used by men than by women and are more likely to be viewed by both as sources of sexual contacts than as places to make friends. Identifying bars as sources of contacts poses a number of problems.

In the first place, bars are often not a source of fruitful social contacts. Second, bars are organized around alcohol consumption, which is uncomfortable and unhealthy for many people. Third, using bars to make contacts requires social skills gays and lesbians who have just come out may not have. Fourth, many gays and lesbians, particularly those who live in small towns or who are concerned about being identified as gay or lesbian, are afraid to be seen entering or leaving such places. Finally, the AIDS epidemic has made bars much less attractive than they may have been at one point. Individuals who are considering using bars or baths for sexual contacts should, of course, be warned about the increased incidence of AIDS, told how this disease is contracted, and urged to take precautions.

SUMMARY AND CONCLUSIONS

Unpartnered gay men and lesbians face some unique and difficult personal tasks and challenges. Those men and women who have never had a gay or lesbian relationship are often struggling with defining and accepting their identities *as* gays or lesbians, even as they are weighing the relative merits for them between being single and entering a relationship. Many of the concerns they have and the issues they face as single persons can be related to this struggle for identity, as well as to the isolation they often feel, to doubts about finding a partner, and to their having inadequate social skills. Previously-partnered and never-partnered gays and lesbians are equally liable to have problems with feelings of loneliness as single members of the gay or lesbian community. The objective of this chapter has been to identify, discuss and, thereby, better sensitize the readers to these difficult and problematic situations that arise in the lives of single gay people. It is hoped that the counseling approaches and resources I have shared will be of considerable use to those readers who, as health care providers, will be sought out by single gays and lesbians for help.

NOTES

1. The term "family of friends" is taken from the song "Don't Lose Heart" on the album *Prairie Fire,* released by Olivia Records. Words and music by Chris Williamson, copyright 1984.

REFERENCES

1. Albro, J.C. and Tully, C. (1979). A study of lesbian lifestyles in the

homosexual micro-culture and the heterosexual macro-culture. *Journal of Homosexuality, 4(4)*, 331-344.

2. Cass, V.C. (1983/1984). Homosexual identity: A concept in need of definition. *Journal of Homosexuality, 9(2/3)*, 91-105.

3. Cass, V.C. (1979). Homosexual identity formation: A theoretical model. *Journal of Homosexuality, 4(3)*, 219-236.

4. Coleman, E. (1981/1982). Developmental stages of the coming out process. *Journal of Homosexuality, 7(2/3)*, 31-43.

5. Jacobs, J.A. and Tedford, W.H., Jr. (1980). Factors affecting the self-esteem of the homosexual individual. *Journal of Homosexuality, 5(4)*, 378-382.

6. Kus, R.J. (1985, May). Stages of coming out: An ethnographic approach. *Western Journal of Nursing Research, 7(2)*, 177-198.

8. Minton, H.L. and McDonald, G.J. (1983/1984). Homosexual identity formation as a developmental process. *Journal of Homosexuality, 9(2/3)*, 91-104.

9. Moses, A.E. (1978). *Identity management in lesbian women.* New York: Praeger.

10. Moses, A.E. (1981, Nov.). *Treatment issues in counseling lesbian women and gay men.* Paper presented at the Seventh Biennial Professional Symposium of the National Association of Social Workers, Philadelphia.

11. Moses, A.E. and Buckner, J.A. (1980). Special problems of rural gay clients. *Human Services in the Rural Environment, 5*, 22-28.

12. Moses, A.E. and Hawkins, R.O., Jr. (1980). *Counseling lesbian women and gay men: A life-issues approach.* St. Louis: C.V. Mosby.

13. Troiden, R.R. and Goode, E. (1980). Variables related to the acquisition of a gay identity. *Journal of Homosexuality, 5(4)*, 383-392.

Chapter 18
The coupled gay

Charles Silverstein

THE COUPLED GAY

Some readers may be surprised to learn that homosexual love has been documented for at least two thousand years. By "homosexual love" we mean romantic feelings and feelings of sexual desire, either transient or permanent, between two males.

Here are some well-known examples from history. The ancient Greek philosopher, Socrates, was said to be the lover of young Alcibiades, who later became a leading politician in Athens. Hephaestion was the lover of Alexander the Great; they fought side by side in Alexander's conquests.(2)

Classical Greek society institutionalized pederastic love. The Dorians of Sparta encouraged relationships between adult males and adolescent boys, using these relationships to train the youngsters for war. Athenians, on the other hand, emphasized youth and beauty, though they did not neglect the moral character of pederasty, as the works of Plato show.(3, 14)

Roman society had its examples of male lovers as well. Julius Caesar was a man who enjoyed a variety of sexual pleasures, and was for a time the lover of King Nicomedes of Bithynia.(2) Caesar's reputation for bisexuality was once used against him in the Senate by the Elder Pliny, who called him "Husband to every man's wife, and wife to every woman's husband."

But perhaps the most prominent Roman example is the love of the Emperor Hadrian for the beautiful youth Antinoüs, who drowned in the Nile, quite possibly having sacrificed himself to save Hadrian from the wrath of the gods, who, many believed, were turning against him. When the distraught Hadrian deified his beloved, Antinoüs' sacrifice so caught the imagination of the ancient world that he became the object of a widespread religion which lasted for centuries and produced some of the greatest art of late antiquity. But this important event in the moral development of the West has been almost totally written out of our histories.

Each era has produced men who were lovers of other men.(4) Richard the Lion-Hearted, who preferred the company of his male friends to that of his wife, went on a crusade to the Holy Land. His opponent, Paladin, the Moslem military commander, is famous for remarking that sleeping with girls is like eating a joint of meat without a bone. Edward II of England was madly in love with Piers Gaveston, who was murdered in a palace intrigue. A second lover of Edward's was murdered as well, because of his potential political influence. Finally, Edward himself was murdered most cruelly. James I of England fared better in his love affair with George Villiers, the duke of Buckingham (James used to call him "My Steenie").

We know best how the royal families lived and with whom the great generals of history bedded, but little of the common man. Much of this history does not exist because the prevailing moral system proscribed sexual relations between men and prevented even the mention of such a grave sin. By the nineteenth century, with the decline of clerical control, the discussion of such matters became possible in a medical setting. Medical science was then composed of equal parts of empiricism, conjecture, and moral beliefs. In the twentieth century, psychoanalysis made its claim to understand the origins of all sexual behavior and defined the normal and the abnormal, in both cases ignoring contrary evidence. Today we know that psychoanalysis was burdened by the same prejudices and inaccurate reasoning as previous generations.

Today, gay couples live in every area of the country. They are found in urban settings and rural farm communities. We find men in loving, lifelong relationships with all the romance and passion found in heterosexual marriage. Gay couples have become an important economic force in many areas of the country. They buy property in common, sign contracts together, and benefit from survivorship. They demand, but have not yet received, full economic parity with heterosexual marriage, e.g. family medical insurance and legal recognition of the union. Nevertheless, for the most part, the lives of gay couples are very much like the lives of other people in their community. Where competition and dynamism are in the air, as in, say, New York City, gay couples compete in that fast-paced society; where time is measured more slowly, as in our rural settings, gay couples mirror the pace of their neighbors.

Our modern gay couples share one trait with the historical examples previously cited: a desire to express both romantic and sexual feelings toward members of the same sex. But modern gay couples differ significantly from the historical examples in a number of important ways. Perhaps the most important difference is the concept of *sexual identity*, the idea that each of us can define ourselves as homosexual, bisexual, or heterosexual. This is a distinctly modern idea.(10, 15) In fact, the term "homosexual" was coined only in 1869.(13, 6) Previous societies did not believe, as we do, that there is this tripartite continuum. They believed, rather, that sexuality was merely behavior. It had nothing to do with what we today call "sexual identity." For instance, when Paul, in Romans 1:26, writes that it is an abomination for one man to sleep with another, he is merely talking about the sex act. In his society there was not a class of people who defined themselves as gay.

At the same time as the homosexual identity developed, medical science rushed in to explain it. Unfortunately for gay people, the explanations were devastating for the development of gay love relationships. Gay men were initially diagnosed as suffering from a mental disease caused either by defective genes or a degeneration of the nervous system.(5) When psychological etiologies replaced physiological ones, such depravity was thought to be the result of psychopathic adults, and later to be the result of a pathological constellation of family relationships.(1) One wonders at how resourceful gay couples had to have been in order to maintain their relationships in the face of so much erroneous thinking, prejudice, and discrimination from family, society, religion, and the state.

With the development of a gay identity, gay communities appeared in the United States. Today most large cities have a gay section, where one can find bars, restaurants, and a variety of businesses catering to gay people. Not surprisingly, one also finds a significant number of gay people living in this area. These gay ghettoes are a haven for couples. In this environment, they can act freely and relax in a public setting with less fear of arrest or harassment. Such gay communities reinforce the concept of the gay identity and support the establishment of long-lasting love relationships.(9)

In summary, today's gay couples share very little with their ancestors, probably only similar feelings of romance and passion. They differ dramatically in their concepts of themselves as gay. Consequently, the male lovers of antiquity felt themselves a part of the larger society, while the gay lovers of today feel themselves as separate and often alienated from it. This sense of alienation, the fear of police brutality and the brutality of average citizens, the condemnation by religious institutions, and perhaps most of all, the hostility of their own families give rise to many of the problems facing gay couples.

THE PROBLEMS OF GAY RELATIONSHIPS

For purposes of this short chapter, we may divide the potential relationship problems into three classes: Those that are externally caused, interpersonal problems within the couple, and individual personality problems that affect the relationship. Though the divisions are somewhat artificial, they are convenient classifications for learning purposes. In reality, these problems seldom occur singly. Most of the time, there is much cross-influencing. The sensitive therapist will notice how these problems affect each other, and how changes in one sphere of influence can alter the others.

Problems Arising from Societal Attitudes

1) *Family Discrimination* — Perhaps no difficulty is as great for many gays as the rejection they face from their own immediate families.(12) The average set of parents look upon their son's gay relationship as unfortunate at best, and at worst as decadent, immoral, abnormal, and doomed to end in misery. Fed for years with faulty information about the immorality of gay love and the belief that the relationship must end in hopeless despair, parents usually make a variety of attempts to interfere with it. One of the first courses of action is to send the son to a therapist. "Cure my son" is the

desperate request. If the son is young enough to be coerced, or wants to please the family, the therapy (useless though it may be) will begin.

A second reaction from parents is a guilt trip they place upon themselves. This is particularly true of mothers who believe, quite incorrectly, that an abnormal relationship with their sons produced a homosexual orientation. A mother may experience this guilt intensely. The gay son who continues his gay relationship may, in turn, assume responsibility for his mother's anguish.

Another problem arises for the gay man, who, for whatever reason, chooses not to tell his parents about his homosexuality. Of course, he could not tell them about developing a love affair with another man, either. An enormous wall of secrecy surrounds his actions, making him a mystery to the family, who quickly learn not to ask questions. In this closet, the couple feel prohibited from spending the usual family holidays together. They separate at holiday time, each going to his own family.

Here the role of a therapist is to break through the barrier that prevents communication between the family and the gay couple. There are two ways to do this. The first is to provide good information about homosexuality to the parents. This material should be given by the son. Most parents want their children to be happy, but believe that a gay lifestyle will end in depression. They are usually willing (though sometimes not at first) to read whatever information is given. They should read this information by themselves, and then should take the opportunity to discuss it with their son and his lover. The second is to have discussions between family members (I am including the lover as a member of the family) to resolve all the barriers to good communication. A full discussion should expose the fear, guilt, and resentment that prevent good communication between the family members and the gay couple.

Some families are destructive, abusive, or alcoholic. One finds fathers, for instance, who will be at a son mercilessly for his homosexual activity. Or one sometimes finds a mother who so wants to control a son that she will persist in trying to make him feel deep guilt for "having done this to me." There is no point in trying to establish communication with a destructive family; it will only end in further hurt for the gay son, and will probably destroy his love relationship. Such families are so narcissistic, so involved with their own feelings of deprivation, that they lack even a primitive capacity for empathy. Though it may sound cold and unfeeling, such families should be avoided by the gay son and his lover.

2) *Social Discrimination* — Job security can be a problem for a gay man, and especially one in a love relationship. There are many documented cases of gay men being fired from their jobs after the employer learns that his employee has moved in with another man. Unfortunately, there are rarely laws to prevent such blatant discrimination. This is truer of smaller communities than of large cities where gay couples have more anonymity. Sometimes gay couples are evicted from their rental housing on grounds of immorality.

While most gay couples, like their heterosexual counterparts, like to invite friends and colleagues over for dinner or for other social events, the gay couples forced into the closet are isolated from all but the gay community. If that gay community is itself small, as one finds in rural and suburban areas, it can increasingly create the feeling that the couples live under a state of siege. This defensiveness is further reinforced when the local police, for reasons that escape logic, begin a vendetta against gay people, arresting them and publishing their names with the full knowledge that these actions will cause some of them to lose their jobs, and perhaps their homes, and will create family embarrassments.

Both family and social discrimination create extraordinary stresses on a gay relationship. Disagreements between the gay men are likely to arise, aggravated by any personality problems, or by any unresolved conflicts in their relationship. Of course, there are also other gay couples who have the strength to turn to each other for guidance and support. These couples will likely turn out to be strengthened by the adversity, rather than crippled by it. The role of a therapist should obviously be to help the two men find strength in themselves and support for each other. It is in the circumstances of facing family and community discrimination that the therapist needs to be sensitive in separating levels of conflict between the men.

Problems Arising from Interpersonal Tensions

A key concept when considering love relationships among gay people (from which all other concepts follow) is that gay relationships are different from straight ones in the sense that two male lovers emphasize masculine traits, and two lesbians emphasize female traits, while heterosexual lovers must compromise between male and female traits. This will undoubtedly sound peculiar in a society that perceives gay men as acting feminine, and lesbians as masculinized women. These ill-informed stereotypes aside, both the strengths and weaknesses of gay love relationships mirror the strengths and weaknesses respectively of masculinity and femininity as these are defined in our society.

1) *Excitement-Seekers and Home-Builders* — One can find two general lifestyles within the masculine framework that contribute either to stability or conflict in a gay relationship. An Excitement-Seeker is one who emphasizes novelty and change, rather than stability and longevity in a relationship, often evaluating other men on their sexual abilities. He avoids dull experiences and values his mobility and independence. The Home-Builder, on the other hand, is one who looks for permanence in a relationship, someone who wants to make future plans with and for his lover. He judges the quality of his relationship more by the degree of intimacy achieved than by the level of sexual excitement.(11)

Common sense would predict that the Home-Builder would be a better lover and more likely to be in a long-lasting relationship. But common sense would be wrong, the factors in human relationships being very complex. It is the compatibility of lifestyles that predicts success or failure. For instance, Excitement-Seekers, though often terrified of (and sometimes terrorized by) the Home-Builder kind of man will find a relationship with another Excitement-Seeker intimate and satisfying. Two Home-Builders are also likely to form lasting relationships. The sparks fly, however, when an Excitement-Seeker and a Home-Builder are matched, the one motivated to increase the level of novelty in his life, the other striving for a more domestic, quieter environment. Sometimes compromises are possible, but often their incompatible goals will mean the relationship will be transient. This is likely to be acceptable to the Excitement-Seeker, but not to the Home-Builder, a fact that only further drives them apart.

2) *Monogamy and Fidelity*—There is probably no one issue in gay relationships that causes more strife than that of sexual fidelity. Conflict between the two men concerning sexual exclusivity is probably the single greatest cause for the breakup of gay couples. Many men are not highly motivated to remain in a monogamous relationship throughout their lives. Some people believe, without a shred of evidence, that this desire to have sex outside the relationship indicates an inability to be intimate and that it is caused by the socialization of men. These critics, however, are usually of the Home-Builder type. This is not to say that fear of intimacy may not motivate some particular gay men to run out for sex, instead of dealing with their fear. But the fact is that very few gay relationships remain sexually exclusive for very long. Before the first year is out, conflicts will arise, and it is a rare couple that has been together for more than a few years that is still sexually exclusive. One should also note that a high percentage of heterosexually married men also have sex outside the marriage. We have every reason to believe that more would do so if they weren't frightened of the consequences.

Sex outside of the love relationship does not cause the breakup of gay couples. What is crucial is the means they use to resolve the crisis. There are innumerable solutions, too many to discuss in this short chapter. Destructive to the relationship is the unconditional demand by the one who has remained sexually exclusive (often acting like a jealous wife) for the other to change his wayward behavior. Indeed, all demands are likely to end up being destructive to a relationship. Winning the battle does not increase intimacy and caring; rather, it most often leads to resentment which only builds to a crescendo and a final explosion. Over time, negotiation and explorations of feelings and reactions will more probably lead to a mutually agreeable resolution. The prudent therapist, working with such a couple in conflict, will do everything possible to prevent quick, and especially retaliatory, actions by either man.

3) *Problems of Jealousy and Envy*— In contrast to straight relationships, gay ones need to differentiate between prob-

lems of jealousy and envy. Let us define them. Jealousy is the fear of abandonment. What is likely to be feared by the jealous lover is that his beloved will leave him for another man. Jealous behavior is but the outward sign of the fear of abandonment and desertion. Such jealous lovers are likely to subscribe to Schopenhauer's dictum that to forgive and forget is to throw away valuable experience!

Envy, on the other hand, is the enmity motivated by competitiveness or covetousness. When envious, we are resentful of our lover's perceived superiority or success. We covet what he has — perhaps his looks, his lifestyle, his money, or his sex appeal. Envy implies a competition between lovers in which one partner perceives himself as second best. The perceived lack of equality by either or both of the lovers is most often a sign of long-standing insecurities. Moreover, envy can be extremely damaging to a relationship, especially since the envious lover is likely to be unaware of his feeling, and then confused by it.

Personality Problems that Interfere with the Relationship

Gay relationships, like straight ones, are subject to all the insecurities that each member of the pair brings to the relationship. Inevitably, these insecurities and fears become intertwined with the couple's ways of functioning, communicating, and resolving conflicts in their relationship. There are no specifically interpersonal issues here, since the fears and insecurities begin their work long before romantic and sexual desires arise. Still, we can discuss some common sources of personal conflict.

1) *Self-hatred* — The first personality problem that can hurt a love relationship is self-hatred for being gay. It is very difficult to grow up in our society without some regret of one's homosexuality. For some, the disappointment of not pleasing the family and community is intense and persistent, leading inevitably to low self-esteem. A chronic depression exists in such men, and any barrier to their plans, or roadblock in their progress, is interpreted as proof of their inferior status. These men typify the quip by Groucho Marx, who once said, "I wouldn't join any club with standards so low that they

would invite me to be a member!" While homophobic gay men do try to establish love relationships, they cannot engage in intimacy because they cannot accept love from another man. Occasionally, one finds a closeted, self-hating gay man in a relationship with another man who is out of the closet and secure in a positive sense of self. A clash is inevitable.

2) *Overvaluation of Sex* — An overvaluation of sex is another personal problem for some gay men. Men, as distinct from women, value sexuality as a primary criterion of a relationship. Any sexual problem between men is often interpreted as an indicator that the relationship is over. This overvaluation also expresses itself by the gay lover using outside sex as a palliative for any frustration he may have in the relationship, or for problems in general. Sex is readily available in the gay world, and some gay men will vent their frustration through sexual encounter rather than by solving the real problem. These gay men live the Yiddish proverb that says, "When the penis is hard, the brains are soft."

3) *Paternal Relations* — The relationship between a gay man and his father may exert a powerful influence on the success or failure of the young man's love relationships. This is a complicated issue, filled with many levels of subtlety. Etiological factors cannot be examined in depth here.(11) The problem expresses itself in the following way: the gay man, quite unconsciously, expects his lover to fulfill two roles, that of lover — and father. The father role is composed of the aspects that were missed by the son during the formative years of his development. It is as if the son were attempting to recover the missed love and caring of prior years by means of his current love affair. It is a restorative venture, but since it is misdirected in its object (the lover instead of the father), it is doomed to failure. The lover soon becomes confused about who he is in the relationship, and this quickly leads to conflicts and resentments that are ill-understood by both parties. This kind of problem usually leads to a feeling of helplessness and futility.

Not all traditionally trained therapists can work with gay couples in crisis. For instance, the therapist who believes that homosexuality is abnormal would serve the couple best by referring them to a colleague who is more sympathetic. But, generally speaking, the techniques of therapy for gay couples are no different than they are for straight ones.

In therapy, the therapist will learn that gay couples have their strengths, as well as special problems. They will find, for instance, that gay couples are unusually honest in their interactions. While deception does exist, it occurs less often in gay than in straight couples. Good therapeutic techniques will always emphasize the strengths of a relationship, rather than dwelling on the weaknesses.

REFERENCES

1. Bieber, I., et al. (1962). *Homosexuality: A psychoanalytic study.* New York: Basic Books.

2. Bullough, V.L. (1976). *Sexual variance in society and history.* New York: John Wiley & Sons.

3. Dover, K.J. (1978). *Greek homosexuality.* Cambridge: Harvard University Press.

4. Hyde, H.M. (1970). *The love that dared not speak its name: A candid history of homosexuality in Britain.* Boston: Little, Brown.

5. Katz, J. (1976). *Gay American history: Lesbians and gay men in the U.S.A. — A documentary.* New York: Thomas Y. Crowell.

6. Lauritsen, J. and Thorstad, D. (1974). *The early homosexual rights movement.* New York: Times Change Press.

7. Lambert, R. (1984). *Beloved and God: The story of Hadrian and Antinoüs.* New York: Viking.

8. Larson, P.C. (1982). Gay male relationships. In W. Paul, J.D. Weinrich, J.C. Gonsiorek, and M.E. Hotvedt (Eds.), *Homosexuality: Social, psychological and biological issues.* Beverly Hills: Sage.

9. Levine, M. (1979). Gay ghetto. In M. Levine (Ed.), *Gay men: The sociology of male homosexuality.* New York: Harper & Row.

10. McIntosh, M. (1968). The homosexual role. *Social Problems, 16,* 32.

11. Silverstein, C. (1981). *Man to man: Gay couples in America.* New York: Morrow.

12. Silverstein, C. (1977). *A family matter: A parents' guide to homosexuality.* New York: McGraw-Hill.

13. Steakley, J. (1975). *The homosexual emancipation movement in Germany.* New York: Arno Press.

14. Vanggard, T. (1975). *Phallos: A symbol and its history in the male world.* New York: International Universities Press.

15. Weeks, J. (1977). *Coming out: Homosexual politics in Britain from the nineteenth century to the present.* New York: Quartet Books.

Chapter 19
The coupled lesbian

Joanne Hall and Pat Stevens

Lesbian couples living in our present culture often believe they have found the best of all possible worlds as women because they are not confined to the traditional woman's role in relationships. Yet, obviously, to be lesbians in this society is not to be in the best of all possible worlds. In fact, because of the difficulties involved in forming and maintaining lesbian relationships, some lesbians might be ambivalent about coupled relationships, while for others, being in coupled relationships is the whole point of being a lesbian. Sounds confusing? It need not be. A look at relationships from the viewpoint of lesbians may be quite useful for the would-be helpers of coupled lesbians.

Lesbian relationships are first of all relationships between women. Lesbians are attracted to other women *because* they are women. Women value relating, and, typically, are very empathetic and nurturing. When women form loving relationships with one another, there is the potential for very fulfilling, emotionally intense, and sexually satisfying interactions.

Finding a partner is usually more difficult for lesbians than for straights. There is no well-known social script for lesbian courtship. There are few social outlets in which lesbians can be fully themselves. For fear of losing economic and social supports, lesbians may conceal themselves. But their identities must be known to meet one another as friends and lovers.

There is no one stereotype for lesbian relationships. Male-female marriage, the only socially supported model for establishing and maintaining long-term sexual and emotional relationships, does not fit. So lesbian lovers must adopt their own models of relating. Of necessity, this requires an atmosphere of creativity, planning, and problem-solving which holds the potential for enhancement of equality, authenticity, mutuality, and respect in relationships.

Few assumptions can be made about lesbian relationships. Feminism has offered some ideas for how women might relate to each other. Ethnicity, religion, family of origin, and previous relationships also affect how each woman views the roles in relationships. For example, many lesbians choose monogamous, long-term unions, while others form open relationships, not emphasizing sexual exclusivity. Some lesbians prefer to live in communal arrangements, while others prefer to live alone and uncoupled. Some are celibate but have close emotional relationships with other women. The one generalization that does hold true for lesbian relationships, however loosely or closely coupled they are, is that the overall communication pattern for lesbian couples usually reflects equality.(1)

Permanence is valued by some women, while others feel it more realistic to expect relationships to end after a time. As an example, since lesbians often are not financially dependent upon each other, each must engage in her own occupation and pursue her own financial resources. Career decisions may cause the end of a very rewarding relationship, through no one's fault. Some couples formalize their commitments to one another by joint investment in property, or by making legal contracts.

Helping persons may be wise to explore their own feelings and beliefs about these issues, as well as their feelings about the value of lesbian relationships in general. Are you focused on permanence, or on one set of rules for all? Do you believe that lesbians will only be more accepted by society if they have permanent relationships? Can you consider a lesbian couple as a family? How do you feel about lesbians rearing children? Can you imagine the grief at the loss of a lesbian lover relationship? Exploring these questions may assist helping persons to appreciate the potential of lesbian relationships as strong, healthy, and worthwhile.

Helping professionals are in a unique position to value and validate lesbian couples by welcoming the partners in these relationships as legitimate members of their clientele. Respect and sensitivity to the facts that a lesbian couple is a primary relationship and that the partners form a family are essential. Caring for a lesbian means including her lover as an important part of the planning and implementation of that care. For example, when a woman becomes seriously ill and is hospitalized in the intensive care unit where visitors are restricted to immediate family, she and her lover deserve to be able to spend time with each other without having to struggle for the privilege.

Many lesbians avoid interaction with helping professionals, or avoid disclosing their lesbian identities to them. Historically, lesbians have suffered negative reactions and abusive treatment from professionals, such as condescension, inappropriate mental health referrals, and voyeuristic questions.(2, 5) The decision to disclose to a professional is not an easy one. Some defensiveness on the part of lesbian clients is natural and can be expected. Through reassurance and a show of knowledge and genuine concern, the helping professional can ease the disclosure situation.

It is important that helping persons make it clear that they do not assume that all women are straight. This can be accomplished by the use of such words as "partner" and "significant relationship" instead of "boyfriend," "husband," "marriage" when inquiring about social support. Careful use of pronouns can indicate an awareness of the possibility of gay, lesbian, or straight relationships. An open and non-judgemental approach creates the atmosphere in which lesbians can disclose their identities if they so choose.

Lesbian couples have concerns similar to those of straight couples, but, in addition, lesbian couples do not have the advantage of legal and social sanction. The social expectations and legal pressures to keep straight couples together do not exist for lesbians. Society grants lesbian partners no status beyond lover, which is far from approximating the legitimizing status given to husband or wife. So lesbian couples must cope with many difficult situations that straight couples may never have to face. A sensitive and aware helping professional may provide a much-needed source of social support in an often hostile environment.

It is important that the helping person look very carefully at the external environment for sources of stress in the relationship as a first step in working with lesbian couples. What is the local community like for lesbians? Are there many resources for lesbians, such as support groups, telephone hotlines, organizations, or meeting places? Is the client, or couple, aware of these? Is there a large lesbian community nearby? What are job and career pressures like? What financial resources does each woman have? What is the attitude of each family of origin toward the couple? What are sources of social support in terms of other lesbians and straights? Are there racial, class, or ethnic differences between the women, or between the couple and the outside community? How much time and privacy is available to the couple for relating? Attempts should first be made to decrease the impact of these outside stressors, before internal problems are assumed.

There are many potential sources of internal stress for lesbian couples. Living in a hostile society prompts lesbians to overload their relationships. For example, if partners get little or no support from families of origin, the media, religion, jobs, and friends, they look to each other to meet their needs for acceptance and caring. The lover becomes family, best friend, confidante, and protector from a damaging environment. Each lover is a reflection and validation of the other's womanhood and lesbianism, a reality that soothes the isolation and loneliness that can be felt in a homophobic society. The intensity of the emotional bond and the fear of abandonment may lead to a "you and me against the world" feeling in the relationship. Since women are likely to empathize easily, the boundaries may become blurred between partners. One or both may identify strongly with the feelings, problems, or needs of the other.

This has been called fusion, or interdependency.(3) The inexperienced helping person may see this as an unhealthy sign and may even begin working toward the goal of terminating the relationship. Actually, this fusion tendency occurs so often in lesbian couples, that it should be considered usual, a natural developmental step.(4) The helping person can support both women, and encourage each in her own way to develop some private time, separate friends, or activities so that the need for a well-defined sense of self does not become a struggle and an internal pressure on the relationship as time goes on.

One or both of the women may consider themselves strong feminists, and may develop guilt feelings about their feelings of jealousy, or abandonment fears. They may feel that possessive feelings are reflective of straight relationships, in which the man dominates and possesses the woman. This could be reframed by a helping professional as "feelings of self-preservation," or "anticipating realistic risks" in relationships.

If the fusion situation is pervasive and one or both of the partners persistently lose a clear sense of self, more investigation is in order. Substance abuse, for example, can emerge under the conditions present in lesbian as well as straight couples. Substance abuse in one partner often leads the other partner to cope with life by focusing on the substance abuser's addictive behavior. She begins to react instead of to act. This is called co-dependency, or relationship addiction. Co-dependency may also develop as a result of leftover childhood patterns, as in the case of adult daughters of alcoholics. In these cases, the substance abuse and co-dependency should be handled first, before other problems are tackled. Specialized counseling or referral to self-help groups such as AA or Al-Anon are needed. Books are always a good starting point to reduce the denial that often comes with these painful wounds. (For further information on co-dependency, please see the co-dependency chapter in this book.)

Other potential internal stresses in lesbian relationships result from the ways in which they develop. For example, the lack of established courtship patterns means that lesbian relationships may develop quickly. There may not be time for each of the partners to explore the meaning of the relationship, and their expectations for its future. They may need help in clarifying these issues later in the relationship. On the other hand, a pair of women may live together for twenty years and never establish a sexually intimate relationship.

First relationships for either or both women may present special needs for support. For many, the discovery of attraction toward other women may be the first realization that they are lesbians. Yet some of these women do not identify themselves as lesbians at this point. They may choose, instead, to see these attractions as "special cases" of same-sex love, which do not necessarily mean they are lesbians. It may be more comfortable for a time to explore relationships without launching whole new identities at the same time. Other lesbians have come to realize their lesbian identities before they become involved in coupled relationships.

Identity formation, one part of coming out, may be one of the first internal issues faced by the lesbian couple. Each partner may be at a different point in her own coming-out process. For instance, the lesbian in a first relationship may experience powerful feelings of affirmation as a woman, and may be relieved to discover at last that fulfillment is possible. She may be just discovering the lesbian community and finding others like herself for the first time. These positive feelings may be hard to separate from her attraction toward her partner. On the other hand, her partner, who has already passed this stage of newness, may be content to focus on other aspects of life.

Another pressure for lesbian couples is the internalization of negative attitudes toward lesbians that abound in society. They may devalue themselves as lesbians, and so devalue the relationship as well. Internalized homophobia can be a nagging source of problems in terms of self-image for both women, since it is not easily cast off once and for all, but reappears particularly at times of stress. The professional might help the couple explore the external origins of the negative images and identify more positive ones.

Another internal difficulty that could develop in any relationship is attraction to a third person. The lesbian couple may seek help because one or the other partner has become attracted to another woman. How does this situation develop? Perhaps one woman seeks to define herself more clearly by expanding her friendships separately. Most of her friends may be women; many may be lesbians. Same-sex friendships always carry the possibility of new attraction. Even association with other lesbian couples may be a source of new attractions. Rarely, a bisexual woman who had falsely believed herself to be a lesbian may become attracted to a man.

Partners may have different levels of comfort with disclosure, and this creates another internal stress. For example, one woman may feel it is best, or "politically correct," to be as open as possible about her identity and about her lover. Her partner may have strong fears that if word passes through the grapevine to her employer or to her family of origin, she will lose her job or her family's support. This could be reframed as a matter that simply needs to be negotiated — that there is no one "right answer."

Lesbians who have children present special needs. They may seek help to determine when and how they should disclose to the children about their lover relationships. In most cases, when given an opportunity for open discussion of sexuality and relationships, children are able to let their parents know how much information they would like to hear at any one time. Disclosure is best viewed in this case as a process, rather than a once-and-for-all event. Lesbian mothers may be facing legal threats, or fears of loss of custody. They may need support in handling the effects of stigma which occur when others vent prejudices at their children.

Many internal problems reflect external realities, as in the case of role-related behavior. In any pair of people, one may seem more intellectual, more talkative, more athletically inclined, more mechanically adept, or more attractive. Straight culture has made it easy to conclude that one of the lesbian partners is in a "masculine" role, while the other is playing the role of "wife." Lesbians are very offended at this assumption. As in the old days of "butch" and "femme," these categorizations are only true for some lesbian couples and, then, true only with regard to superficial appearances.

As in any relationship, crises may arise in the course of lesbian relationships, causing stress and tension. Acute illness or the death of a loved one, such as a parent, ex-lover, or sibling can be disruptive to both partners. Chronic illness represents a prolonged stress which may also be critical.

What about sex? Being a lesbian is more than a matter of sexual orientation, but there are some potential internal problems in this area, too. For example, a woman may believe that she knows what pleases her partner, since physiologically they are similar to each other. Beyond this basic level, sexual likes and dislikes can vary a great deal among women. Helping persons who feel comfortable and secure with their own sexuality should encourage and even initiate open dialogues about intimacy and sexual behavior.

Frequency and initiation of touching, as well as the meanings of these occurrences, present possible differences of opinion between partners. Many lesbians have a heterosexual history. For some it was short-lived. Others have been married and, perhaps, have raised families. These circumstances can affect sexual relationships. Since many persons, lesbian, gay, and straight, have been victims of sexual abuse, incest, and domestic violence, these wounds may also surface in intimate relationships with their partners, and may affect feelings about sexuality in general. Past traumas often heal in stages. The involved couple may need support in talking over these memories and reassurance that the healing process will continue.

Sometimes one or both women feel a loss of sexual desire. One may find it difficult to bring this up for fear of hurting the other. In these cases, many factors may be involved. Substance abuse, depression, overwork, overstress, physical illness of many kinds, and side-effects of some medications may be possible areas to check out.

When relationships end, both women usually experience grief, which takes time to get over. In some cases, it is better to take the time to reflect on this loss and re-evaluate goals and needs. In other cases, if a new relationship is developing, it should be explored without much delay. This is best decided by the women involved, with the understanding that each is an expert at being herself.

One might say that lesbian couples are engaged in important cultural developments. By their creativity and courage, and also out of plain old necessity, they are exploring new ways of relating. They do a great deal of reflecting on their instincts, their perceptions of their environment, and their hopes for the future. They live the "examined life." For most lesbians, this is an asset — a means of strengthening their abilities to cope with the unexpected. This is like a journey without a map, a road that is made by walking. In this sense, all people can benefit from the insights of lesbians who, in their lives together as couples, are changing and expanding our culture's concept of relationship.

REFERENCES

1. Day, C.L. and Morse, B.W. (1981). Communication patterns in established lesbian relationships. In J.W. Chesbro (Ed.), *Gayspeak: Gay male and lesbian communication* (pp. 80-86). New York: Pilgrim Press.

2. Johnson, S., Guenther, S., Laube,D., and Keettel, W. (1981). Factors influencing lesbian gynecological care: A preliminary study. *American Journal of Obstetrics and Gynecology, 140(1)*, 20-28.

3. Krestan, J. and Bepko, C.S. (1980). The problem of fusion in the lesbian relationship. *Family Process, 19*, 277-289.

4. McCandlish, B.M. (1985). Therapeutic issues with lesbian couples. In J.C. Gonsiorek (Ed.), *A guide to psychotherapy with gay and lesbian clients* (pp. 71-78). New York: Harrington Park Press.

5. Smith, E., Johnson, S., and Guenther, S. (1985). Health care attitudes and experiences during gynecological care among lesbians and bisexuals. *American Journal of Public Health, 75(9)*, 1085-1087.

Chapter 20
Gay and lesbian widowhood

Judith M. Saunders

BACKGROUND

Gay men and lesbians establish loving relationships that endure until death. Experiencing the death of a loved one produces anguish for the one who is left to struggle with the effects of that loss. The pain of acute bereavement involves body, mind, soul, and more. The "more" is that grieving individuals are also vulnerable to illnesses and other negative consequences. Though deprived of the legal sanctions of marriage, gays and lesbians who have lost their partners of loving relationships through death are ushered into widowhood, and will experience, in full, the anguish and negative consequences of spouse grief. As the AIDS epidemic continues to take its heavy toll in the gay community, all too many will know personally the anguish of widowhood.

Death of a loved one is a threatening event that is dreaded. Even thinking of our lover's dying is avoided by most of us, just as we avoid thoughts of our own death. Death involves multiple, interwoven losses that reach beyond the already terrible loss of a partner in a loving relationship. Some of these losses are concrete, such as finances; others are less tangible, such as the loss of a status. Holmes and Rahe identified a list of life-change events that produced major changes in one's life and one's view of the world; when a sufficient number of these changes were experienced, an individual was considered to be at risk for subsequent illness. They specified death of a spouse to be the most powerful life-change event that an individual could experience.(9) Severe consequences of acute bereavement have been identified to include an increased natural death rate; a variety of psychosomatic illnesses; increased life-threatening disorders, especially cardiovascular disease; reduced financial resources; and increased rate of consultation for mental health problems.(21) A classic study of mortality associated with bereavement found that, of all the close relatives studied, widowed people had the highest mortality rate.(19) It is clear, then, that bereavement leaves individuals vulnerable to major distress, some illnesses, and even, potentially, to death. Some clinicians and researchers have taken the view that bereavement itself is an illness.(7, 11) While not sharing the belief that bereavement is an illness, I certainly believe it is a time of intense pain and heightened vulnerability.

People in helping relationships need to know the nature of this anguish of acute bereavement and how it might be mitigated in gay and lesbian widowhood. Only when an understanding of bereavement as a process has been achieved can helping professionals consider the particular strategies or interventions most useful to their gay and lesbian clients who are in the midst of such a bereavement.

BEREAVEMENT: THE PROCESS

Whether the death was expected, or whether it happened abruptly and without warning, the surviving partner of a loving relationship will realize this loss slowly, over months, and perhaps years. The realization unfolds little by little, as habits change, emotions shift, and life itself is redefined; rarely is the full impact of the loss perceived immediately after the loss. Typically, spouse bereavement, in its acute form, will last eighteen to twenty-four months before one's life is seen to have settled down and returned to where life is not dominated by memories of the deceased lover. This gradual realization of the loss is the essence of the bereavement process.(17) Bereavement progresses slowly and involves readjustments in relationships and activities, as well as in meanings of events. Some theorists have organized the phenomenon of bereavement into phases, while others have organized them into the symptoms of grief.

Bereavement also fits into the broader scheme of adaptation to threatening events as proposed by Taylor, who argues that adjustment centers around three themes: searching for meaning in the experience, regaining mastery over the specific event and one's life, and restoring self-esteem.(26) I will follow, in part, the conceptualization of grief established by Parkes, who organized bereavement around three large components, instead of phases. The components serve to cluster the behaviors, feelings, and phenomenon of grief. They are arranged into different clusters by different authors. While Parkes organized grief into the components of Searching-Pining, Assumptive World, and Symptomatology,[17] I have found the following components to be most useful in understanding the phenomenon of bereavement as a process: Seeking, Finding Meaning, and Balancing Activity-Affect.

Seeking: Seeking is the component of bereavement in which the widowed person can say the words, "She is dead" or "He is dead" but the words are empty. Saying the words cannot stop the impulse to continue to look for reasons the death has occurred and to pursue clues about the impact of this death. Parkes has insisted that the acute anxiety found in Searching-Pining is the predominant emotion early in acute grief and is akin to separation anxiety.[1, 16] Without doubt, the seeking originates from the intense longing for the person who has died, a longing so intense that despite telling oneself that Mary, or Joe, has died, the grieving lover will continue to scan crowds looking for that familiar face. The lover reviews, over and over, the events around the death, as though a loophole will emerge that will undo the dying and expose the unbearable reality as a vanished nightmare. Early in widowhood, the grieving lover may resent interruptions while interacting with memories, as the memories can sometimes blunt the full impact of the loss. John Denver sings a song with the refrain, "Hold on tightly, let go lightly. It's only surrender, it's all in the game." Letting go will have to wait until later.

One feature of Seeking involves a sense of the continued presence of the person who has died. This awareness is more than the usual memory; the presence seems real — as if the person were still alive and nearby, although congnitively the grieving person knows the lover is dead. I have called this type of presence a friendly presence, as it is always positive. It is experienced frequently in spouse bereavement and invariably is described by those experiencing it as comforting. In my study of heterosexual widow bereavement, several women described successful efforts to evoke this friendly presence through wearing an article of clothing that had belonged to the husband, such as his bathrobe or the shirt he wore hiking.(21) Friendly presence relieves suffering and provides comfort in acute grief.

Seeking is fueled by the need to have the loved one alive again, even while being unable to deny the reality of the death. Seeking behaviors can extend to mistakenly identifying someone as the recently deceased lover and even going to the person to speak before realizing the illusory perception of the person. Occasionally, seeking behaviors have involved hearing the voice of the deceased lover while alone, or seeing the lover in a chair or doorway, only to realize several moments later that the chair is empty, or the doorway unoccupied. While, technically, these last two examples qualify as hallucinations, they are both considered normal in the context of acute bereavement.

Finding Meaning: A second component of bereavement is Finding Meaning, called Assumptive World by Parkes.(18) Finding Meaning focuses on how the gay and lesbian widows relate to the world and make sense of how death changes this relationship. In his discussion of the Assumptive World, Parkes points out that we make assumptions about the world according to our past experiences and knowledge, and through these assumptions we make sense of things. With the death of a lover-partner, assumptions become invalidated; we become aware of the discrepancy between how the world is and how it should be.(13) Finding meaning involves alterations in meaning of how the widowed gay and lesbian relates to the world. Daily activities provide the stimulus for needing to reassess meanings, but they also provide the opportunities for finding new meanings.(22) This process produces growth, but its pathway is a mixture of more painful than pleasant experiences. Habits and behaviors have to be reformed. The grieving person feels lost, helpless, frightened, and bewildered. Scenes and situations that should seem familiar and comforting appear strange or tense, as with a dinner with friends in which the grieving person will have moments of discomfort, of being out of focus.

The most critical relationship that widowhood changes is that of being part of a couple into one of being a person alone. Some experiences and activities are necessary to allow widowed men and women to readjust their self-concepts and reform their social roles in order to confront the reality and implications of their lovers' deaths. Experiences which facilitate this shift in identity include sorting the personal belongings of their lovers, dating, and altering socializing patterns. Personal belongings are infused with special meanings, and deciding what to do with them is a pivotal identity task which aids in the individual's identity transition from being coupled to being uncoupled.(22)

Dating is not an activity that simply begins to happen to the recently widowed. Rather, it is chosen by them when they feel the need for romantic social interactions. Dating is taking a step toward building lives without their lovers. And regarding changes in socializing patterns, many, though not all, widowed lesbians and gays will find they do not feel comfortable interacting with their friends who are coupled. Being with other couples constantly provides the widowed gay or lesbian with proof that their partner is missing. Sometimes feelings of envy and resentment appear and have to be dealt with. Also, newly single persons often feel as though they no longer belong in activities peopled by couples. Feeling different in this way gives one the sense of being the "fifth wheel" in the situation — both unneeded and out of place. But, gradually, socializing patterns evolve. Lonely evenings push men and women into seeking social patterns that match their status as a single person. Reforming internal self-concepts and social roles are critical in helping widowed persons move through bereavement toward evolving an uncoupled identity.

Many situations are encountered which allow the bereaved one's meanings to be reassessed. One important factor in a variety of situations that causes major changes in meaning can be regarded as different sorts of a sense of a continued presence. One such continued presence is the Constraining Force, which may be experienced negatively, yet still aids in reassessing values and meanings. Constraining Force may be evoked by any situation that had been a source of conflict during the couple's relationship, and that involves feeling judged and disapproved of. A consideration of going to the bars, when this had been an area of conflict during the relationship, might provoke the lover's presence as a Constraining Force, so that the widowed man or woman feels inhibited from actually going out to the bars. Another type of continued presence is the Consulting Guide. It is a positive experience, and may occur as a feature of Finding Meaning. Consulting Guide occurs where activities were formerly the responsibility of the lover, but are now left to the widowed woman or man to resolve. In these situations, the widowed person experiences the lover's presence in a way that allows review of how the lover would have managed the situation, step by step. Rather than imitating the problem-solving steps employed by the lover, widowed persons will use this mental dialogue with the deceased lover to think through the steps involved and find an approach by themselves. The Consulting Guide is a positive influence which aids in bridging a gap of knowledge and skill, and it contributes to a sense of pride in handling a new situation.

Balancing Activity-Affect: The third component of bereavement is Balancing Activity-Affect. For grieving spouses of heterosexual marriages, the early weeks of bereavement are characterized by a recurrent sense of numbness interposed with a tremendous flurry of activity. For some gay and lesbian couples, on the other hand, there is often a paucity of activity, as the surviving lover is usurped by "real family" who use their legal status to disclaim the loving relationship that had existed. More often today, however, the surviving lover will be involved fully in planning the funeral or memorial service, notifying friends and relatives, taking care of shared belongings, completing the unending forms for insurance, government, and employers. These early activities protect the bereaved ones by preventing them from being overwhelmed with intense and painful emotions. As the number of activities subsides, emotions come more to the forefront. Even during the busiest of activity-times, emotions are experienced with intensity, but the activities do serve to blunt the experience. These activities tend to subside within a few weeks after the death.

Several feelings and behaviors are characteristic of grief. Initially people respond to death with a sense of numbness, disbelief, or unreality, even when the death was expected. A depressed feeling, described variously as sadness, despair, or painful dejection, is probably the best known and most expected feature of grief. Although sadness may diminish over time, unexpected encounters with people, objects, or holidays may trigger these feelings with surprising strength much later in bereavement. Crying, a behavior which often accompanies sadness, is characteristic for both men and women and occurs in almost all culture groups. The widowed also experience disruptions in their sleep pattern during the first few weeks and months of bereavement. Another common feeling, anger, can be directed at oneself, at the deceased, or at others. Anger can range from mild anger to persistent irritability to rage, and can persist over time. Anger is difficult for people to acknowledge, and it may appear indirectly; for example, in an overreaction to a frustration at work or with friends. Guilt may range from mild self-reproach to feeling responsible for the death. Most bereaved spouses will describe a feeling of disruption in their own bodily integrity, ranging from feeling empty to feeling as though a part of them has been torn away. Anxiety, grief's most prominent, early feature, is characterized by feelings of unrest and fear, and is coupled with restless activity. People describe walking from room to room for no apparent purpose, just to move because they could not bear to not move. Also expressed are fears of loss of control, and even fears of losing one's hold on reality, if the floodgates of feelings were really unleashed. Another characteristic of grief is that an idealization of the person who died begins to take shape and can become the replaced image of the person.

After six months or so, in spouse bereavement, a surge of increased activity is reported by some individuals, and does not seem related to the restlessness of the early separation anxiety or the need to handle a press of activities imposed by the death. Rather, this surge seems related to Finding Meaning, when surviving spouses realize they must move ahead with life and try to find new activities and patterns.

Activities can be sought and used in order to avoid

encountering the anguish of bereavement. Avoidance activities may include losing oneself in work or beginning a rash of dating before one has "let go lightly" of the partner who died. These activities may be effective in erecting a temporary barrier to the pain, but they will only postpone the process of grief until some later occasion triggers the release of feelings that have not been dealt with.

It is less important to consider whether a particular activity is helpful or unhelpful, than to evaluate the relative balance of activity with affect. The activity level can be a healthy buffer against feelings that are too intense, or feelings that are untimely. However, these temporary protective measures should give way to the expression of feelings soon, and should not become a safe "prison" where the grieving spouse is locked away from the pain that is natural to bereavement.

ADDITIONAL FACTORS AFFECTING GRIEF

While the three components — Seeking, Finding Meaning, and Balancing Activity-Affect — contain the major features of bereavement, other factors will interact to alter the grief that is experienced. Certainly, the person's past experiences, psychological makeup, and coping styles have a major impact on the personal grief experience. For example, although both are gay, a seventy-year-old widowed man is likely to mourn his loss differently than a twenty-year-old man. They will have become widowed while involved in different developmental life tasks. How mode of death (natural, accidental, homicidal, or suicidal) interacts with grief is not well understood, yet mode of death has been linked with social interaction patterns. This includes experiencing rejection from friends and from the spouse's family when the death was suicide.(22, 25) If mode of death interacts with stigma to influence grief, then gay men and lesbians may be more sensitive to these variations, since they already are identified as being in a stigmatized group. Five factors which do influence the grief experience will be discussed briefly: nature of the relationship, social worth of being gay or lesbian, suddenness and unexpectedness of the death, personal support network, and practical problems.

Nature of the Relationship: The nature of the relationship that couples have established will influence the grief experience during widowhood. McWhirter and Mattison(14) have told us that longevity itself in a relationship reveals little about that relationship; rather, information is needed about the complexity of the relationship. They provided guidelines for interpreting that complexity through their discussion of the six stages of a relationship: (1) Blending, (2) Nesting, (3) Maintaining, (4) Building, (5) Releasing, and (6) Renewing. Widowhood will differ, in part, according to the relationship's developmental stage at the time of death. These stages may not apply well to lesbian couples, since they were derived from studying gay couples only, but it is logical to assume that lesbian couples also will have a developmental evolution of their relationships which would also affect lesbian widowhood. Couple relationships which were characterized by unexpressed, ambivalent feelings may set the stage for difficulties for the surviving spouse.(5)

Social Worth: At best, the social worth of lesbians and gays, in the eyes of society at large, can be viewed as moving from negative toward neutral. Many of us gay people have internalized some of these negative societal values. Until we find ways to develop a positive identity, this internalized homophobia increases vulnerability through reducing self-esteem. Additionally, researchers have shown that threatening events, such as the death of a loved one, can reduce one's self-regard.(3, 2) Siegal and Holfer consider gays and lesbians who are grieving as being doubly stigmatized: first from being gay, and secondly from being bereaved.(24) Reduced social worth also contributes to reduced accessibility to existing community resources because gays and lesbians are in relationships not sanctioned by society. This is most noticeable through such practices as bereavement leave (paid time off from work when there is a death in the "family"), and inheritance rights. Many nightmare stories are available which document society's ability to impede access to joint acquisitions or rights to death benefits, practices which clearly invalidate being regarded as a couple.(6, 4) Rarely is it reported that a trade union has negotiated a policy of bereavement leave for the death of a "roommate" for its lesbian and gay members.(12)

Suddenness and Unexpectedness: The more sudden and unexpected the death, the more difficulty the survivors have in trying to cope during bereavement.(5, 18) Even being able to anticipate the death by a few weeks may provide a man or woman with some time to overcome the immediate shock and to begin to plan for and grapple with the upcoming loss. Grief begins when one knows the death will happen; it does not wait for the physician to pronounce death. Practically, there may be an opportunity for the couple to share some of the dying experience together, and to plan for the time when one will continue alone. When the death has been sudden and unexpected, couples cannot say goodbye to each other, and this is a source of frustration and regret that extends throughout widowhood.

Personal Support Network: Personal support network consists of those people who may provide support during widowhood: friends, families, neighbors, colleagues, and professional helpers. The more accessible and rich the support network, the easier the bereavement. This does not mean more people; rather, it means access to a variety of people who will "be there" for the bereaved person. This access is the heart of a rich personal support network. Early in grief, those in the personal support network who knew the deceased will be more valued, as sharing the grief is so important. Later, those who can support the widowed in their attempts to find meaning and balance activity-affect are needed. All too often, supporting friends and relatives try to comfort through encouraging the grieving spouse to stop living in the past and to start going out more, and to find someone else. Though well intended, this attitude will cause the grief to be repressed by the widowed gay or lesbian.

Practical Problems: Practical problems associated with bereavement can quickly become overwhelming. The very diversity of the gay and lesbian communities precludes a quick summary of the types of problems most likely to be experienced, but they may include immediate custody of children, eviction from the home that had been shared with the deceased lover, lack of money for immediate living expenses, relationship strain with families and friends, and lack of skills to carry out everyday living tasks the deceased lover used to perform. Although more gay couples are seeking legal action to protect themselves, their children, and their belongings, the typical situation continues to elude a solution that provides adequate protection. The practical problems of living in bereavement are both many and complex. Although they are painful for all persons suffering from spousal loss, such problems are inevitable and realizing the necessity to deal with them is an important part of the bereavement process.

PROBLEM AREAS

Although bereavement is a painful process through which most people progress without encountering major complications or hurdles, some do encounter problem areas. It is those problems which will be discussed in this section. First, we will consider some of the characteristics of the gay and lesbian communities which form a context for understanding widowhood among lesbians and gay men. The fact that we are a hidden population means we cannot know how many men and women are struggling with widowhood. Little is known about how gay people manage bereavement and what help they might need. Few gay and lesbian resource services include support groups for bereaved lesbians and gay men among their identified services, but this does not mean these services are not needed.

For those individuals who are closeted, added pressures exist through not being able to share their grief. Beyond not sharing, there is the need to hide being upset from colleagues, family, and friends. Even this strain is compounded, since many of the people from whom the grief is hidden comprise the basic personal support network for the grieving spouse, and these people are now cut off from providing critical support during bereavement. Already mentioned were the problems resulting from society's allocating a low social worth to gay and lesbian couples. This has resulted in their being excluded from those systems and agencies which provide access to legal and financial benefits offered to those involved in male-female relationships. What a couple has accumulated together can be devastated quickly by a family which disapproves of the relationship, unless the partners have legally protected themselves adequately before the death.

Another general issue lies within the nature of the gay and lesbian communities. In some ways, our communities have not come of age. Not surprisingly, the communities are uneven — perhaps immature in some directions, while undeveloped totally in other directions. The gay and lesbian communities have created few traditions, or resources, to aid with developmental issues of growing old and dying. Our current, tragic crisis of AIDS has mobilized services and directed resources toward providing support during the dying process. Only now are we beginning to address the aftermath for lovers, family, and friends who continue living. Our only traditions around dying, death, and mourning are those brought from our own backgrounds.

Characteristics of the gay and lesbian communities provide a context of invisibility, of a community "youth" with no traditions and few resources for bereavement, and of social pressures which keep many closeted. Gay individuals may move from the typical grieving process to one of troubled grief, i.e., problem areas — characterized by symptoms and behaviors which may require professional assistance to guide the grieving lover back into the more typical bereavement processes. Parkes and Weiss identified three syndromes associated with what I have termed troubled grief: Unexpected Loss Syndrome, Conflicted Grief Syndrome, and Dependent Grief Syndrome.(18)

Substance Abuse: To relieve the anguish of acute bereavement, many people increase their reliance on drugs. The drugs involved include those prescribed by physicians as well as alcohol, marijuana, and cocaine.

Unfortunately, physicians sometimes add to the problem by encouraging the use of mood-altering drugs and sedatives for people experiencing despair, anxiety, and sleep-pattern disruptions. Some of these drugs may be used excessively to blot out all feelings, rather than to make feelings manageable so grief can proceed. The use of drugs must be monitored carefully, as it is very easy for excesses to develop. When this occurs, the pain of grief is supplanted by the pain of addiction. Alcohol use should be watched with special care because problems with alcohol abuse are associated with troubled grief for the general population. The adult gay and lesbian communities have estimates of alcohol abuse far in excess of the rates found in the heterosexual population even without the added burden of widowhood.(8)

Depression-Suicide: The sadness of grief may be difficult to distinguish from depression, i.e., depression as a treatable clinical entity. Close monitoring of symptoms, such as alterations of moods or sleep patterns, emergence of feelings of hopelessness and helplessness, interference in ability to carry out everyday activities, and a significant reduction in self-esteem is mandatory to help separate grief from depression. As time continues, the acuity of bereavement should become blunted, not progressively more profound. To monitor bereavement, it is critical to be alert for clues that the depression, helplessness, and hopelessness triad has not extended to thoughts of suicide. If any suicide clues exist, or if there is any suspicion of suicidal thoughts, then the widowed gay man or lesbian should be assessed for suicidal thoughts and plans.

Stalled Grief: Some people can get "stalled in their grief"; that is, they may defend themselves against the grief through total denial that the death has occurred — a very rare and extreme problem. More likely, they may fail to progress through the bereavement process, and instead reach a plateau within one of the components. In this case, they fail to move through subsequent features and components. An example of this would be the lover's combination of idealization of the dead person and failure to completely uncouple his or her own identity, so that the bereaved never is able to let go of the dead lover sufficiently to engage in new, intimate relationships.

THE HELPING PROFESSIONAL

Necessary Areas of Knowledge: To be effective in easing the anguish of widowhood, helping professionals must temper their competence with caring, and their flexibility with assertiveness. Two areas of expertise will be needed to assist with gay and lesbian widowhood: knowledge about bereavement and knowledge of gay and lesbian lifestyles. Without knowledge of these two areas, the helping professional can become the harmful professional. Since studies specifically of bereavement among gays and lesbians have not been reported, the professional must use creative efforts to blend and apply knowledge of the two areas mentioned. Accomplishing this blending requires that the professional be comfortable with lesbians, with gay men, and with the legitimacy of their being and their grieving. Remembering that widowhood is a time of increased risk will guide the professional to direct efforts toward careful monitoring of several important issues. Foremost among the areas to monitor throughout bereavement is the general state of physical and mental health. While anxious overreaction to every sniffle or sore throat is not warranted, the professional should encourage health-maintenance practices. Health problems and illnesses that develop should be treated promptly. Both quality and quantity of social interactions should be watched to ensure there are people available to listen and to share in the grieving. If the social support is not adequate, then the professional could explore ways the client might increase the social support. This is not a time for slipping into isolation. Exploring how and where social interactions occurred before the partner died may provide clues which can be used in directing the widowed lesbian or gay man for further assistance.

Monitoring the client's mood is especially important. While some instability of mood initially is typical, getting locked into a mood and having it intensify over time will lead to problems, whether the mood is anger or depression. Monitoring for mood also involves being alert to clues of potential suicide. Minimal assessment of suicide risk potential will include noting the intensity of the bereaved's moods, inquiring directly of the bereaved exactly how bad they feel, and judging the likelihood that any mentioned suicide plan will be executed. If the client is only moderately suicidal, the helping professional usually will be able to form a contract in which the client promises to phone the professional, or the local suicide prevention center if the professional is not available, instead of acting on suicidal feelings. If the client is severely suicidal, then a protective, nurturing environment may be needed for a brief period of time. Moderate suicide risk is more common; severe suicide risk is rare. Whether gay men and lesbians are more vulnerable to suicide risk has not been established.(20, 23)

Often professionals will fail to monitor practical problems that arise during widowhood because these are outside of the usual sphere of health care. Adequate money, housing, transportation, child care, information about procedures with agencies and insurance companies, and legal protection are major, baseline necessities. Response to difficulties in maintaining these necessities may provide clues for how well the lesbian or gay man is coping with widowhood through meeting the hassles of grief.(10)

Finally, an important area for the professional to monitor involves physical, intimate, and sexual touch. Intimacy is expressed partially through our sexual relationships, and loss of both intimate touch and sexual touch are major losses of the spouse in bereavement. Intimate touch involves hugging, holding hands, standing with an arm around someone's shoulder. Intimate touch can be initiated by friends and is separate from that which invites sexual touch. The helping professional would be wise to aid lesbians and gay men in exploring the meaning of loss of touch in their lives, as well as exploring the ways they are comfortable experiencing touch. For gay men who were not sexually exclusive with their lovers, seeking sexual touch may not provoke the same level of conflict as for men who were monogamous and sexually exclusive. Many lesbians expect to know a woman well before exploring a sexual relationship. Other lesbians will see sexual relationships and loving relationships as more distinct from each other. Masturbation can be explored as a supplemental sexual activity among men and women; this form of sexual activity generally is more accepted within the gay and lesbian population than it is among heterosexual women. Rather than assume that any particular attitude prevails, however, the helping professional will want to initiate open exploration of the widowed man or woman's accessibility to both intimate and sexual touch.

Counseling: Those characteristics of counseling that make it effective for other problems are the same characteristics needed to aid gays and lesbians through widowhood. Helping professionals will guide clients through the painful experiences of grieving, and will avoid the temptation to seek prescriptions for tranquilizers and sedatives to anesthetize them to the experiences. Painful memories and feelings need to be encountered and experienced, not shoved aside or chemically mollified. The helping professional will want to provide a safe and accepting climate where the gay or lesbian client will feel protected and safe enough to allow feelings to emerge. For those clients who are especially concerned with maintaining and not losing control of feelings, the professional may want to encourage them to telephone when and if they feel things moving out of control, in order to preclude their being overwhelmed by their feelings. The offer of telephone contact in between scheduled sessions provides access to a safety valve that may not ever be used, but remains important for having been offered. Also, some clients may benefit from being taught relaxation exercises to aid in their own tension reduction.

While constructing a climate that allows for the safe expression of negative emotions, the professional will also need to be alert to the client's need to have the freedom to share joy, success, and humor. Often, widows reported feeling very frustrated because everyone expected them to be constantly sad and bereft.(21) Sharing successes is important for facilitating growth and recovery. Active involvement in discussing and listing accomplishments is helpful in validating the progress the client is making.

Movement through the bereavement process is accomplished largely by revisiting memories and experiencing the feelings connected with them. It is also necessary to confront situations where old meanings are found inadequate, and to begin to forge new meanings and behaviors. The professional will want to encourage interaction with memories, and may use pictures and other articles to facilitate focusing on specific memories. This will be especially useful in aiding with feelings and behaviors during the Seeking component of spouse grief.

Many widows reported not being able to trust their own perceptions and judgments. In these instances, the professional will assist clients to evaluate their perceptions and judgments about specific situations, and not rush to reassure them that their perceptions have remained adequate. Neither will the professional want to provide alternative perceptions before exploring the client's own perceptions of the situation. The underlying issue is likely to be diminished self-esteem, presented through the questioning of judgment in specific situations.

Many gay men and lesbians who are widowed will not have experienced personal grief before, and may have little knowledge of what to expect of the grief they are to experience. Even when personal grief has been experienced, that grief will likely have been qualitatively different from the current experience of loss of a loving partner. To the extent possible, the professional should guide the bereaved clients' knowledge about grief not in a manner that dictates or confines responses, but in a manner that informs them of the general components and features, as they are ready to know them. While it would be helpful to find other gay men or lesbians who have experienced spouse bereavement, few resources such as these exist, and they would be known only through a personal network. Visible role models for grieving in the gay and lesbian community often do not exist. Reading materials about grief in general, and spouse grief in particular, may be helpful to some.

The professional may need to be more directive than usual by making it explicit to the client that it is acceptable to feel whatever is being felt. This should not be confused with the traditionalist approach in which the professional decides what is best for the client. Rather, it is important for the professional to acknowledge that feelings are not rational, and that it is okay to feel sexual feelings, or anger, or pride of accomplishment. Likewise, the gentle encouragement to try something new, or even the more directive "I think it is worth trying" may be warranted.

Community: In working with the widowed gay man or lesbian individually, the professional must be aware of resources available in the community at large, and in the gay and lesbian community specifically. In cities where the gay and lesbian population is large and fairly well integrated, widowed lesbians and gays may be able to use traditional health resources openly. These will probably also be the cities with the greatest wealth of gay and lesbian resources, such as gay community centers. Resources will vary from city to city, and from region to region. Many traditional support services may exclude lesbians and gays from access because of the nature of their eligibility requirements.(24) Gays and lesbians risk rejection and misunderstanding when they openly grieve for loving partners in groups traditionally designed for the widowed heterosexual. A national group which offers support to people with terminal illnesses, and extends that support to those grieving the loss of loved ones, is Make Today Count. This is a group traditionally used by heterosexuals; how welcome a gay man or lesbian would be is likely to vary from one locale to another. Whether such a group would be open and supportive for a gay or lesbian client should be checked out before a referral is made for the client.

One group which targets an outreach to the gay and lesbian community is Shanti. This group, with branches in many cities in America, offers psychosocial counseling to people with life-threatening illnesses. Some Shanti groups do not direct their services exclusively to persons with AIDS. Where they exist, gay and lesbian community service centers should have information available about groups and individuals in that area that offer relevant services and that are appropriate for gays and lesbians. Some of the centers will offer direct services themselves. Many communities now have one of the many religious groups which serve the gay and lesbian communities, such as Metropolitan Community Church, Dignity, Integrity, or gay temples. Professionals will need to build their own network of referral resources appropriate for gay men and women to use.

The helping professional will want to extend some effort to educate other professionals about bereavement in general, and about particular needs of gays and lesbians in widowhood. The professional can disseminate information from and about new resources, as the need for this is identified.

Gay widowhood will increase in very visible ways, as more of our men are lost through AIDS, and their lovers left to grieve that loss. Women will continue to be widowed through the deaths of their loving partners, whether we can identify those who are bereaved, or whether they grieve in invisible silence. Studies of grief in the gay and lesbian communities are needed to find out how the bereavement process is affected by those factors inherent in our gay identities and lifestyles.

REFERENCES

1. Bowlby, J. and Parkes, C.M. (1970). Separation and loss. In E.G. Anthony and C. Koupernick (Eds.), *International Yearbook of Child Psychiatry & Allied Disciplines, Vol. 1.* New York: John Wiley & Sons.

2. Briar, S. (1966). Welfare from below: Recipients' views of the public welfare system. *California Law Review, 54,* 370-385.

3. Chodoff, P., Friedman, P.B., and Hamburg, D.A. (1964). Stress, defenses, and coping behavior: Observations in parents of children with malignant disease. *American Journal of Psychiatry, 120,* 743-749.

4. Cort, J. (1984, December 11). $22,000 check arrives for death benefits — 8 years late. *Advocate,* p. 30.

5. Demi, A., (1978). *Adjustment to widowhood after a sudden death: Suicide and non-suicide survivors compared.* Unpublished dissertation, University of California, San Francisco.

6. Dlugos, T. (1980, February). Gay widows. *Christopher Street,* 19-24.

7. Engle, G.L. (1961). Is grief a disease? *Psychosomatic Medicine, 23,* 18-22.

8. Fifield, L. (1975). *On my way to nowhere: Alienated, isolated, drunk.* Los Angeles: Gay Community Center.

9. Holmes, T. and Rahe, R. (1967). The social readjustment rating scale. *Journal of Psychosomatic Research, 2,* 213-218.

10. Kanner, A.D., Coyne, J.C., Shaefer, C., and Lazarus, R.S. (1981). Comparison of two modes of stress measurement: Daily hassles and uplifts versus major life events. *Journal of Behavioral Medicine, 4,* 1-39.

11. Kutscher, A.H. (1970). Practical aspects of bereavement. In B. Schoenberg, A.C. Carr, D. Peretz, and A.H. Kutscher (Eds.), *Loss and grief: Psychological management in medical practice,* (280-297). New York: Columbia University Press.

12. MacLean, J. (1984, September 4). Lesbians and unions. *Advocate,* pp. 24-25.

13. Marris, P. (1974). *Loss and change.* New York: Pantheon Books.

14. McWhirter, D.P. and Mattison, A.M. (1984). *The male couple: How relationships develop.* Englewood Cliffs, NJ: Prentice-Hall.

15. Parkes, C.M. (1971). Psychosocial transitions: A field for study. *Social Science and Medicine, 5,* 101-115.

16. Parkes, C.M. (1972). *Bereavement. Studies of grief in adult life.* New York: International Universities Press.

17. Parkes, C.M. (1979, September 29). *The bereavement process.*

Paper presented at a workshop on Bereavement: Loss & Grief. University of California, Los Angeles.

18. Parkes, C.M. and Weiss, R.S. (1983). *Recovery from bereavement.* New York: Basic Books.

19. Rees, W.D. and Lutkins, S.G. (1967). Mortality of bereavement. *British Medical Journal, 4,* 13-16.

20. Rofes, E.E. (1983). *"I thought people like that killed themselves": Lesbians, gay men, and suicide.* San Francisco: Grey Fox Press.

21. Saunders, J.M. (1979). *A clinical study of widow bereavement involving various modes of death.* Unpublished dissertation, University of California, San Francisco.

22. Saunders, J.J. (1981, October). A process of bereavement resolution: Uncoupled identity. *Western Journal of Nursing Research, 3(4),* 517-525.

23. Saunders, J.M. and Valente, S.M. (1987). Suicide risk among gay man and lesbians: A review. *Death Studies, 11,* 1-23.

24. Siegal, R.L. and Hoeffer, D.D. (1981, October). Bereavement counseling for gay individuals. *American Journal of Psychotherapy, 35(4),* 517-525.

25. Silverman, P.R. (1972). Intervention with the widow of a suicide. In A.C. Cain (Ed.), *Survivors of Suicide.* Springfield: Charles C. Thomas.

26. Taylor, S.E. (1983, November). Adjustments to threatening events: A theory of cognitive adaptation. *American Psychologist,* 1161-1173.

IV

Spiritual Journeys
of Gay and Lesbian Clients

Chapter 21
Gay and lesbian Roman Catholics

Mary E. Hunt

WITHIN THE CATHOLIC TRADITION

The bereaved parents of a man who died from AIDS wanted a memorial mass for their son, whose body was cremated immediately after his death. The sermon, a subtle but sure condemnation of the gay man's lifestyle, came complete with Irish brogue. At communion time, the many non-Catholic mourners were told to steer clear of the altar. Even the Catholics gathered were left to wonder if they were worthy to receive the Body of Christ in memory of their brother.

This is an all-too-typical experience of contemporary Roman Catholic treatment of self-affirming, sexually responsible Catholic gay men and women. Many, like this man, have long since stopped going to church. They feel that the institutional church has left them. However, the religion's hold on even the most disillusioned cradle Catholic (one brought up in the tradition) is legend. To be Catholic is not measured by mass attendance or by subscription to the institutional church's position on issues like birth control, abortion, or even homosexuality. It is not experienced as a belief in the infallibility of the pope or the virginity of Mary. Rather, to be Catholic, especially for those of us who were brought up Catholic (and more so for those who lived, studied, and ate in Irish, Italian, Polish and, now, Hispanic communities) is to respond in a physical way to the sights, sounds, tastes, and smells of a religious tradition.

Catholicism, stereotypes notwithstanding, is a dynamic tradition which interacts, whether some of its leaders like it or not, with the times and cultures in which it is set. Root values of love and justice, as spelled out in the Gospels, are part of our heritage; emphasis on community and service is integrated early on by Catholic children. Ours is a *sacramen-*

tal faith; one which is expressed by liturgy and ritual, by processions and gestures, by art and music. We are attuned to the symbolic world, to body language, and to touch.

Ours is a *justice-oriented* faith, one which puts a high premium on work with the poor and marginalized. We are especially attentive to the needs of those who are mistreated by society. Above all, ours is a *relational* faith, one which takes seriously the bonds of family and community as a starting point for living in "right relation."(2) We value fidelity and commitment, and relationships of substance and challenge, whether these are among family members and friends or within a religious community. Finally, ours is a *global* faith, one which understands the People of God from around the world and on a pilgrimage throughout history. We present-day Catholics are simply one more generation trying to live faithfully to the Gospel by trying to embody it in our lives.

Why, then, all of the well-publicized opposition by the institutional Roman Catholic Church toward gay men and women? Why the many serious problems of guilt and insecurity, of self-hatred and confusion felt by so many lesbian and gay Catholics? With this kind of religious tradition, would it not seem that same-sex relationships would be welcomed and celebrated, now that science has found them common, and psychology has found them healthy? After all, Jesus did say to love one another!

An optimistic view is that the Roman Catholic institution simply has not done its homework yet. In time it will incorporate the valuable insights of its gay and lesbian members, learning from our lives about how to love, seeing in us a reflection of the goodness of God. A pessimistic view is that the Roman Catholic institution is so thoroughly homophobic that it will never permit us sexually responsible gay people to be whole on our own terms or to be members in good standing of the Church. The only option, according to this view, is for gay people to leave the Church in order to be healthy.

I am candid about the fact that contemporary evidence favors the latter view. The Vatican continues to insist that same-sex orientation is morally neutral, while homosexual behavior is always wrong. Bishops have used their influence to affect public policy against gays and lesbians, and horror stories abound about the responses gay Catholics get in the confessional. Sadly, the official teaching is so far off the mark that, according to its own internal logic, it is better to sin occasionally and to confess it, resolving time after time not to be sexually active again, than to live in a healthy, stable, committed relationship with a person of the same sex.

A realistic view of all of this is that the official position is not softening, but that the *sensus fidelium*, the sense of the faithful, the lived and very trustworthy experience of faithful Catholics, is changing rapidly. People are realizing that the Catholic Church has its share of gay and lesbian members. Fine studies like that done by John Boswell show that discrimination has not always been the norm.(1) In fact, current discussion of homosexuality among clergy and the religious reveals that some of the very people to whom most Catholics look for leadership and for models of Christian behavior are gay in their sexual orientation, though they have taken vows of chastity or made promises of celibacy. This revelation, shocking for some, is a helpful step toward seeing sisters, brothers, and priests as genuine human beings complete with sexuality, even though they have made public commitments to communities which include, per force by the canons of the institutional church, a life of sexual abstinence. Some of these people are being looked to for effective ministry in the Church on these issues. But we must recognize the difficult and, in some cases, dangerous position in which it places them vis-à-vis the institution. Luckily, the many people in religious education and ministry who are concerned with these issues include gay and lesbian lay people whose positions are not especially vulnerable (though some have felt reprisals). Included also are sexually active and celibate heterosexual people who simply see this as one more area where the Church must be brought into the modern world.

This background helps the sensitive professional to appreciate the complexity of the Roman Catholic situation, as well as to see the particularity of coming out in this context. Living as an openly lesbian or gay person presents its own set of challenges. What rituals will mark passage and commitment if the sacrament of matrimony is limited to heterosexual people? How will the children of same-sex couples be welcomed into the Catholic community, if baptism is seen in a narrow way as a reward for the parents who live according to the rules? How will well-qualified gay men and lesbians find employment in Catholic schools, in social service agencies run by the institutional church, or even in ministry itself, if policies restricting our participation continue to be enforced? These are the kinds of questions which try lesbian and gay Catholics' souls. In fact, these are the kinds of situations which need healing and help. There are also more common issues which have a special Catholic twist to them and which the caring professional will want to consider in order to function effectively with gay and lesbian Catholics. The key is to look at those situations which all lesbian and gay people face in a heterosexist and homophobic society, and then to see how the Catholic factor makes them different.

TO BE GAY AND CATHOLIC

Lesbian and gay Catholics approach coming out and disclosure in the same way as gay people in general do. The big questions are the same: Am I the only one? What will my parents say? and Does this mean that I will never be happy? But, for Catholics, each of these questions has at least one extra layer of guilt and certain anxieties which need to be recognized. Further, it is precisely in these critical events of coming out and disclosure that we see the differences between lesbians and gay men.

As gay Catholics, we have been brought up in a patriarchal church; one which does not take women's experiences on their own terms seriously, and one which will co-opt men's experiences to fit its patterns as often as possible. Lesbian and gay Catholics are taught that same-sex experience is intrinsically evil. This is but one more negative message on sexuality set alongside birth control, abortion, and masturbation. Except in the context of marriage with heterosexual intercourse always open to procreation, the Church maintains a negative view of sexuality. Our starting point, then, for coming to a mature, healthy integration of sexuality is not auspicious. Gay men are treated to the "fear of the Lord" when they consider being homosexually active. Lesbians pick up

– 249 –

the same message, though it is merely implied, since homo-sexuality is understood on the basis of male experience. Misogyny is so deep that we rarely hear the word "lesbian," yet gay women get the message. No matter how liberated we lesbian and gay Catholics are from our backgrounds, these messages still plague us. In short, helping professionals should not assume that even the most studied casual but politically-correct gay Catholic is free from the heavy pressure of dogmatic morality.

While working out all of this, gay Catholics are plagued by the fear of being the one and only. For gay men, this often fosters feelings of being unlovable and of being unworthy of a substantive relationship with another human being. For lesbians, this is seen as an additional negative dimension of female sexuality foisted upon yet another group of women. While these are generalizations which may not apply to specific clients, they are all too often exhibited in the lives of those gay Catholics who seek help. Many turn to priests for spiritual direction, hoping either for the grace to change their sexual orientation (unlikely, but in a moment of despair many revert to bargaining with God) or for some sanction, some ecclesiastical stamp of approval which will validate their feelings. Receiving neither, and in many cases receiving condemnation, many gay Catholics leave their church. Thus, in times of illness, accident, or personal loss, when the response of a Catholic is to call a priest, the gay person may well not be interested. Sensitivity to this is important for the helping professional, who can make matters worse by push-ing religious help when it will really be a hindrance.

The problem created by the institutional church's rigid position on same-sex genital expression is not just the con-tent of its position but the fact that once having stated it, it is closed to other perspectives. This means that thoughtful, faithful Catholics have few religious professionals with whom to talk and pray about particular relationships. For example, with whom does John talk if he is having trouble in a committed relationship with Steve, who is too busy to give him the kind of time and energy for housework, companion-ship, and fun that he needs? With whom shall Jane discuss her love for Barbara, especially when it is this very love which has helped her to see herself as a valuable and holy person? How should Tom go about coping with a home, children, and a loving wife, when he is really attracted to Father Bob? These are common occurrences in daily life. And the need by gay Catholics for helpful and healthy pastoral ministry and attention through the Church is considerable. Fortunately, lay men and women are increasingly involved in ministry, and many priests are becoming sensitized to the various needs of gay Catholics for effective pastoral ministry. Groups like Dignity, New Ways Ministry, and the Conference of Catholic Lesbians (which I will return to later) are springing up, so that calling a priest is not the only option at hand.

It is not naive to say that things are changing in the Roman Catholic Church. The face of the clergy is being lifted, if you will, and the possibility of engaging effective religious professionals on teams with health care folks is not as remote as it once was. But these changes involve years of study and training which we are just beginning to offer to ministers other than priests, so it will take time. Meanwhile, I would suggest that health care and other helping professionals recommend clergy and other ministerial personnel only after the most careful screening as to attitudes, openness, and ability to be free of the constraints of a very confining institution.

Coming out to parents, another source of tension for gay people, may be especially difficult for gay Catholics. When the coming-out process is initiated by illness, as in the case of AIDS, or when it is precipitated by a third party's disclosure in a breach of confidence, the situation is difficult, to say the least. Often, faced with the sudden and unexpected discovery of a son's or daughter's homosexuality, parents find themselves feeling either that their child is dishonest, or does not trust them, or both. Such stress in a family requires competent care for both parents and children. It should not be forgotten that often this same stress can be transformed into an occasion for celebrating and deepening family ties, and for firmly establishing the honesty which most families try to achieve.

In a Catholic family (of course, any generalization will have limited value) emphasis on the nuclear as well as on the extended family will caution most gay sons and daughters against coming out hastily. But peace at all costs is sometimes a camouflage, a game of keeping the lid on what everyone knows anyway, which sets the child up for rejection for both being gay and being dishonest. Being honest is so drilled into the heads and hearts of Catholics that feelings of being dishonest are invariably associated with any feelings of guilt. Likewise, there are some very traditional families and parents who believe that "the family that prays together stays together." In these households, the suspicion that grown children do not attend mass is enough in itself to produce shock waves. "How can such a family possibly handle my sexual orientation?" wonder many gay Catholic offspring, and not without reason.

Another coming-out issue for gay Catholics is related to a rather peculiarly Catholic notion of what "honor thy father and thy mother" means. For Catholics, this admonition includes protecting the elderly not only from the common hardships of life, such as hunger and loneliness, but from those personal matters that Catholics believe God has commanded siblings not to trouble their parents with, such as a sibling's alcoholism or homosexual orientation — from those matters that are viewed as sinful. For many gay Catholics, the question as to whether their parents have sufficient knowledge to deal with their child's homosexuality looms larger and more frightening when joined with the question of how their parents will react to their son's or daughter's being a sinner, and an unrepentant one, at that. Sexually active gay people are perceived as detestable sinners by the vast majority of Catholics, if not by the majority of gay Catholics themselves. Gay Catholics assume that their parents share this perception, making Catholic children ready prey for such anxiety-inducing warnings as "Your father will die of a heart attack if you tell him." For a variety of reasons, then, the Catholic family environment is hardly conducive to gay and lesbian offspring coming out to their parents.

Knowing that many Catholic parents will turn to the Church first, last, and always, and knowing that too few Catholic clergy are able to help, casts some doubt on the prudence of gay Catholics coming out to their families. The prospect of a reconciliation of a gay Catholic with his parents and family is further reduced by the fact that Catholics are used to solving their moral and ethical dilemmas individually or with the priest in confession or in spiritual direction, and not in groups. So suggesting such fine secular groups as Parents and Friends of Lesbians and Gays may not be the most welcome advice. Suspicion of going "outside the Church" for insight, coupled with the group setting, will discourage some traditionalists; conversely, looking beyond the confines, and making common cause with other people, will hearten some of the progressives. Again, the watchword for professionals in the helping fields is caution, with a healthy dose of risk. They should mention several options to parents and let them decide which one seems appropriate. The professional should get as much information on the parents' particular brand of Catholicism as possible before deciding on a counseling approach.

To balance the bleak report I have made, I offer this encouragement. The very factors which mitigate against gay Catholics coming out can be the motivating factors behind such action. Compelled by the faith's stress on honesty, and seeking stronger and deeper family bonds, many gay and lesbian Catholics take the risk of disclosing their homosexuality. The results for some have been sufficiently positive to motivate others, under the rationale that if even a gay friend's Irish Catholic parents can cope, so can my own.

But there are other cases of chance discovery at the time of death or of critical illness or injury, or at the time of arrest or the loss of a job, which are painful beyond words. There are stories of unpleasant scenes when a friend or lover is brought to a family function and treated rudely. Many are the occasions when gay people are asked not to bring a friend to a wedding, funeral, or other family gathering. Often gay Catholics experience not only the hurt of family rejection, but the deep alienation which comes when actions fly in the face of professed belief. Not unreasonably they ask, "What ever happened to unconditional love? What about 'love one another as I have loved you'? What about the Church as an inclusive community?" What falls by the wayside is one of the strongest glues that hold a family together, namely, shared belief. This is a time when effective counseling is necessary. To help parents integrate the Good News of their children's honesty, even if they cannot accept the reality of their sexual orientation, is a therapeutic challenge that, unfortunately, most Catholic professionals cannot or will not assume.

DEALING WITH CHURCH REJECTION

Coming-out issues get so much attention that little is paid to what I consider an equally critical concern for gay people, the question of "Will I ever be happy?" It is, of course, a generic question faced by every human being. For gay people, it is the one which long after a lover has been found, and parents have been told, still continues to surface. It is the focus of attention, if one is without a lover and if one's parents have not been told. Regardless of one's life situation, this question pops up from time to time. It is one of the basic questions which religions are designed to answer. And Catholics, no less than others, seek to find the answer.

For us gay Catholics, the question has particular pathos. Old tapes of the famous *Baltimore Catechism* linger in the minds of many of us. We were taught that we were created "to know, love and serve God, and to be happy with Him (sic) in heaven." But most of us would admit to a lingering doubt or two about this precept when faced with the overwhelming and intransigent rejection by the Church of our experience of being gay or lesbian as healthy and good. Even without the Church's pressure, when life simply takes its twists and turns of lost jobs, switched partners, boredom, or bad weather, we all suffer the pains which correspond. But for gay Catholics who honestly cultivate and value the celebratory mode of the liturgy, for whom the music and dancing, the incense and the kiss of peace break into the routine of life like a mountain stream, cleansing, refreshing, and fortifying for the pilgrimage, any melancholy is serious. We face it with extra doubt, rooted not just in the whimsy of existence but in the dread that rejection is God's plan for us — that they were right after all and we are condemned. Fortunately this is not epidemic, but flames of such self-doubt are fueled by the nature of the Catholic's faith. Thus the everyday problems of life get blown out of proportion for some

Catholics.

I have discovered these overreactions again and again in counseling, when I have found myself telling a person that, while signs might point toward an ominous future, there are equally revealing indications that she is managing just fine. Education is necessary to get rid of the ingrained negative attitudes and beliefs, but Catholics are notorious for stopping their religious education in early adolescence. Yet there are increasing opportunities for support and community which make the daily grind enjoyable enough to celebrate. Reminding gay Catholics of the real values of friendship, beauty, meaningful work, good health, and a deep spirituality help them to pass over the harmful emphasis placed on sexual orientation, on fitting in, and on being the "good Catholic girl (or boy)" that they have been schooled to be. Encouraging them to find people and places for relaxation, and reminding them that friends and lovers, hobbies, political involvement, sports, volunteer work, and prayer and meditation are all consistent with the best of the Catholic tradition, will go a long way toward removing the religious taboo about homosexuality.

Several case studies will give a flavor for how these issues get played out and what the concrete needs of Catholics tend to be.

Barbara had been a nun for many years when she decided to leave her order and live with a lover. Her parents have all of the usual issues to cope with, but added to them is the special difficulty of seeing their youngest daughter leave religious life after six years. Now in her late twenties, she is, for them, a sexual being for the first time. Their local priest has no idea of what to advise. His "hate the sin but love the sinner" line falls on deaf ears, as Barbara's parents cannot separate their daughter from her actions. Barbara makes it clear that she is very happy, that religious life with women has given her a deep appreciation for the goodness and strength of women, and that her lover is a woman, a lawyer working with the poor. For Barbara, this relationship seemed natural and good. Where do Barbara's parents turn?

George is married and the father of three children. He and his wife are straight from the cover of any good Catholic magazine at Christmas time. The children go to Catholic schools; George is an usher and his wife, Marge, is the treasurer of the parish. George thought he might be gay in high school but buried the thought long enough to get through military service and into his current job as a printer. But he has begun to find sexual partners outside of his marriage — other men his age, with whom he spends time. He worries about being found out, struggles with whether to tell his wife, and wishes at times that he could start all over again and forget his past. As he and his wife, with two children trailing behind, take the offertory gifts to the altar, he wonders if Jesus will come down from the crucifix and say "hypocrite."

Katherine is single and a teacher by profession. She has the full range of interests of a feminist of her generation. Her male friends tend to be gay; her women friends, married. Then she meets Suzanne. Their shared love for music and poetry, for travel and pottery, make them quick friends. Two years later, they settle into a lovely home together, but begin to wonder if this is all there is. Both families have been understanding, happy to see their daughters happy. But the women are restless — now is the time when "What's it all about?" questions plague both of them. Life is a little boring; the house is spotless, but only the plants are flourishing. Having both been brought up Catholic, they wonder if God is punishing them, even though their well-honed feminist insights have led them away from the Church.

Paul is a middle-aged government worker who likes to make the bar scene on alternate weekends. Although he has other interests, it is fun to socialize in an atmosphere of fraternal affection. He finds Dave attractive, caring, and fun. But when they get up the next morning, Dave mentions that he has to say mass at noon, so cannot stay for brunch. Weeks later, Paul is diagnosed with AIDS. Though he has had several other sexual partners, the only one he can think of is Dave. Will Dave be the one to give him the Last Rites?

These cases, purposely inconclusive, show the range of issues that everyday Catholics face. Difficult issues are present, and the resources for sorting them out often elude us. But the realistic perspective on all of this is a hopeful one.

Many committed Catholics love their gay Catholic sisters and brothers enough to try to transform the institution in its practice and in its theology, so that future generations of gay Catholics will find affirmation within the Church. Groups like Dignity (with chapters in many dioceses throughout the country) and the Conference of Catholic Lesbians are proof that Catholics are moving. Masses are held weekly by many Dignity chapters, providing gay Catholics a place to meet, pray, and ponder. Some bishops are very accepting of Dignity chapters, even to the point of celebrating mass with them, occasionally; others are openly hostile. But this does not deter Dignity leaders and chaplains from fulfilling their ministry. While Dignity does not confront the institutional Church as directly as it might on its inadequate teachings on homosexuality, the very existence of Dignity provides the nurture, community, and challenge that individuals need from the Church. Sacramental life is key for Catholics, and Dignity makes that possible in a way that recognizes the reality of gays and lesbians in the Church.

The Conference of Catholic Lesbians is a network of women who *are* church to each other. Through a newsletter, local contact people, and occasional national gatherings, CCL gives Catholic women a context in which to be church. Since lesbian Catholics share with all Catholic women the experience of sexism in the Church, many Catholic women find that women's base communities, which are growing up throughout the country, are comfortable places in which to worship. This means that many women, including lesbians, have left the Church altogether, preferring instead to form Women Church, a movement of thousands of Catholic women to renew and recreate the Catholic tradition. CCL people include a range of perspectives, and some are simultaneously part of Dignity chapters. All are searching for ways to be Catholic and to develop feminist spirituality. Both CCL and Dignity are highly recommended as starting points for gay Catholics.

New Ways Ministry is an educational group which serves the needs of gay and lesbian Catholics, their families, and friends. Based in the Washington, D.C. area, NWM provides workshops, counseling, spiritual direction, and publications.

As a sign of their effectiveness, the co-founders, Father Robert Nugent and Sister Jeannine Gramick, were forced to leave the archdiocese because the archbishop felt that they did not faithfully present just the institution's position on homosexuality to the exclusion of all other positions. While it has long been the case that responsible dissenting positions are part of Catholic discussion, New Ways was deprived of its excellent leadership. Nonetheless, under the direction of a lay board, it continues its pioneering work to understand, support, and counsel gay Catholics. In recent work, the NWM has even addressed the difficult theme of lesbian nuns, gay priests, and gay brothers, something which surely does not please the archbishop, but which helps thousands of people to better cope with their lives.

The Consultation on Homosexuality, Social Justice, and Roman Catholic Theology, directed by Kevin Gordon, is a very promising think tank. Scholars who work on religious issues surrounding homosexuality meet to listen to the experiences, struggles, and questions of gay Catholics and then to write theological essays which relate to the traditional Church teachings from a cumulative and honest gay Catholic perspective. Such an unbiased process stands in sharp contrast to the way the Vatican develops theology from abstract concepts, rather than from people's lives. Persons beyond the Catholic faith will undoubtedly benefit from the work of the Consultation, when eventually we have a body of literature which reflects adequately and meaningfully the experiences of faithful gay people. Widespread dissemination of such materials will assure that the next generation will benefit.

Hopefully, this overview of Roman Catholic issues and problems gives the reader a sense of how diverse and complicated are the lives of faithful gay Roman Catholics. But caring professionals should keep several things in mind: We gays and lesbians who come from the Roman Catholic tradition have generally been well steeped in it. Most of us gay people harbor a certain love for the Church, despite its position regarding homosexual sex and homosexual relationships. And many (possibly even most) of us lesbians and gays retain our faith and are trying to make the Catholic tradition a loving and accepting home for us against great odds. Those of us who remain within the Church are confident, however, that our faith is not futile. And this confidence takes us a long way toward personal health and wholeness.

REFERENCES

1. Boswell, J. (1980). *Christianity, social tolerance, and homosexuality: Gay people in western Europe from the beginning of the Christian era to the fourteenth century.* Chicago: University of Chicago Press.

2. Heyward, C. (1982). *The redemption of God.* Washington, D.C.: University Press of America.

Chapter 22
Gay and lesbian Jews

Montana Christmas

A Star of David painted on the window of a corner deli. Corned beef on rye. The smell of freshly baked challah being taken from the oven. Hanukkah candles glowing in the window of a home on a snowy winter's night. Colorful prayer shawls and yarmulkes of participants in synagogue. The sound of the shofar, or ram's horn, indicating the start of the High Holy Days. The sights and sounds of Judaism and Jewish ethnicity: an ancient faith and an ancient people. The Chosen People.

There are other aspects of the Jewish experience, too. Documentaries depicting the Holocaust. Swastikas spray-painted on subway walls. Bombings in Israel by hostile nations. Reports of Jewish persecution behind the Iron Curtain.

Because most of us in American society are not Jewish, a glimpse into this religion and its followers is provided. Some of the following questions will be answered. How does the Jew worship and perform rituals? What are the festivals celebrated during the Jewish year? What is the Halakhah or "the Way?" What are the present-day branches of Judaism? How does Judaism see homosexuality and same-sex sexual behavior?

We will also look at some problems which might be faced by gay and lesbian Jews and offer some ways helping professionals may be of help.

THE FAITH

Overview: What is a Jew? Jewish scholars have grappled with this question for centuries. For some, Jews are all persons who consider themselves to be Jews and believe in the religion, Judaism. For others, being Jewish means belonging to the Jewish ethnic group, even while rejecting the teachings of the Jewish religion. For simplicity's sake, in this chapter Jews will be defined as all persons who consider themselves to be Jews and who believe in Judaism as a religion.

Judaism is an ancient belief system rich in traditions and rituals, colorful symbols, and tasty foods. Unlike some other religions, it has no supreme ecclesiastical authority. Thus, Judaism has never been a unified belief system, at least since the second destruction of the Temple at Jerusalem in A.D. 70. Rather, the belief system of the Jews is based on the teachings of the Old Testament books, the interpretations of this material by Jewish scholars down through the ages, and the interpretations of the individual believers.

Two of the three branches of Judaism existing today had their roots in the nineteenth century; they are Reform and Conservative Judaism. The third branch, Orthodox Judaism, goes back to antiquity. *Reform Judaism* is the most liberal branch and the one in which many gay and lesbian Jews find their greatest acceptance. It believes in progressive revelation and the idea that traditional ceremonies should be maintained only if they are meaningful to modern Jews. In sum, they believe in keeping to the "spirit of the times." *Orthodox Judaism,* on the other hand, places great emphasis on the letter of the law and holds to beliefs rejected by Reform Judaism, beliefs such as the resurrection of the dead, the belief in a personal Messiah, and the idea that ultimately the Temple will be rebuilt and sacrifice as done in ancient times will prevail. In Orthodox Judaism, all services are conducted in Hebrew, dietary laws are followed to the letter, and strict differentiation of the sexes is mandated. Finally, *Conservative Judaism* is a belief system standing in the middle of Reform and Orthodox Judaism. It values traditions while being open to new interpretations based on modern life and modern thinking.

Because Judaism is not a monolithic belief system and recognizes no central authority, individual Jews are supposed to study the Scriptures on their own and to weigh their interpretations against the generally accepted beliefs of the Scriptures. Because there is no longer a temple or priests (persons who offer sacrifice), the religion is basically a layperson's religion. In fact, a rabbi is simply a teacher, and the synagogue is simply a school. Many of the religious observances and rituals are conducted by the family around the table in the home; no clergy is required for these ceremonies. Because it is up to the mother to pass the religion and its rituals down to the children, many persons see Judaism as having a strong female-centered nature.

The Halakhah: The Halakhah, or "the Way," refers to the Jewish style of living. This "way" refers to all actions done by the Jew from sunset to sundown, actions such as prayer, study, charitable works, eating, hospitality, and work.

All Jewish beliefs and actions flow from the heart of Judaism — love. This love is for two sources, God (Deut. 6:5) and one's neighbor (Lev. 19:18). How one follows the dietary laws and daily prayer routines, for example, is determined by one's individual sanctity, as well as to which branch of Judaism one adheres. For example, the dietary laws were created to inculcate holiness through self-discipline. They were not, contrary to popular mythology, designed to protect health, although certain ones coincidentally accomplish that. Orthodox Jews will follow the original dietary laws to the letter, while Reform Jews probably will not.

Scholarly study is given high priority in Judaism. In fact, it is considered a form of worship. The saying, "the ignorant person cannot be truly pious," is taken to heart. The spiritual rejuvenation, which is supposed to be done on the Sabbath, is achieved not only through rest and prayer, but also through study.

Hospitality, likewise, is seen as critical, for it is by showing hospitality toward guests that one partially meets the requirement of "love your neighbor as yourself." We will see later how the sin of inhospitality led to the destruction seen in the story of Sodom and Gomorrah.

The Festivals: The Jewish calendar is based on festivals which were originally part of specific agricultural and seasonal events, such as grape harvesting. However, through the ages, many of the festivals lost their agricultural origins and meanings, while retaining and, often, expanding their historical and specifically religious significance.

It is important to note that a Jewish day begins at sundown. For example, if your calendar says that Rosh Ha-shanah is on September 16 this year, it begins to be celebrated at sundown on September 15.

Shabbat, or **Sabbath,** is a weekly observance beginning at sundown on Friday and continuing until sundown on Saturday. On this day, one is supposed to rest as God rested on the seventh day of creation. Sabbath is a family day and celebrated as a day of light and joy for Israel. At Friday evening's meal, tradition has it that egg bread, called hallah or challah, be served and a piece given to each person at table.

Rosh Ha-shanah is New Year's Day or the Day of Memorial. It is a day of solemn joy, celebrating the birthday of the world as well as reflecting on the judgement day when God will decide the fate of both individuals and nations. Rosh Ha-shanah introduces the Days of Awe, or High Holy Days, which culminate in the Day of Atonement, or Yom Kippur. The worship service of Rosh Ha-shanah is designed to arouse the Jew to introspection in preparation for the Day of Atonement.

Yom Kippur, or Yom Ha-Kippurim, is the **Day of Atonement.** This day, the most solemn of the Jewish calendar, marks the end of the High Holy Days, the ten-day period from Rosh Ha-shanah to Yom Kippur. On this day, one fasts for twenty-four hours. It begins at sundown with the recital of Kol Nidre (All Vows), which asks God to release the individual from obligations to God which he or she cannot fulfill. The meditation and prayers of that day focus on introspection, self-examination, confession, contrition, and resolution.

Pesah, or **Passover,** is considered by many to be the most special of the Jewish festivals. Originally a farmer's spring festival, it now commemorates the Jews' exodus from Egypt and celebrates the ideal of freedom. Passover finds family and friends gathering for an elaborate seder, or meal. At this meal, there are many different types of foods such as matza (unleavened bread) and bitter herbs, each symbolic of Jewish experiences. Also at this meal one hears the Haggadah, which describes the exodus and explains the significance of the Passover foods and symbols.

Shavuoth, or **Pentecost,** is the Festival of Revelation commemorating the giving of the Ten Commandments by God to Moses. Originally, this was known as the Feast of the First Fruits.

Sukkoth, or the **Feast of the Tabernacles,** was originally a festival of harvest and vintage. Today it is celebrated in commemoration of God's caring for the Jews during their desert wanderings.

The Ninth Day of Av commemorates the destruction of both Temples of Jerusalem and other calamities which have befallen the Jewish people in their long history.

Purim, a minor holiday, is a carnival celebration based on the Book of Esther.

Hanukkah, the Feast of Dedication, is also known as the Festival of Lights. It celebrates the rededication of the Temple after the Maccabean victory in 165 B.C. At that dedication, there was only enough oil to last for one day. However, miraculously it burned for eight days. Thus, on the eight days of Hanukkah, candles on the menorah, or candelabrum, are lighted one at a time. So, for example, on the first night of Hanukkah only one candle shines, two shine on the second night, etc. Although it is a minor festival like Purim, its significance in the United States has grown because of its occurrence around Christmas time. In some Jewish homes, gifts are exchanged each night of Hanukkah, special foods are prepared, the house is decorated with candles, and company is invited over. A "Hanukkah bush," a version of the Christmas tree, is sometimes seen in Jewish homes, much to the dismay of many rabbis and those following a stricter form of Judaism.

JUDAISM, HOMOSEXUALITY, AND SAME-SEX SEXUAL BEHAVIOR

Like most religions, Judaism holds homosexuality, a non-chosen state of being, to be morally neutral. But like many other religions, Judaism has struggled with same-sex sexual behavior. The stricter Jews have always interpreted same-sex sexual behavior to be wrong, while more progressive scholars have come to interpret it as morally okay. One's scholarship comes into play here.

Those who see same-sex sexual behavior as wrong base their beliefs on the Bible. But as modern scholars such as Bailey(1), Boswell(2), McNeill(3), and Treese(4) point out, most Biblical passages used by persons to condemn same-sex sexual activity have been mistranslated or have been taken out of the historical and cultural contexts in which they were written.

For example, many people believe that the cities of Sodom and Gomorrah were destroyed because God was angry that same-sex sexual activity was going on among the men of the village. There is not a shred of evidence to back up such a claim. In the Bible, the story was that God wanted to destroy the cities of Sodom and Gomorrah because the people were sinning gravely. (What the "grave sins" were is never discussed.) But Abraham begged God to give the people another chance. So, God agreed and sent two male angels to Sodom to find ten righteous men. If ten could be found, God would spare the cities. The angels spent the night at the home of Lot, Abraham's nephew. As it happened, the men of the village came to Lot's house and asked him to bring out his visitors so they could come "to know" them. Lot refused and offered his daughters instead. The men of the town became angry at Lot's refusal and would have harmed Lot had not the angels struck the men blind. Lot and his family fled, and God destroyed the city.

Scholars maintain that the word to examine closely in this story is the verb "to know." Those who are ready to read this story as an anti-gay diatribe would define "yadha" or "to know" as referring to same-sex sexual activity. But as Bailey and other biblical scholars point out, the verb yadha, to know, is used 943 times in the Old Testament and at least 10 times it refers to heterosexual coitus. Why would it be translated only once to refer to same-sex sexual activity out of 943 times? It is more likely that the men of the village wanted simply to "make the acquaintance" of the strangers. Their sin was that of inhospitality for getting angry at Lot's trying to protect his visitors' rest.

In addition to mistranslations of Scripture, many persons have taken parts of the Scriptures out of their historical and cultural context. For example, it is highly doubtful that the ancient Jews understood the concept of sexual orientation. In fact, the term "homosexuality" did not even come into our language until the nineteenth century. Rather, it was assumed that all persons were created as heterosexuals, in harmony with what has become known as "natural law." Thus, any sexual behavior outside of natural law would be considered "unnatural." But as we know today, not all persons are created as heterosexuals; some are created homosexual. Thus, same-sex sexual behavior would be a natural act for a gay or lesbian person, while opposite-sex sexual behavior would be an unnatural act, being out of sync with the person's sexual orientation.

POTENTIAL PROBLEMS

To be Jewish in America is to be a member of a minority. To be gay or lesbian and Jewish is to be a minority within a minority. One is the target of both homophobia and anti-Semitism.

Anti-Semitism ranges from anti-Jewish jokes to outright violence against Jews. Bigotry, whether it is anti-Jewish, anti-Catholic, anti-male, anti-female, anti-black, or homophobic, can be internalized by the victim through time and can manifest itself in negative ways. For example, some Jews have internalized this anti-Semitism so completely that they change their Jewish-sounding names, abandon Judaism and its trappings completely, and even go so far as to have plastic surgery to get rid of their Jewish look. This is a tragic abandoning of one's heritage. But being the lifelong victim of bigotry can have another, more positive effect on people. It can make them very strong and intensely proud of their heritage.

Homophobia and its resultant discrimination has been seen down through the ages. The anti-gay term "faggot," for example, originally referred to faggots, the bundles of sticks put at the base of crosses on which gays and lesbians were burned at the stake. The term "flaming faggot," referring to a stereotypical gay man, takes on added significance when the origins of the symbolism are understood. Likewise, homophobia dramatically showed itself in the Holocaust as Hitler began exterminating gay men, the men who were forced to wear the pink triangle. The term "final solution" to refer to an extermination of a people was first used by the Nazis to refer to gay men; only later was it expanded to include Jews, Catholic priests, gypsies, and others.

In some Jewish homes, especially in Orthodox ones, one of the most devastating homophobic acts is the sitting of shiva. This custom is a seven-day period of mourning following the death of a loved one. Unfortunately, sitting of shiva has been used when gay or lesbian children have come out to their parents. Following the sitting of shiva, the child is considered dead and the child's name is never again spoken in the home. This use of the custom, which flies in the face of the twin Jewish concepts of "quality of justice" and "quality of mercy," is becoming less and less. Sitting of shiva, it should be pointed out, has also been used by parents when their child marries a gentile; such a portrayal is seen in the musical play, *Fiddler on the Roof*.

For those gay and lesbian Jews who have a gentile lover or who are estranged from their families, or both, the celebration of Jewish holidays may become less and less frequent. Likewise, these same persons may find themselves hospitalized with no one around to share with them the celebration of their holidays. For example, in this society Christmas is so powerful a holiday that it overshadows Hanukkah just as Easter can overshadow Passover.

But rather than dwelling on problem areas, let us look at some ways helping professionals such as counselors, nurses, physicians, social workers, and others can be of help.

WHAT HELPING PROFESSIONALS CAN DO TO HELP

In this section, I offer some suggestions for the helping professional to consider in providing care for gay and lesbian clients who follow Judaism. Suggestions one through six are geared for the client in the community, while suggestions seven through ten are designed more for the care of the hospitalized client. The final suggestion is relevant for both hospitalized and non-hospitalized Jewish clients.

One, if the family has rejected the client because of disclosure of sexual orientation, consider family counseling.

Two, encourage gay and lesbian Jews to celebrate the

Jewish festivals in their homes with their gay or lesbian family, not just with their biological one, and give them liberal doses of positive strokes for doing so. Celebrations and rituals add a rich dimension to life, provide a sense of community, and remind one of one's heritage. And one does not have to be Jewish to partake in the celebrations. For example, while living in the wonderful city of Seattle, I often celebrated Hanukkah at my friend Michael's house. At the celebration were men and women, Jews and gentiles, gays, lesbians, and straights, old and young. Then when Christmas came, my Jewish friends would come to my house because as a Roman Catholic and an intensely devoted Child of Christmas, I would celebrate that holy day. Often, when the days of Hanukkah fell at Christmas, the Jewish guests would bring their menorah, light the menorah in the living room with my Christmas tree in the background, and recite the Jewish prayers. Then we would share in the Christmas festivities with gifts and good food. The same type of happening would occur at the house of my friends, Katy and Tim, where Passover would find a wide variety of persons from Jesuit priests to lesbian nuns to little children to old folks.

Three, not only should you encourage your Jewish gay clients to continue their religious rituals, but you yourself should learn more about them through active participation. This is a fascinating way to learn of another culture and to come to the realization of how similar are all religious celebrations.

Four, encourage your clients' significant others to participate in Jewish rituals. In some instances, the gay's or lesbian's lover is non-Jewish and does not understand the notion that the primary rituals of the religion are celebrated at table, not at synagogue. Thus, they may need a word of encouragement to participate and learn of their lover's customs.

Five, for those Jewish gay clients exhibiting low self-esteem from guilt stemming from religious beliefs, there are many things the helping professional should consider. Consider referring the client to a rabbi after discerning that the rabbi is non-homophobic, skilled in pastoral counseling, and knowledgeable about the gay and lesbian coming-out process. Use biblical passages featuring love and mercy, rather than those focusing on vengeance and justice. Encourage the client to see God as a loving, gentle, humorous, caring being, rather than as a judgmental, vindictive, punishing sort of being. Encourage the client to read positive gay or lesbian literature and, especially, to look at modern biblical scholars' works which deal with the gay and lesbian issue. Encourage such clients to attend gay and lesbian synagogues, if there are any around, and to attend gay and lesbian Jewish conferences.

Six, encourage gays and lesbians to provide educational programs to Jewish groups on the needs of gay people. For example, imagine the feelings of rejection a gay Jewish college student would feel if he were accepted by and joined a Jewish fraternity on campus, but then was thrown out when his fraternity brothers learned he was gay.

Seven, if your Jewish gay client is hospitalized, determine if there are any special dietary requirements and make the necessary arrangements with the dietary department.

Eight, provide for hospitalized clients to celebrate the festivals. For example, on one psychiatric ward where I worked, Jewish staff would come in and celebrate Passover or other holidays with our Jewish clients if no family or friends were in the picture.

Nine, if a hospitalized client cannot go home for important celebrations, make arrangements for the client to at least make a phone call to loved ones.

Ten, in the case of death, learn if there are any special body-handling requirements to consider. If there are, see that they are followed.

Finally, be open to new learning and demonstrate a caring attitude. A friendly attitude is far more important in establishing trust and being therapeutic with a client, than is a head full of knowledge of each little custom a person might celebrate. In short, a warm, caring attitude is the most important ingredient in serving your Jewish client — or any other type of client, for that matter!

REFERENCES

1. Bailey, D.S. (1955). *Homosexuality and the Western Christian tradition.* New York: Longmans, Green.

2. Boswell, J. (1980). *Christianity, social tolerance, and homosexuality: Gay people in western Europe from the beginning of the Christian era to the fourteenth century.* Chicago: University of Chicago Press.

3. McNeill, J.J. (1976). *The church and the homosexual.* Kansas City: Sheed Andrews and McMeel.

4. Treese, R.L. (1974). Homosexuality: A contemporary view of the biblical perspective. In S. Gearhart and W.R. Johnson (Eds.), *Loving women, loving men: Gay liberation and the church.* San Francisco: Glide.

ENDNOTE

Material for this chapter was obtained from Jewish friends and colleagues, the author's participation in festivals, and the sections on Judaism in Grolier's Collegiate Encyclopedia of 1970.

Chapter 23
Gay and lesbian Protestants

Betty Havey

As a minister (Endnote 1) and therapist, I have had the privilege of counseling many individuals in coming out as gays or lesbians. These people have found themselves struggling with their faith and have shared journeys of confusion as well as journeys of self-discovery and acceptance. Additionally, there are families and friends who also experience confusion, anger, and denial. Finding spiritual support can be awkward, and finding sympathetic ministers, difficult. Following are examples of clients' stories.

• My pastor told me it was bad enough I was thinking of leaving my husband after twenty years, but that any strong feelings for women were more than he could accept.

• I want to go home and visit my parents for Christmas, but since I came out to them, they have said they feel I don't belong in the church.

• I've been a pastor for seventeen years. I've always been gay but I'm just now beginning to openly acknowledge it and to accept myself. In doing so, I'm beginning to realize there may no longer be room in the church for me — that I may have to leave.

• I could never go to my pastor about my son. My son seems happier than ever since he told us he's gay. I have no confidence that my friends in the church will be able to accept this.

• I tried to be patient. I thought the church would accept me. Now, for my own protection, I've come to reject the church that has rejected me.

• Our 23-year-old son is dying of AIDS. My pastor will not perform the funeral and he refuses to visit him in the hospital. We've known each other for years. Why is he so afraid? Who can we turn to, if not to our church?

Why do some gays and lesbians continue to struggle, sometimes desperately, with their church affiliation or sense of identity with a religious community? Is total rejection of the church a positive goal for people who have faced ostracism by their religious community because of sexual orientation? What constitutes healthy spirituality?

On the one hand, gay people with strong religious identifications sometimes choose to maintain close relationships with their churches or spiritual communities, even though most denominations of the Protestant church still reject and remain unsupportive of its gay and lesbian members, unless they are sexually abstinent. The nearly consistent message of most denominations is: "We love you, but we consider what you do to be sinful." If the need for community identification is strong enough, some will choose to stay by closeting themselves. The result of this choice can be a painful series of lies and cover-ups.

As an alternative, many have chosen to leave their church, rejecting the institution that rejects them and their lifestyle. Frequently, all ties to church or religious community are severed. This helps the individuals disassociate themselves from the sources of oppression and criticism.

Many lesbians and gays, once aware of the role religion has played in their own self-loathing and homophobia, will go through an intense period of hatred and anger. This is an important step in separating their identity from the church, while, perhaps, developing a healthy rapport with those aspects of the church which may still carry meaning and significance for them. The psychological task is to maintain a vision of reclaiming rituals, relationships, and history that are positive. The gay person who totally rejects the past eliminates not only the negative aspects of such experience, but the positive as well. This baby-out-with-the-bathwater mentality, which is understandably common among gays and lesbians, can be a sign of emotional vulnerability, rather than of emotional autonomy. Ideally, significant aspects of the person's religious experience are reclaimed and integrated in new and more productive ways, once the feelings of anger and betrayal subside. An unfortunate alternative is for gay individuals to entirely reject all spiritual pursuits and totally separate themselves from all rituals and activities which were formerly meaningful.

GETTING OVER THE CHURCH; GETTING ON WITH SPIRITUALITY

Not all persons consciously acknowledge the importance spirituality plays in their lives. Many of us consider the religious or transpersonal dimension of our lives to be secondary or superfluous. Some of us who have left the church consider spirituality to be past history. It is my belief that healthy personhood includes an openness to exploring spiritual meaning in our lives. Full psychological integration includes both the emotional *and* the spiritual freedom to act without constraint in our culture. Therapy is a process which provides permission to explore new options. Even though clients see no use for religion or consider their previous experiences to be disappointing, further exploration often reveals an inner awareness of the importance of spiritual anchors.

Clients who seem mute or closed to the subject frequently share significant feelings when asked what role spirituality has played in their lives. Often, behind the anger of feeling excluded, there is revealed a longing to replace the sense of family, community, and acceptance felt in the church. Assisting clients in finding appropriate ways to replace such important connections is an important therapeutic task.

Many clients have expressed fear over feeling a choice must be made between the church and their gay or lesbian lifestyle. Separating from the church, while preserving a commitment to one's spiritual needs, can be a positive step toward healthy autonomy. Clients need reassurance that there are numerous options for fellowship with alternative groups, many of which have a spiritual dimension. Some gays and lesbians who have a need for approval from the church can benefit from seeking association with these communities where there is a greater likelihood of acceptance and support. This is crucial to self-esteem.

Clients with a strong past or present identification with the church confront the same issues as other gays and lesbians in the coming-out process. However, often the confusion, anger, or pain are more intense when deeply felt anti-gay religious convictions are a part of the personal background. Such convictions can exacerbate self-loathing and guilt to an almost unbearable level.

Because of the extreme nature of religious homophobia, gays and lesbians who have had meaningful relationships with religious communities are vulnerable to the persuasive arguments of some groups about what they perceive to be the immorality of a "homosexuality identity." Some clients will go to great lengths to convince themselves they are not gay, while concurrently participating in same-sex relationships. This kind of contradictory behavior contributes to a confused identity, and often the disowning of one's sexual life. Clients vulnerable to such self-negation need assistance in forming their own view of those biblical passages that are widely used to condemn homosexual behavior.

Major biblical scholarship suggests passages such as that found in Romans, Chapter 1 have been misinterpreted. Such passages do not refer to "homosexual" identity or relationships, but rather to the pagan practice of same-sex sexual activity by heterosexuals. Many theological reflections now include attempts at gay-positive interpretations. (Endnote 2)

The therapeutic task of encouraging alternative ways of looking at profoundly homophobic information is a complex but important one. Providing permission to question traditional religious teachings is crucial in working with clients who have rigidly incorporated religious taboos against same-sex relationships. At the same time, it is important to affirm the importance of a healthy spirituality, enabling clients to come to the new images and understandings of their spirituality.

Another common difficulty among gays and lesbians is the emotional constriction caused by keeping oneself in check, out of fear that others will "find them out." Changing pronouns when talking about a vacation with a significant other, always referring to a lover as a roommate, and holding back enthusiasm about friends and activities, are all ways of hiding the truth. Sometimes the need to conceal is real. Gays and lesbians have been disowned from families, threatened by parents, and fired from jobs. No matter how necessary, such caution extracts the cost of blunted emotional depth. To stay safe and out of trouble also requires being out of touch. Spontaneity in all relationships suffers when living a guarded life.

Because of homophobia, some gays and lesbians lead double lives, behaving straight in society while maintaining a network of friends and activities in the gay subculture. Gay men have especially borne the brunt of homophobia evident since the AIDS crisis has emerged. Because of the pervasive fear of AIDS in today's society, gay men with the disease are sometimes denied the basic personal and spiritual considerations needed in times of distress: the support of ministers, physicians, and therapists who are sympathetic; a community to fall back on; a place to live out one's last days; and the guarantee of a funeral with dignity. Fundamentalist religious groups were quick to brand AIDS as the "gay plague." Other groups have been slower to lash out, but are unmistakably condemnatory by their silence. The inability to speak freely of anxiety and fear is just one form of increasing stress in the lives of gay men today.

To be fair, my observation is that the Protestant church has responded to us gays and lesbians in different ways. In some cases, we have been embraced by this church, encouraged in our commitment to remain involved, and appreciated for the unique contributions we offer, as people who understand the path of healing and wholeness that emerges out of the struggle with alienation, confusion, and rejection.

In other cases, we have been ignored by the church and have been told in a multitude of ways to keep silent and private the fullness of our lives. At times, the church finds it equally difficult to understand our deep need for love and community, as well as the overwhelming joy we have discovered in our sexual and social identity.

In still other cases, we have found ourselves intentionally alienated from the church. Instead of words of love and grace from the church, we have been judged by it. When we reached out for community, we were shunned. Some of us have found more love and acceptance from gay brothers and lesbian sisters than we have found in the church. In many cases, we have not left because our spirituality and the church are unimportant to us, but because we have been forced out. Our identity as gays and lesbians is perceived as the cause of our ostracism. In reality, it is the blatant homophobia that most people carry toward us which has caused our alienation. Where our spiritual values and insights have been discounted, we have moved on and sought new ways to nurture ourselves.

TURNING BACK TO THE CHURCH

Most of us desire our spirituality to be positively integrated in such a way that we can draw on it as a resource, especially during crises. However, finding meaningful spiritual support to complement a gay or lesbian identity is often difficult. Finding positive affirmation of gay and lesbian sexuality and of the unique and special spiritual strengths and tasks of being gay are important steps toward wholeness and integration. To help in this search, there is a vast network of peer and professional support in the religious community. Learning to identify resources and to tap into the network is an important task for those of us seeking social and spiritual support, counseling, and community. Local chapters of support groups for gay and lesbian Protestants have sprung up all across the United States. These groups meet regularly for social events, education, and worship. Often, they are aware of local ministers whose counseling expertise can be trusted.

Unfortunately, gay and lesbian caucuses of Protestant denominations have a tendency to move frequently, taking the address of the newly-elected president, for example. Therefore, any address list of such groups is quickly outdated. To get complete listings for local, regional, state, and national addresses, helping professionals should call the local churches of the denomination's gay and lesbian caucus they are seeking. For mainstream Protestant denominations, such as Episcopals and Presbyterians, this is an easy task. For denominations noted for their particularly harsh anti-gay stance, however, it will be more difficult. For example, local Mormon stakes may not provide information on how to get in touch with Affirmation (Gay Mormon Underground). When this occurs, contact mainstream Protestant groups; they will often have this information.

Some of the Protestant support groups are: American Baptists Concerned, Disciples of Christ Task Force on Human Sexuality, Kindred (Seventh-Day Adventists), Integrity (Episcopal), Lutherans Concerned, Moravians Concerned, Presbyterians for Gay Concerns, Unitarian Office for Gay Concerns, Brethren Mennonite Caucus, Friends Committee for Gay Concerns, United Church of Christ, United Methodists for Gay Concerns, Universal Fellowship of Metropolitan Community Churches, Evangelicals Concerned, and Affirmation (Gay Mormon Underground). Although not technically Protestant, Unitarian-Universalists and Mormons are included here.

To find a minister who is competent, as well as aware of and sensitive to the particular issues of gay and lesbian clients, can also be difficult. Although more and more ministers are confronting their own homophobia, finding gay-sensitive ministers does require some perseverance.

In addition to gay-sensitive ministers, there are gay clergy and others who are willing to be helpful when contacted. Helpers who have successfully navigated the turbulent waters of coming out while maintaining some religious or spiritual identification can provide important role models.

Some of us have certainly transcended the limitations of traditional theology and the self-loathing it fostered with a renewed understanding of the Gospel and its inclusion of people dispossessed by the dominant culture. This journey of healing and spiritual renewal has been profoundly important in our lives. Many of us are willing to verbalize our experiences of a Creator, who loves and accepts us, in the hope that others will be encouraged along the way.

Gay and lesbian ministers who are willing to counsel others who are coming out often identify themselves to local psychotherapists, women's centers, gay community centers, and hotlines. This informal network serves the function of referring people to capable and sympathetic ministers. Other gay-sensitive ministers are those clergy who are inclusive in their sermons and supportive in their ministry with gays and lesbians.

What about the parents and families of lesbians and gays?

When children come out to their parents, the announcement is often met with denial, shock, and anger. Parents ordinarily have not heard words of understanding and compassion from the church. Consequently, the parents often feel alienated from what could be a primary source of support, the faith community. The silence (if not overt condemnation) from the pulpit connotes intolerance for the church's gay and lesbian members. Parents and families, as well as their gay sons and brothers and lesbian daughters and sisters, feel that they lack available sources of spiritual support.

A helpful resource for families confronted with the news that a member is lesbian or gay is P-FLAG, Parents and Friends of Lesbians and Gays. The goal of P-FLAG is to help parents and their gay children to understand and love one another and to offer support to both parties. Local chapters are already formed in over a hundred communities. These groups meet monthly for support and to develop goals relevant to their communities. Sometimes they have a parent hotline. Some are developing groups for parents of AIDS patients. Local chapter contacts, information, and a helpful booklet, entitled *About Our Children,* can be obtained by writing: Federation of Parents and Friends of Lesbians and Gays, Inc., P.O. Box 27605, Washington, DC 20038, or by calling them at (202) 638-4200.

To be lesbian or gay is to be given one of life's most complex *and* most inspiring challenges. To be gay or lesbian is a gift and a paradox: from the difference and alienation emerge the hope and possibility of accepting who we are in spite of rejection by others.

Many of us gays and lesbians have responded to the ambivalence and rejection of parents, friends, family members, and the church with realism and integrity. Together, we have found creative ways to meet our spiritual needs when we have felt unwelcome in the church. Our collective experience is valuable to us and, in the gay and lesbian communities, is a source of hope to others who are just setting out on the journey of self-discovery. But even within the religious community, there are many positive resources for gays and lesbians who are setting out on the journey or coming to new and deeper understandings of self. (Endnote 4).

ENDNOTES

1. In this chapter, the term "minister" refers to both lay and ordained persons in professional ministry.

2. See James B. Nelson's comments in *Embodiment, An Approach to Sexuality and Christian Theology*, Minneapolis, MN: Augsburg Publishing House, 1978.

3. Following the example of the predominantly-gay Metropolitan Community Church, the Unitarian-Universalist Association in 1984 approved religious blessings for gay and lesbian unions. Ministers in other denominations who advocate full inclusion for gays and lesbians in the church are willing to provide pastoral counseling, support, and ceremonies to acknowledge commitment to a relationship.

4. The author has been collecting reports from lesbian and gay Protestants in ministry who have stories to share of their self-discovery, relationship to the church, and current spiritual paths.

Chapter 24
Spirituality for unaffiliated gay and lesbian clients

Vivian B. Larsen*

In the development of the culture and society of the United States, institutions to be embraced and protected by the majority of its people have emerged: families, schools, governments, and churches. Being civilized and gregarious peoples, we Americans join together, in most instances, to provide for the meeting of our needs. To create order, we organize regionally and nationally. We identify ourselves with groupings of people for economic, social, psychological, and spiritual reasons. We exclude from our groupings those people whom we view as threatening to our existence. Usually those from whom we feel estranged are people unknown to us, or those whose values are at great odds with our own. Those unknown to the larger society are minorities who tend, of course, to group together for their own preservation.

This article is concerned with the growing American minority communities comprised of gay men and lesbian women and, in particular, with the issue of spirituality for

---

* *Author's note:* Whether we understand the nature of the process or the result, it is my belief that everything in the universe that happens unfolds exactly as it should, and that the good force will prevail. This is offered honestly because I am fully aware of being a novice in the area of unaffiliated spirituality. To give full credit to the hundreds of brilliant and sensitive lesbians and gay men who have practiced, researched, and written about spirituality is not practical here. It would also be impossible, since many of us feel that we must remain in the closet. Additionally, reference to an author does not imply sexual preference. Reference to available writings is listed at the end of the chapter for those who desire further reading.

those in these communities who consider themselves as unaffiliated. For the purposes of this article, "unaffiliated" means both those who do not identify themselves as practicing members of formalized religions and those who are involved in non-mainstream belief systems. I find defining "spirituality" a little harder. Strictly speaking, we might say that anything that is not concerned with the physical bodies of people is concerned with their spirits. However, holistic health has helped us to understand the intrinsic link between the body and mind. And the more knowledge we gain from the arts and sciences, the easier it is to understand that the separation of body and spirit is an illusion. For the purpose of communication, I use "spirituality" in this chapter to mean the conscious and unconscious dimension of life inherently present in human beings and that appears to set them apart from other forms of life. Spirit refers to the undefinable soul, or psyche, which is beyond known physical processes. I will not attempt to set the spirits or psyches of people aside from their bodies.

("History" is a very valuable word of communication in our language, but as with many words used in our culture, it is sexist. This author, to communicate the same meaning, will use the word "ourstory." Please note that for the same reason, the words "person" and "human" are generally not used.)

As far back as we look in the recordings of ourstory, we find references to peoples organizing for nurturance of their spirits through religions. There appear to be two primary differences in these religious organizations. One is found in the Judeo-Christian, Islam, and Hindu approach, which purports that people will be united with God in an afterlife. The other approach, found in a larger and more diversified grouping, purports that union with God, or a higher power, is available to everyone now in this life. Those who believe in yoga, Taoism, Buddhism, Goddess and womyn's spiritualism, Sufism, Wicca, Indian spirituality, and others are in this grouping. In the former approach, we find the patriarchal foundation debasing to womyn and even depreciating to men. Both sexes are restricted in their self-realizations to very limiting traditional sex roles. Within this grouping, even when theologians explain the misinterpretations of the Bible and other recognized books of religious authority, masses of people cling to their condemnation of homosexuals to insure heterosexuals' preference in the sight of their higher power. Churches, to remain organized (wisely or not), need power; and that means a number of people and their monies. Thus, "the welcoming back to the folds" of gays and lesbians, by some of the sects and denominations within this grouping, is an example of this need. In the other grouping, too, we find both matriarchal and patriarchal foundations for beliefs that some people experience as limiting.

Along the passage of time in the experience of ourstory, many people remained in the areas of paganism or witchcraft, or fell from the folds of Judeo-Christian or Eastern religions and returned to pagan practices or witchcraft. There are present in America countless groupings of pagans and occultists, and covens of witches and warlocks. Many people, discouraged from affiliating with formal religions because of their disdainful attitudes toward gays and lesbians, found their way into these non-mainstream belief systems.

As we look back over ourstory and see the repetitive and massive accounts of torture and death of those affiliated and unaffiliated, it sometimes appears more than remarkable that people pursue spiritual nurturance. The pagans were slain, the Jews gassed, the Native Americans massacred, the witches burned, the "deviants" electro- and insulin-shocked, and on and on, in the name of religion or moral righteousness. Yet people persist in their search for spiritual meaning. This searching for the mystical state of oneness, whether that is with oneself or with a higher power, seems to be an inextinguishable force within people.

All people need to experience their basic self-worth. But when we are oppressed through shunning or degradation, and through deprivation of our fundamental rights to housing, jobs, social services, education, and religious pursuits because of our sex, age, skin color, national origin, or sexual orientation, we do not receive the warm personal regard for our individual worth that each of us must have in order to be healthy, productive individuals. When our worth is denigrated, we become angry and hurt. To survive and find meaning for life, many have disassociated themselves from those seen as oppressors.

As a helping professional, it is not difficult for you to assist your lesbian and gay clients in their searches for spiritual oneness, if they are affiliated. You can refer them to their local gay newspaper. There they will find many different churches listing special services or programs for them. But what do you do if your client is not inclined, for whatever reason, toward an organized religion? It would seem important for you to know a few of the avenues being taken by gays and lesbians who consider themselves unaffiliated.

In 1978 a very interesting development for gay men began, which is now known as the Radical Fairies Movement. Encouraged by Harry Hayes, the founder of the Mattachine Society, and Mitch Walker, author of *Men Loving Men* and *Visionary Love*, a retreat for unaffiliated men was organized in the desert of Arizona. That gathering of 250 men, identifying themselves as gays, was what some gay historians consider to be the beginning of a period of new consciousness. In 1979, a very eclectic group of 300 mostly unaffiliated men, among them witches, Shamans, radical Christians, and Zen Buddhists, gathered in the mountains of Colorado to pursue their spiritual search together. Recently, there was a Pagan Spirit gathering in Wisconsin, and two of the happenings included a Native American purification ritual and a Sweat-Lodge ceremony. This represents one non-traditional approach to communal spirituality. There are also many totally unaffiliated men who consider themselves solitaries, who deepen their own spirituality through transcendental meditation, yoga, guided imagery, and self-hypnosis. Some of them prefer to pursue the deepening of their spirits individually, and some, from time to time, gather together with other men to share in ritual ceremonies which they create for themselves.

Lesbians who are unaffiliated have also taken many diverse pathways in their spiritual pursuits. In Madison, Wisconsin, a womyn named Salina Fox conducts rituals for womyn. A group in Wisconsin, called the Circle, and in Florida a group called the Pagoda, are alternative womyn's religions. Some lesbians, as some gay men, have attached themselves to non-mainstream belief systems such as astrology, psychic readings, psychic healing, witchcraft, and paganism. Others choose no affiliation and either remain totally independent or gather from time to time with others, for rituals like the celebration of the solstices of the seasons or for affirmation and bonding ceremonies. However, my experience suggests that whether one is a pagan, a witch, a member of the order of St. Martinique, Pagoda, the Circle, or a visionary, a Shaman, a radical Christian or Jew, a Zen Buddhist, a Goddess Worshipper, a Native American, a member of the Radical Fairies Movement, or even a worshipper of the devil, one finds oneself associated with others in a more or less ritualized way before long.

Many womyn, and particularly lesbians, find affirmation and spiritual bonding through womyn's music. They may listen to it at home, in their cars, while jogging, at gatherings with friends, or at concerts or music festivals that bring them together in local areas by the hundreds or that gather them together from round the world by the thousands. The womyn's music culture has been developing in this country for over twenty years, but it experienced an explosion in 1975 when four extremely talented womyn did a tour in California called Women on Wheels. Holly Near, Margie Adam, Meg Christian, and Chris Williamson joined forces to do that tour, and the emotional power of their music still reaches the hearts and spirits of womyn today, uplifting them and giving them a spiritual bonding. The womyn's music culture addresses itself to far more than what will sell today. Womyn's music is concerned with the issues of living. This music addresses hunger, war, the environment, politics, love, religion, play, work, aging, and all oppression. Artists such as Betsy Rose, Toshi Reagan, Alix Dobkin, Teresa Trull, Barbara Higbie, Ferron, Chevere, Debbie Fier, Rhiannon, Linda Tillery, Casselberry & DuPree, Nancy Vogl, Holly Near, Chris Williamson, Christin Lems, Ginni Clemmens, Nancy Day, Meg Christian, Margie Adam, to name only some, usually write their own music and poetry, or sing and play that of other womyn, to raise the consciousness of our society to matters of importance. The comedians Kate Clinton and Robin Tyler, and the actors Nan Brooks, Judy Sloan, and Susan Freundlich, all address the issues of life and stir us to more feeling and more caring than we had before we heard them. This is perhaps the essence of all spiritualism. That when our minds are raised to a new awareness, we will rise up, join together, and take action to make this world a better place to live for all people, a place that not only allows or tolerates differences, but that actually honors the differences.

If your clients would like to locate others who are pursuing their spiritual development, either through non-mainstream affiliations or through unstructured and more spontaneous types of gatherings, they might best start their searches through their local lesbian and gay bookstores. Our society, in all of its complexities, has not lost touch with the power of what might be called underground networking. Asking some-one who knows someone through the trust system of rela-tionships is how to get where you want to go in an oppressed subculture, particularly one that is made up of as many sub-strata groups as are the lesbian and gay communities.

REFERENCES

1. Alder, M. (1981). *Drawing down the moon: Witches, Druids, goddess-worshipers, and other pagans in America today.* Boston: Beacon Press.

2. Bolden, J.S. (1979). *The goddesses in everywoman.* Los Angeles: J.P. Tarcher.

3. Budapest, Z. (1979). *The holy book of women's mysteries* (2 volumes). Oakland, CA: Susan B. Anthony Coven No. 1.

4. Capra, F. (1981). *The turning point.* New York: Simon & Schuster.

5. Chesler, P. (1972). *Women and madness.* Garden City, NY: Doubleday.

6. Chew, W. (1977). *The goddess faith.* Hicksville, NY: Exposition Press.

7. Chicago, J. (1979). *The dinner party: A symbol of our heritage.* Garden City, NY: Doubleday.

8. Clark, D. (1977). *Loving someone gay.* Millbrae, CA: Celestial Arts.

9. Daly, M. (1978). *Beyond God the father: Toward a philosophy of women's liberation.* Boston: Beacon Press.

10. Grahn, J. (1981). *Another mother tongue: Stories from the ancient gay tradition.* Watertown, MA: Persephone Press.

11. Lorde, A. (1978). *The black unicorn.* New York: W.W. Norton.

12. Rich, A. (1979). *On lies, secrets and silence: Selected prose, 1966-1978.* New York: W.W. Norton.

13. Spretnak, C. (Ed.) (1982). *The politics of women's spirituality: Essays on the rise of spiritual power within the feminist movement.* Garden City, NY: Anchor Press/Doubleday.

14. Starhawk. (1982). *Dreaming the dark: Magic, sex and politics.* Boston: Beacon Press.

15. Walker, M. (1977). *Men loving men.* San Francisco: Gay Sunshine Press.

16. Wallace, A. and Henkin, B. (1978). *The psychic healing book.* New York: Delacorte Press.

17. Woodman, N.J. and Lenna, H. (1980). *Counseling with gay men and women.* San Francisco: Jossey-Bass.

Chapter 25
Wicca: A healing religion

Jan Bearwoman*

The word "Wicca" is derived from an Anglo-Saxon word for "Wise One." Wicca's roots are in nature worship. In Wicca, we revere the connection between all things, the force that binds us as creatures of the same god and goddess.

Wicca is not a dead religion, but one that is very active today. Many lesbians are involved, as are gay men, because it is one of the very few religions that allows us gay people dignity and a sense of worth. Women are given the honor of being life-bringers and the source of life itself. Men are thought of as the catalysts to the life-bringing process, and they are encouraged to allow their female sides to shine through the tough-guy façades. Both sexes are encouraged to let the other sex, the other part of us, out. Just as Jung believed that we are all female and male, so Wiccans believe. We are a combination of goddess and god. We Wiccans believe that people are happier if they are in touch with their duality. Historical examples of such people from within our tradition are the shamans. Shamans were ancient medicine women and men. They lived totally in the world of androgyny. The shaman was either a woman who dressed and acted like a man and even took a "wife," or a man who took a "husband" and acted like a woman. This was thought of as normal, and gay and lesbian sex was a fact of life. Of course, missionaries forced a radical change in these views with a vengeance when they Christianized the Native Americans.

---

* *Editor's Note:* In between those gays and lesbians who have abandoned all forms of religion and those who believe in mainstream religions, there are those who find themselves in non-mainstream religions or belief systems. In this chapter, we see an example of one such non-mainstream religion, Wicca, as discussed by an Iowa maverick Wiccan priestess.

Most Wiccans (Neo-Pagans) today borrow from European traditions, but Wicca remains eclectic. Goddesses and gods are brought in from India, Greece, Africa, and Native North America. In my group, or coven (consisting of thirteen members), we have a similar mix to that. We call on Athena, the warrior Amazon who did not need to be protected by a husband. We admire her strength and courage. Diana is the goddess of the moon, and like Athena, she is a strong goddess who needs no one, and yet she is loving toward women. The legend is that she married her brother and produced history's only female messiah, Aradia. Aradia was the first Wiccan. She taught us how to use cards for divination, how to use herbs to heal, and how to help our sisters and brothers who are less fortunate. The Wiccan religion is not a group of crazies out to hex people, or worship a devil. We were the first healers, midwives, and nurses.

The Christian religion tried, as did its predecessor, Judaism, to usurp the Old Religion (Wicca) by calling the Horned One (Wicca's male deity) the devil. Cerrunnos and Pan are but two of his names. The Horned One was not only horned but had cloven hooves. He was frisky and liked to sport with maidens in the woods.

The converts to the new religion of Christianity tried to rid themselves of their past and, no doubt, of their guilt. They did away with the "pagans," as we were branded (Pagan means "country dweller"). To rid themselves of the pagans, Christians tortured, murdered, and plundered Wiccans.

The Middle Ages continued the zealous persecution of the Old Religion, and especially its female devotees. Women-hating Inquisition members sent beautiful, old, straight, and lesbian women to the stake or gallows. A woman was accused of being a witch if she refused to sleep with a duke, if she practiced herbology, or if she was a maverick in some way. A woman who was independent was intolerable in those days and was thought to be in league with the devil. One accusation could be enough to have her burned alive or hanged from the gallows.

This hatred of Wicca continued both in the United States and Europe until the 1700s. Today, the hatred of Wiccans continues, thanks to Falwell, Inquisitor Supreme, and his minions. Not only is he guilty of conducting a witch-hunt, but a gay hunt as well. Wiccans today, especially gay and lesbian Wiccans, still live in fear of the stake.

Most of the problem is that our faith is misunderstood. I recently was accused of being a Satanist in a letter written by a rabid born-againer. It is hard to combat narrow and closed-minded thinking. If nothing else, I can only hope that someday these people will break out of auto-pilot and start thinking for themselves.

Wiccans today, as in the past, still use herbs. Wicca has given to medicine some of its greatest "inventions." It is ironic that physicians were credited with the miracle cures, when it was wise women over the centuries who discovered the proper herbs and dosages. The ancients knew that foxglove was a good medicine for the heart. Physicians invented digitalis, which is a derivative from foxglove. Bread mold had curative power and today it is called penicillin. Anesthetics were fashioned from poppies, teas, and liquors, having similar bases as anesthetics do today. Women had control of their own fertility by visiting the local wise women, who could mix up a fertility drug or induce abortion.

Today, medicine ridicules herbal healing and seeks to have people gobble dangerous chemicals such as birth control pills, mood elevators, and tranquilizers. Midwives offered more than herbs. They also gave women support, which is something many physicians do not. Some physicians today are taking a more enlightened view toward herbology, finally recognizing its healing properties.

Modern medicine is also looking at the effect sound has on the body, mind, and spirit, something that has long been accepted and appreciated by Wiccans. Loud noises not only jar our physical bodies, but they can also drag the spirit down. Loud rock music has been linked to violence at rock concerts. Sound can also kill. A French scientist has developed a sonic weapon that can knock down buildings. Music has been used to charge up soldiers, and to lead them into battle.

Music can also inspire us to look within. Witness the sheer poetry of a Ravi Shankar concert, where the fans do not riot, but go on inner journeys. The bamboo flute music of Japan can also take us to higher consciousness and relaxation. Through music, when we achieve this inner peace, stress is reduced, and we can attain better health because the body and mind are not separate but together. Both need to work together for us to be healthy individuals.

Ritual is not only a powerful religious tool, but it is also used as a healing technique. Ritual is important for us Wiccans because all of our energies are combined. Each person brings her own energy, enthusiasm, and ideas to our coven, and these blend as one big idea and one power.

The techniques vary for setting up a ritual. Z. Budapest, in her book *The Feminist Book of Lights & Shadows*, describes a ritual like this:

1. Determining the boundaries of the circle.
2. Consecrating the grounds with fire and air (incense), water and salt.
3. Drawing of the circle — separating the grounds of worship.
4. Purification of those who enter the circle.
5. Closing the circle after all are admitted.
6. Invocations to the corners of the universe.
7. Sealing the circle.
8. Raising witches' power.
9. Inviting the Goddess.
10. Blessing on all tools, food, people.
11. Ritual work appropriate to the event.
12. Feast; first thanks and libation to the Goddess, then personal business with the Goddess.
13. Dancing and "Pleasure Now!" celebration.
14. Dismissing the spirits.

Our coven draws the circle as she described, and we also invoke our helpers or guardians, our spirit-guides. We think of them as being on a higher plane, and from their elevated status we believe they can give advice on the right healing choices for us. They can suggest professional help, too.

We use candles at our rituals to help us focus on our intents. Blue candles are lit to help us attain mental clarity on an issue; red is for more energy; white, gold, and silver are for more spiritual power; and green is for health and growth. Each time a candle is lit, it is a reminder to work on or toward that specific goal. Candle-burning is practical psychology. It helps a person to think positively and to realize his mental, physical, or spiritual potential.

Another ritual tool is Tarot. It comes from a Latin word for wheel, Rota. No one knows its exact origins. A fanciful idea is that it came from ancient Egypt. The first extant deck we have is from 1329.(3)

Tarot can be used to look at options, to avoid pitfalls, and to clearly map out one's life. I think that Tarot is a very helpful, insightful path. I use it with clients to help them look at their lives and to identify what could possibly happen ahead. It is so much more than mere fortune-telling. It is reaching into clients' feelings, thoughts, and lives, helping them to help themselves in understanding these better.

Healing is often accompanied by touch. Humans respond to touch. Nothing can make a throbbing knee stop hurting faster than a mother's gentle kiss. Nothing can replace the stroke of a lover's hand and a backrub or footrub after a particularly harried day. It is heaven! Polarity massage, a technique equalizing energy flows in the body, and "the laying on of hands" are techniques to help bring the body into synchrony. Touch, working together with love, are two of the most powerful remedies humankind knows. A psychologist made the claim that we need to be hugged every day in order to survive; and tests have shown that an infant monkey who is not held or loved loses the will to live — refusing food and wasting away.

The other type of healing that Wiccans use is color, or rainbow therapy. A person is told to visualize his pain as pulsing red. Then he is told the pain is lessening as the color becomes orange. Each color of the rainbow from yellow to green to blue to violet reduces the pain, until finally it vanishes as the color sequence reaches white. This is one technique that can give dramatic results. It can be illustrated by the following examples:

A co-worker of mine had always had migraine headaches, the kind that required her to lie down in a darkened room, and that made any amount of noise seem like a jackhammer or a drum solo by the late Keith Moon. We sat down. I told her to take some deep breaths, and to imagine red light around her head. That light was to have a life of its own. I told her to imagine that it was growing, pulsing just as her pain appeared to pulse. The next step was orange, yellow, green, blue, violet, and white. She went through all the colors and noticed that her headache was feeling less intense with each one. When she opened her eyes at the end of the exercise, her pain was gone. She was able to keep working for the rest of the day.

A student in one of my classes had been bothered by severe menstrual cramps and heavy bleeding. She tried the rainbow technique and was able to avoid a D&C, which was her usual cure for the ailment.

Another student used not only the rainbow technique, but all of the healing techniques, especially the love therapy. The spots which had shown up on a liver scan were gone at her next appointment. Perhaps love *can* conquer all.

I do not pretend to be a physician, nor did I represent myself as one. The techniques described here will not work well for everyone, just as penicillin will not work well for everyone. But these techniques do give you the ability to help your body in its attempt to heal itself.

Why do Wiccans avoid AMA-approved medicine? The main problem is that many of us want to be able to include our medicinal cures in the program a physician prescribes for us. Let us say that I am undergoing chemotherapy. I want freedom to use herbs to control my nausea, and I also want freedom to try meditation, sound and color therapy, and love, and to have a shaman and my coven involved with my therapy. To me they are *as* important, if not more important, than conventional medical techniques. These beliefs are very basic to Wicca. We control our own destiny, we control our own healing, and it is very difficult to surrender ourselves to a professional who may ridicule our chanting, even if the ridicule is done with subtlety, as in the case of male physicians' parentalism.

I am not going to let female physicians go unchastised either. They have been enculturated to play the game by the Big Boys' rules. I fervently hope that they can find more compassion for a patient, but they are still trained in the same science-worshipping manner.

Physicians and other professionals expect to be treated as authority figures. If someone else wants to be heard, we have to raise our hands for permission to speak. Physicians keep patients in crowded rooms, or cold examining rooms, until they are ready. Who else but the medical professionals are allowed these obnoxious mannerisms and attitudes? Is it any wonder, then, that Wiccans, who are mostly self-sufficient women who can heal, stay away from this sort of contemptuous behavior and the people who exhibit it?

The physicians and medical staff are not the only problem. Ministers view our religion as amusing at best, as satanic at worst. Satanism and Wicca have always been lumped together; yet, as I have pointed out, they are totally different. Satanism is Christianity reversed. It is a mockery of the Catholic Mass and uses Christian symbols reversed: a black host and an inverted cross, for examples. Our religion is far older than the Catholic Mass. Until people understand that we too want nothing to do with satanic human sacrifices, killing of animals, and other such horrible acts, we will be wrongly referred to as devil-worshipers. We have a saying in Wicca, that everything comes to us in threes, so it is much for the better to do good for someone and be rewarded three times rather than to be hit by an evil action three times over.

A problem a professional will face is non-recognition of a Wiccan. We have learned to hide, and we can do so very well. We hide to avoid the ridicule and abuse we receive from the many who misunderstand our faith. We hide out of the fear of losing our jobs because of our religious views. The similarity between Wiccans' hiding their beliefs and gays' their orientation is striking. For many Wiccans, both religious intolerance and homophobia are reasons for hiding.

If your client does tell you that she is a Wiccan, why not join in and celebrate? Wiccan ceremonies are fun, free-spirited, and usually combined with good music and good food. Foods for rituals reflect the pagan influences by being seasonal: pumpkin bread for Halloween, or strawberries for May Day.

The main holidays for Wiccans are Halloween and May Day, both occurring six months from each other. To us, they are times of transition. On Halloween, the departed spirits return to bring messages. The worlds of the living and the dead come together as one. In Europe, bonfires are burned to keep the spirits warm and to welcome them with light. The fire also serves a useful purpose as something over which to cook the food during the ritual.

May Day is the same event, only in the spring. To Wiccans, the world is ruled by the male aspect-god for six months, and the female aspect-goddess for six months. The Male ascends on Halloween, the Female on May Day. We celebrate not only the spirits, but also the harvest on Halloween and the planting on May Day. The ancients relied on their land to sustain them. Modern humans have foolishly polluted Mother Earth. Wiccans lead the battle against the rape of Mother Earth, for we respect Her as did our ancestors.

By joining in a celebration, not only will you have fun, but you will learn what is important to a Wiccan. It will be clear that we have our own belief system. We also have our clergy, priestesses and priests. In my coven, the clergy is not a hierarchy; we all take turns being leader. We have our dogma, no matter how eclectic it may be, and we use our dogma of goddess and god, or even of a gender-neutral force, for positive magic. We do not curse anyone, or hex them; we use our knowledge and power for healing. We do not attack, but we will protect ourselves.

If you have Wiccan patients, allow them to practice not only their religion, but also their holistic practices of massage, herbs, and meditation. Most of us may be distrustful of modern medicine due to its parental and authoritarian nature, but we feel that a balance between our ways and the ways of the AMA may be wise.

In conclusion, I will leave the reader with two requests on behalf of all Wiccans. We ask for the freedom to practice our joyful and loving religion without fear of reprisals. And, from our gay Christian and Jewish brothers and sisters, we ask for their support, and that they not shun us as straight Christians and Jews have shunned them.

REFERENCES

1. Budapest, Z. (1976). *The feminist book of lights & shadows*. California: Luna Publications.

2. Grahn, J. (1984). *Another mother tongue: Gay words, gay worlds.* Boston: Beacon Press.

3. Hall, A. (1975). *Signs of things to come.* London: Danbury Press.

V

Helping the Client with Legal Issues

Chapter 26

Legal issues I: Power of attorney, wills, lovers' rights

Duane L. Rohovit

Legal considerations may seem to be the last thing a person who is ill or who has been injured would find important. My experience is that legal concerns are often the most troubling aspect of a hospital stay. The reason is that patients often lose the ability to actively manage their affairs, which continue on in the world outside the hospital. The questions of who will manage these affairs, with what authority, and how well, are often foremost in the patient's mind. This is especially true for gay men and lesbians whose close friends and lovers may not be known to their business colleagues, bankers, and biological family members. The ignorance and insensitivity of health professionals often compound the problems. Lovers are denied visitation rights or even information about the condition of the patient. When a gay man or lesbian loses control of life because of illness or accident, the consequences can be disastrous.

A recent Minnesota case, which received wide publicity, demonstrates many of the problems that can be caused by sudden injury. Sharon Kowalski suffered massive brain damage in an auto accident. Karen Thompson visited her every day. The Kowalski family went to court to limit Karen's access. The Kowalskis were not aware of Karen's relationship with their daughter until Karen wrote a letter explaining that she was Sharon's lover. The Kowalskis denied that their daughter was a lesbian, even though members of Handicapped Services interviewed Sharon, asked her if she was gay, and she responded by typing "yes." According to their report, they also asked Sharon if she had a lover; Sharon typed "karen t." Litigation continues, as of September 1989, between Sharon's lover and family to determine who finally will have access to her.

This situation underscores the anxieties of many lesbians and gays about sudden illness or injury. The health professional must be prepared for these problems and should be able to give advice on how situations like the Minnesota case can be avoided. Also, when the patient knows that death is possible or imminent, there are additional concerns over disposition of property, funeral arrangements, and providing for loved ones.

There are a variety of solutions to the problems faced by lesbian and gay patients. Health professionals must be prepared to provide advice about these solutions, and about how and what kind of lawyer should be contacted. The choice of a lawyer is a crucial one. Many lawyers have no expertise or interest in developing expertise in this area of the law. The best way to approach the problem of choosing a lawyer is to get names of lawyers from local lesbian and gay organizations, the local chapter of the American Civil Liberties Union, or the National Lawyers Guild. These sources can generally provide the names of lawyers who will be sympathetic to the special needs of the gay or lesbian person and who also have the knowledge to give the proper legal advice.

After a list of potential lawyers is acquired, the next step is to interview the lawyers. This should be done in person, if possible, but a telephone conference will also provide enough information to make a decision about which one to hire. The patient should be encouraged to be very forthright and direct in the interviews. Initially, it should be determined how much, if anything, will be charged for an initial contact. If the lawyer is unwilling to answer inquiries about prices, avoid that lawyer. In an initial interview or phone consultation, the following questions may be helpful as a guide for determining whether to hire a particular lawyer:

1. Does the lawyer have any experience with lesbian and gay clients?

2. If so, in what areas of the law?

3. Is the lawyer comfortable with working with lesbian and gay clients?

The final decision should rest on an evaluation of the lawyer's answers to the client's questions, and on whether the client feels comfortable with the lawyer. However, the latter consideration should not be primary; there are many affable lawyers who know nothing about this area of the law.

The most important legal problem for persons who will not be able to handle their affairs for some period of time is to be able to transfer their authority to someone who can do this for them. The document which must be prepared is called a Power of Attorney in most jurisdictions. This particular instrument allows a person to name another to act in his place in specified situations for a certain period of time. For example, if a person wanted his lover to be able to pay the bills, collect the rent from tenants, and transfer funds for a mortgage payment, a Power of Attorney could be drafted which would authorize those specific actions.

A Power of Attorney can be very specific or very general. A person's specific needs should be discussed with a lawyer so that the proper provisions can be included. Other problems can be addressed by use of this document. A person may designate who shall be allowed to visit or who shall be allowed to make decisions regarding medical procedures in the event that the person becomes mentally unable to make these decisions himself. Hospital personnel will often assume that biological relatives or spouses are automatically the best qualified persons to be consulted regarding these decisions. It is important that health professionals realize that close friends and lovers may have a great deal more information about the gay or lesbian patient than biological relatives or married spouses.

The Power of Attorney is also important for a patient who faces the possibility of death. It allows the patient to name someone to take care of funeral or memorial arrangements and other plans for the disposition of the body. This avoids situations which the author has experienced where a tug-of-war takes place in the hospital morgue between family members and lovers or friends of the deceased. The biological family often wants to return the body to the family home town and to have a service in the local church. This plan, of course, leaves out any participation by, or sometimes even knowledge of, lovers and friends. The Power of Attorney provides an excellent method to insure that the affairs of a person who is incapacitated will be managed by someone who is trusted, and it also allows for planning of events after death.

A patient facing a life-threatening illness, or who must undergo risky medical procedures, *must* have a will. If a person has no will, the state has, in effect, a ready-made one in the form of inheritance laws, imposed automatically, which give all property to biological relatives or to a spouse. No matter what the wishes of the deceased were, the property will be disposed of by the Court according to the law. Anyone who has experience with the practice of law with gay and lesbian clients has either personally experienced or heard stories about the horror of relatives walking into a house or apartment that was inhabited by the deceased and his lover and literally stripping the place or, if the house was owned by the deceased, throwing the bereaved lover out immediately.

To avoid this situation, it is necessary to draft a will. Many people believe that this is a very expensive legal service. It is generally one of the cheaper services provided by lawyers. Large fees are made when the will is probated.

The will is a document which in some states can be hand-written (in other states it may be typed) and prepared without a lawyer. It is my opinion that lesbians and gays should not draft their own wills or use do-it-yourself kits. Because lesbians and gay men are more likely to have their wills challenged in court, it is important that they be correctly drafted. If the will is properly prepared, the chances are less that a challenge will be made to the disposition of the property under the will. The author has participated in litigation involving do-it-yourself wills which ended unhappily for the deceased's lover. The do-it-yourself will kit lacked a residuary clause. The residuary clause designates to which person or persons will be given the rest and residue of the property not specifically willed to someone else. This clause becomes very important if a person acquires property after writing the will, or if property is sold or exchanged for other property. In one case, a couple took all of their assets and bought property in the name of the partner who died first. The will was never changed to reflect the change in property. So the result was that the property passed to biological relatives, rather than to the lifelong lover for whom it was intended.

A will is a document which consists of a number of clauses or paragraphs that provide direction to a person who is called the Executor (male) or Executrix (female) and who carries out the provisions of the will. This person hires an attorney who represents the estate and who processes the will through the court. This is referred to as probating a will. The person writing the will should choose someone trustworthy to be the Executor or Executrix, and should make sure that the person knows the specifics of the will-maker's wishes, including which lawyer should be hired to probate the will. The Executor or Executrix must be prepared to act if family members, who assume that they will inherit the deceased's property, begin to take possession of property.

The person making a will may give specific items to specific people (specific bequests) or may give percentages of the value of possessions which would be sold by the Executor or Executrix (general bequest). It is possible to do a combination of both. The will may also be used to set up trust funds for the benefit of beneficiaries.

Some states recognize what are termed "living wills." But even in states which do not recognize these wills, inclusion of them as part of a general will may be a helpful guide to the patient's wishes. A living will directs that artificial means shall not be used to prolong life when death is imminent and the body is merely being kept alive through the use of machines.

There are a variety of other matters that may be provided for in the will, including the person's wishes regarding custody of children, the donation of memorial money to certain sources, and funeral or other memorial arrangements. The author recommends that these arrangements also be covered in a Power of Attorney. This chapter does not pretend to be a complete guide to writing a will, and it must be emphasized that health professionals should encourage lesbians and gay men to seek competent professional advice.

The existence of a Power of Attorney and a will is often the best peacemaker between biological relatives and a patient's lover or friends. The documents establish who will be in charge. Once that is established, it has been the author's experience that often real cooperation and communication among the various parties involved can take place. The health professional can be very helpful in promoting harmony among those parties by being knowledgeable about these basic legal documents.

What is most important is that the execution of these documents can ease many anxieties of lesbian and gay patients, and can allow them to concentrate on getting well, knowing that their affairs outside the hospital are being properly cared for by persons they know and trust. Many times this will be an important aid to a quick recovery or to a peaceful death.

Chapter 27

Legal issues II: Probate, body disposition, funeral arrangements

by Karl G. Rubesh

Gertrude and Alice were lovers for many years. They lived together, acquired property together, and had many close friends. Neither Gertrude's nor Alice's family said anything disparaging about their apparent lover relationship. Both women had made many plans and had discussed what each would like the surviving partner to do in the case of death. They discussed arrangements regarding their funerals and disposition of property, but no formal action was ever taken.

Upon Gertrude's death, her biological family threw Alice out of her own home, as only Gertrude's name was on the title. The family refused to honor Gertrude's last wishes because of the lesbian overtones of her requests, overtones which would have publicly affirmed her lover relationship with Alice. Gertrude's family were able to do as they wished; not only did they not have to follow Gertrude's last wishes, they did not have to accommodate Alice. Rather, they ignored completely the relationship which had endured and succeeded through the years despite many hardships, and which had brought both women much happiness. The family was able to take all of Gertrude's property, as well as some property which the two women acquired jointly but which was held in Gertrude's name only.

Their friends said Alice never really recovered from the death of her lover, Gertrude. This story happened years ago, but it is repeated with regularity today all across our land. Perhaps more than others, gays and lesbians must prepare for the distribution of their effects and implementation of their last wishes.

This chapter deals with probate, body disposition, and funeral arrangements. We will deal with two different concepts of family. Many times you may find that a gay or lesbian client has developed a family outside of the biological one. The new family often results from estrangement from the biological family due to non-acceptance of the gay person's sexual orientation or lifestyle. This new family is no less loving. Indeed, it may be more so. Thus, the grief associated with death will affect this family's members as profoundly as it does blood relatives. It is imperative for legal and other professionals to understand this in order to effectively help gay and lesbian clients.

Probate is the process by which the court determines who shall be granted particular property, and once that determination has been made, the court gives legal title to that individual. This process can be either extremely complicated or quite simple. Factors determining the complexity or simplicity of the process include the size of the person's estate, whether the person has left a will defining his or her wishes, whether the will, if there is one, is contested, and possible tax ramifications.

If the deceased did not have a will, the laws of the deceased's state of residence will determine who receives the property and in what proportions. The percentages and the persons receiving property vary from state to state and are defined by statute. Some states provide for a spouse to receive one-half of the estate, with the other half going to the children. If there are no children, then all goes to the spouse. If the deceased is not survived by a spouse or children, the property is transferred to the parents. If the parents themselves are dead, and the deceased has no spouse or children, property is then distributed along a particular order, regardless of the intent, desire, or wishes of the deceased. Individual state laws will apply, unless there is a will.

A will is a testamentary document, meaning it has no effect until the party is deceased, and it can be changed as long as the party is mentally competent. At death, the will is admitted to probate, the process whereby it is registered with the court. Thereafter, the wishes of the deceased are to be followed by the executor named in the will. Many times it is not necessary to have a full probate of an estate. Many states have enacted laws allowing the deceased's wishes to be carried out without the necessity of any court action, if it is a small estate as determined by a dollar limit set by the state. While this process is meant to simplify and streamline, it is usually necessary to employ a lawyer to prepare the proper documentation in order to transfer a deceased's property. The attorney's fees are much lower here than for a full probate.

When a full probate (court proceeding) is necessary to effectuate, or carry out, the desires of the deceased, it is generally necessary to employ an attorney to prepare the documentation to be submitted to the court. When looking for an attorney, a client must find one with whom she is comfortable. By the same token, an attorney with a gay or lesbian client must realize and be sensitive to the special problems which may arise between the two families — the biological one and the gay or lesbian one. One such problem is the biological family's contesting or ignoring the will of the deceased, especially where property is left to a friend or lover, or to a gay or lesbian organization. A recent case in the East illustrates this point. A gay man had a will which left all of his property to gay organizations. His nieces, the closest relatives in this situation, contested the will. The National Gay Rights Advocates and a local attorney defended the will. In this situation, a small monetary settlement was given to the nieces, rather than litigating the matter. The cost of defense of the contest would have exceeded the amount given the relatives as settlement. The result of any litigation is never one hundred percent predictable. In this case, the nieces decided to take settlement, and the defense counsel thought it best to pay them, rather than leave anything to chance.

The moral of the story is this: While it is extremely important to have a will drawn up, and while it is very important that it be drawn up properly, doing so does not always prevent a court battle. As stated earlier, a will is intended to effectuate the desires of the deceased with the least amount of conflict and uncertainty. Many times it is important to consult an attorney as soon as possible after a death to fully effectuate the deceased's desires and limit possible tax liability.

Potential problems exist regarding the disposition of the body. Many states have adopted a Uniform Anatomical Gift

Act. The laws of each state must be checked to see what that particular jurisdiction has done. If the state has adopted the Uniform Anatomical Gift Act, there are provisions whereby the donor may make a gift of all or parts of his or her body in a written document other than a will. The statement should be specific as to the extent of the donation. For example, if the donor wishes only to leave a cornea, that should be stated; or, if the donor wishes to leave his entire body, that should be made clear. The document should indicate who is to be the recipient of the organ or body. It should attest to the mental competence of the donor. And it should indicate that the donor is making the donation freely. Most states require this documentation to be signed by the donor in the presence of two witnesses. Certain organizations provide donor cards upon request. The gift of an organ or body can also be stipulated in a will.

If the deceased has not made plans for the disposal of her remains, the law allows for others to decide what to do. The Uniform Anatomical Gift Act delineates a priority for those who have a right to make a gift after death. The list includes the administrator or executor named, or any person authorized or obligated to dispose of the body. Most states give precedence to the estate administrator, the deceased's spouse, children, parents, and next of kin, in that order. The Act also includes a section stating that a gift shall not be made or accepted when a member of the same or a higher priority objects. If, for example, a wife were to object to the gift of a deceased's body to a medical school by the executor of the estate, the medical school should refuse the gift.

If the deceased has died without leaving a will or a specific gift under the Anatomical Gift Act, the right of burial belongs to the next of kin. Here, too, the law defines a priority, or pecking order, which is used to determine who may plan funeral arrangements. A lover is not included in this pecking order in any way. The pecking order applies not only to the ability to make gifts of the body and organs, but also to the right to determine funeral arrangements, including place of burial, type of ceremony, whether services will be held, and who may attend.

The duty of burial becomes a problem where the deceased

is financially insolvent and neither friends nor relatives are willing or able to assume the financial obligation of the funeral. Some states provide for burial expenses through their Public Aid Offices where necessary. In some cases where the deceased is under a certain age (as defined by state law), the parent may be legally responsible for funeral expenses. If the deceased has entered into a legal marriage, the spouse may be legally obligated to pay funeral expenses. Funeral expenses are generally only the obligation of the deceased's estate.

The executor is legally empowered to dispose of the body without a court order. Legislators were sensible enough to realize that it would be practically impossible for an executor to take the will, file it with the court, and have the executor formally appointed prior to making funeral arrangements or making gifts of the deceased's body. In situations not requiring court action, the named executor is not liable for funeral expenses unless he personally guarantees payment.

As laws continue to develop in this area, they become more and more complicated, particularly in regard to relationships not recognized by church or state. The only way for an individual to be reasonably assured that her wishes will be fulfilled after death is to leave a will that follows the letter of the law. A pamphlet issued by the National Gay Rights Advocates retells the anecdote which opens this chapter. Not only did Alice B. Toklas receive nothing from Gertrude Stein's estate, she also lost much of her own property which the two women had acquired together. The best recommendation which can be made to someone dealing with a lover's death is this: GET LEGAL HELP! While a lawyer is never able to guarantee that you will not be sued, an attorney will be able to make clear the risks incumbent to your actions. A fully informed client is likely to be able to deal with the emotionally charged issues of death and property settlement more logically than an uninformed one. When choosing a lawyer, it is important to find one who can deal with gay or lesbian relationships and who understands and realizes that in many cases gay and lesbian relationships take emotional priority over biological ties. The lawyer must be willing to go into court and defend gay and lesbian relationships and, especially, the rights of lovers over blood relatives. Many local and national organizations can make referrals or provide a list of attorneys who have exhibited sensitivity and understanding in dealing with gay-related legal problems. Clients must feel comfortable discussing all aspects of their relationship with a lawyer. When dealing with the grief associated with the death of a loved one, no one needs to be judged by the person from whom help is being sought.

VI

Alternative Gay and Lesbian Helping Resources

Chapter 28

Gay and lesbian counseling centers: History and functions

Charna Klein

BACKGROUND AND FUNCTIONS OF GAY AND LESBIAN COUNSELING CENTERS

This chapter is based on seven years of on-site research at the Seattle Counseling Service for Sexual Minorities from 1973 to 1980, two national field trips to visit gay counseling services, a questionnaire of gay counseling services, and a follow-up telephone survey. The results of this research are fully written up and available in a research monograph entitled *Counseling Our Own: The Lesbian/Gay Subculture Meets the Mental Health System* (1986).

The topics discussed in this chapter are the following: the background and functions of gay counseling services, the nature of gay counseling services and typical services provided to gay and lesbian clients, client referral, the limitations of gay counseling services to the mainstream mental health system, and client problems and perspectives.

Social theorists and radical activists of the 1960s spoke of a sense of alienation induced by a modern technological society and of a need to return to a sense of individual worth and community. Return to a community concept was evidenced in the overall culture and in community mental health care. It was also evidenced subculturally, and in alternative social services in which people tried to gain more say in decision-making about mental health treatment.

A process occurred whereby unmet needs among subcultural peoples led to social movements, then movement organizations, and finally to health and social services and to a variety of other kinds of organizations. Gay and lesbian counseling services developed out of both the Gay Liberation Movement and, later, the Lesbian Feminist Movement. A gay movement in the 1950s, known as the Homophile Movement, had as its goal the achievement of acceptance for the gays and lesbians in society. A major function of this movement was counseling, to help gay and lesbian individuals adjust to society. By the early 1960s, a struggle surfaced between homophile factions over how to view homosexuality. The Society for Individual Rights looked to mental health professionals to redefine homosexuality as good. The Mattachine Society split, one faction advocating study by mental health professionals to find out whether homosexuality is good, and the other faction defining gay as good. By 1965, Mattachine formally opposed the American Psychiatric Association's classification of homosexuality as an illness.

In 1969, with the birth of the Gay Liberation Movement, adjustment of gays and lesbians to society was no longer called for; rather, the call was for society to change. The onus of the problem was redefined as one not of gays and lesbians but of societal homophobia. Confrontation tactics to change professional mental health providers' views of homosexuality in the early 1970s resulted in the American Psychiatric Association's resolution in 1973 to reclassify homosexuality. It was now to be called a "sexual orientation disturbance" only for those "who are either bothered by, in conflict with, or wish to change their sexual orientation." The APA decided that self-accepting persons should not be labeled as sick. Despite the fact that the APA and other professional organizations declassified homosexuality as an illness, many practitioners continued to treat such clients as mentally ill.

The mental health field is a key arena in which culturally homophobic and subculturally gay and lesbian dissonances and accepting views are played out. While sectors of the larger society continue to label gayness as a sickness, the gay and lesbian subcultures view lesbians and gays as healthy.

Gays and lesbians often experience difficulty in traditionally-oriented mental health settings, where a sick label is slapped on them. The assumption of a sick role may not be accepted by the client, and such an assumption is neither useful nor desirable. A sick role can only keep people believing they are sick and encourage them to continue to act sick. Homosexuality is not "cured," and gay and lesbian people normally do not want to change their sexual orientation. Such clients often have experienced inappropriate treatment from practitioners who focused on changing their clients' sexual orientations, rather than on dealing with their actually presented problems. The mental health system and its practitioners have often been perceived by gays and lesbians as the enemies. A need developed among these clients for their own mental health delivery systems, ones based on the premise that we gay people have legitimate mental health needs, rather than on the premise that homosexuality is a sickness.

Alternative gay and lesbian counseling centers sprang up in cities all over the country. The first of these centers began in Seattle in 1969, and it is flourishing today. Other centers developed in the early 1970s.

The impetus for starting the centers came directly or indirectly from the Gay Liberation Movement. The founders of these centers were themselves in, or were influenced by, this movement. Centers were started through the valiant efforts of one or more individuals. They recruited other talented persons, wrote grants, developed community credibility, and made their organizations work. They began without support from the larger society and mental health systems, facing many barriers and a dearth of funds.

Most centers combine peer and professional counseling, with the majority of counselors being peer counselors. The philosophy behind peer counseling is that persons who are on a par and share similar life experiences can most comfortably and effectively relate to one another in therapeutic interaction. This is especially applicable to minority, stigmatized, and oppressed people, such as gays and lesbians.

The argument for peer counseling is sound. Studies of therapeutic outcome indicate similar results for peer and professional counseling. Peer counselors usually recognize their limitations and refer clients to professional therapists when necessary, and peer counseling centers refer as a matter of course as needed.

While gay and lesbian counselors are invariably accepting and supportive of homosexuality, this may not be the case for heterosexual counselors. But heterosexual counselors

who overcome homophobia can be good, empathetic counselors for gay and lesbian clients. In fact, one gay counseling
center stated a desire to balance its staff with gay and straight
counselors.

TYPICAL SERVICES PROVIDED FOR THE GAY AND LESBIAN CLIENT

Services for lesbian and gay clients have in common an
ethic of acceptance of and a purpose to provide positive
services to lesbians and gay men. Organizations which provide mental health or social services to these clients may be
either sexually integrated or sexually separated. Typical services offered are telephone, drop-in, in-person, and group
counseling, education, and consultation, and often alcohol
and drug abuse treatment and advocacy services.

Such counseling centers take a client-oriented approach
to counseling, according to which clients are not labeled. The
clients present their problems and seek assistance from the
counselor to better define and work on them.

Services typically offered to lesbian and gay clients are
individual, couple, and group counseling. The telephone is
sometimes a significant medium used for informational requests about gay and lesbian community resources, the
nature of counseling services available, or for counseling
itself. Clients who wish to maintain anonymity, or who are
simply too frightened to come in person, may prefer telephone
counseling. Counseling is often delivered on an emergency
drop-in basis, while in-person counseling by prearranged
appointment is the main service modality. Group services
range from open rap groups to closed, intensive therapy
groups. Groups may be for women, men, older or younger
gays, bisexuals, or persons in mixed-orientation marriages.
Or the groups may have a functional, topical, or technical
focus, such as alcoholism, assertiveness training, self-hypnosis, coming out, couple relationships, or a variety of lifestyle issues.

These centers typically offer education and consultation
services to such audiences as mental health providers,
various professionals, students, and the general public. The
purposes of these services are to improve treatment and

increase knowledge and understanding of gays and lesbians.

Centers may offer alcoholism and drug abuse counseling and client advocacy services. Client advocacy services may involve contact with community agencies, hospitals, police, or government. Advocacy has been done in the legal, medical, and social services areas. Advocates assist their clients in receiving non-biased, positive services when dealing with mainstream agencies and personnel. Alcohol and drug abuse is a major problem in gay and lesbian communities, so this is an important area of counseling. These particular services are sometimes offered in separate centers.

Obviously, the delivery of a wide variety of needed services requires a capable staff. An advantage of gay and lesbian counseling service centers is that clients can draw from staff who are individually and collectively knowledgeable and experienced in meeting a variety of needs, including the provision of information on community resources, individual and group counseling, counseling in healthful living as lesbians and gays, and counseling in adjustment to society-at-large. Counselors usually represent a diversity of sex, age, ethnic group, class, lifestyle, counseling style, and experience in being gay or lesbian.

LIMITATIONS OF THE AGENCIES

With all the positive services these counseling centers provide, they are limited in several ways due to financial constraints. Because these counseling services do not partake of the regular government funding for mental health services, they have had to struggle for adequate and stable funding. Inadequate funding effectively limits paid professional personnel, adequate facilities, and coverage, especially in rural areas.

The Comprehensive Mental Health Care Act provides for community mental health centers on the basis of area and population. Although the CMHC are supposedly "comprehensive" and "community based," they are not mandated to provide services specific to the gay and lesbian populations.

The services vacuum filled by gay and lesbian counseling services is not necessarily supported financially. In answer to our questionnaire, financial problems were perceived as the main problem by most of the centers. In the course of their development, some of the service agencies were willing and able to obtain government funding. Others were either unwilling to accept the strings attached to government money or unable to obtain it. Other sources of funds have been foundation grants, fund raisers, client fees, donations, pledges, CETA jobs, and third-party payments.

While the government-supported community mental health centers can afford to have paid, professional mental health staffs, gay and lesbian counseling services are lucky if at least core staff members are paid a survival salary to keep things going. Most staffs are part-time volunteers who may or may not be professionally trained mental health workers. The essential job of counseling, particularly of the seriously disturbed, is, therefore, met in an uneven way. When one compares the paid staff members at a CMHC and the unpaid staff members at a gay and lesbian counseling agency across the street, one might also raise questions of quality and equality of services for straight vs. gay and lesbian clients. Interestingly enough, gay and lesbian counseling services seem to do a praiseworthy job, with peer counselors performing feats a paid professional across the street may not be qualified to do.

Other effects of financial constraints are inadequate facilities and geographic coverage. Old, ill-repaired, and crowded counseling service facilities often do not compare favorably with government-funded facilities, and gay and lesbian counseling services are generally limited to large cities and are lacking in rural areas altogether.

RELATIONSHIPS TO MAINSTREAM AGENCIES

As gay and lesbian counseling services grew and gained credibility as professional mental health agencies, many turned to and were able to get public funding, or otherwise became affiliated with mainstream agencies. Association with the mainstream mental health system enabled economic survival and a chance to have a positive influence for gays and lesbians.

Concomitant with government funding came formal and hierarchical structures, rules and regulations, increased record-keeping, paid staff positions, more professionally educated staff, agency directors, and boards of directors. The necessity of maintaining and developing funding resulted in increased numbers and power of paid administrative staff.

On the negative side, government funding meant the loss of full ownership of gay and lesbian counseling services by adult gay and lesbian communities, and the imposition of government authority. On the positive side, government funding meant a better organized, more professional approach to running these agencies, and the provision of a source of income for staff workers, enabling staff to make longer time commitments and to perform the jobs that volunteers are loath to do, such as record-keeping.

Centers which received government funding both enjoyed and suffered the consequences, for, given a boost, they were also vulnerable to a fall. Such was the case with Pittsburgh's Persad Center. Persad's fifteen-thousand-dollar annual county funding was cut off, causing financial distress. Despite support of the governor, the National Association of Social Workers, the Greater Pittsburgh Psychological Association, the county administrator, and the Board of Mental Health and Mental Retardation, eighty percent of the mental health system in the area, and thousands of petition signatures, Persad lost its court battle against the two county commissioners who were responsible for the funding cutoff in a legally correct, if unjust, decision. The ruling was based on the non-existence of a right of agencies, as distinguished from individuals, to any government funds.

Centers might also experience the problem of getting too much money too fast. The Gay Community Services Center in Los Angles began in 1971 with staff sometimes having to panhandle the $250 rent. Two years later, with large federal and county government grants, the budget climbed to almost half a million dollars in four months. Financial, structural, and personnel problems led to a crisis which threatened the existence of the Center, a crisis finally overcome.

Another case story is that in San Francisco, gays and lesbians were unsuccessful in bids for government funding. As an alternative, they got themselves on the staffs of public agencies, including Mission Mental Health, Fort Help, the

Center for Special Problems, and the Berkeley Free Clinic.

In general, the advantages for gay and lesbian counseling services having mainstream status, or mainstream affiliation, outweigh the disadvantages. Acceptance and respect from the larger mental health systems are important to most gay and lesbian counseling centers for reasons of funding, client referral, and education and consultation work with providers. By having this status, gay counseling services personnel feel they are having a positive impact on the larger mental health system.

HOW TO REFER CLIENTS

Where no gay or lesbian counseling services exist, especially in rural areas, professionals can consider a number of options: hire gay and lesbian mental health personnel for existing mental health facilities, train existing personnel by local or non-local gay and lesbian counselors, refer clients to a local gay or lesbian private therapist or to a heterosexual therapist who has a reputation for providing positive services to lesbians and gays, refer clients to the least distant gay and lesbian counseling center, refer them to someone who will counsel by telephone or letter, or refer the clients to gay and lesbian service groups that are other than mental health agencies in a nearby area. If referring professionals are not knowledgeable about pertinent gay resources, they should contact local gay hotlines or organizations, or the National Gay and Lesbian Task Force in New York City. (For further help in referral, see Chapter 31 in this book.)

In considering whether to make a referral, professionals can ask themselves these questions:

1. Am I homophobic to an extent that will negatively impact my ability to provide positive services to a lesbian or gay client?

2. Am I knowledgeable about gay and lesbian lifestyles, issues, and resources?

If professionals are either homophobic or ignorant about gay persons, they should refer their clients to someone else. Professionals should be open and straightforward with their clients in discussing any personal prejudices they may have toward gays and lesbians. Referrals should be made with the express permission of the client and in consideration of the client's readiness to accept gay or lesbian counseling. Referrals should then be made to a private therapist or a gay counseling service. However, the reputability of both should first be checked out with and confirmed by several gay organizations within the community the therapist or gay counseling group serves.

REFERENCE

1. Klein, C. (1986). *Counseling our own: The lesbian/gay subculture meets the mental health system.* Renton, WA: Publication Services, Inc.

Chapter 29

The emerging gay and lesbian hospice movement

Donald J. Catalano

"Hospice" is a term that was used in the Middle Ages to describe a way station where travelers, pilgrims, and ill people could stop, rest, and depend on receiving humane care. It comes from the same root word as hospital and hospitality. The term "hospice" has also come to mean a philosophy of caregiving for terminally ill persons, their families, and friends, which includes a choice of receiving care in the home rather than in an institution, though in some instances care in a special hospice facility is also available.

Each hospice program is unique to the special needs of its own community, but all hospices have in common these features: an emphasis on controlling pain and other symptoms of the disease, the availability of nursing services twenty-four hours a day, a focus on dying individuals and their social networks as the unit of care, a multidisciplinary and professional team approach to service delivery assisted by trained volunteers, and a recognition that follow-up bereavement services are integral to helping the survivors complete the process of grieving and adjusting to the loss.

The hospice philosophy recognizes that death is the ultimate bio-psychosocial crisis, and that all persons involved at one time or another may require or desire physical relief, emotional support, and understanding for coping with the changes and losses occurring in their personal and social lives. For gay men and lesbians, these feelings and needs may be underrecognized and unmet by traditional service-providing organizations. This may occur for a variety of reasons. Sometimes gay individuals live in self-imposed isolation as a result of not disclosing information about their social networks, for fear of exposing themselves or their friends as being gay or lesbian. The expulsion by family and friends, or the effects of institutionalized homophobia are yet other reasons. For gay men and lesbians who no longer wish to accept second-class treatment in life or in death, the prospect of developing specific hospice services for lesbians and gay men facing terminal illness is rapidly gaining momentum.

The involvement of gays and lesbians in the hospice movement has increased recently because so many are confronted with the impact of the AIDS crisis. Its swift onset, ravaging course, and fatal outcome make AIDS a modern scourge which affects more young gay persons, their families, and friends than has any other biological or social affliction affected them in our history. This epidemic places tremendous strains on individuals and groups who may be ill prepared — emotionally, financially, socially, or physically — to confront mortality and all its ramifications for survivorship. The unexpectedness and suddenness of AIDS precipitates a crisis for many individuals and their loved ones, as well as for the health and social welfare institutions to which they turn for help. Hospice care provides an important alternative response to the needs of people and institutions caught up in the AIDS crisis.

This chapter will examine trends in the hospice movement which have special appeal to lesbians and gays. It will also describe efforts to develop specific lesbian and gay hospice services. Special attention will be given to the need for lesbian-and-gay-identified hospice services to work collaboratively with mainstream organizations in order to meet current needs, as well as to gain experience for developing specific services for the future needs of our gay communities.

TRENDS IN THE HOSPICE MOVEMENT

The first American hospice was founded in Connecticut in 1974. Since then, over 1,200 hospice programs have been established in this country. The emphasis then, as now, is to have the hospice caregivers provide their care to dying individuals and their social networks in the comfort, familiarity, and privacy of their own homes. In certain situations, however, it is necessary to care for individuals at an inpatient hospice unit. These units are designed to be as homelike as possible, allowing for unrestricted visiting twenty-four hours a day, the use of kitchen facilities, and even visits by favorite pets. Whether at home or at an inpatient unit, every effort is made to give the dying persons control over their own lives. Allowing these individuals to decide for themselves when to eat, bathe, receive visitors, take medications, or move about, helps them maintain their sense of dignity, humanity, and self-esteem.

While it has long been recognized that terminal illness and death affect family members and close friends, the hospice movement from its outset paid special attention to the fact that grieving is a natural response which begins before the loved one dies. To address the needs of these care-giving survivors, hospice programs offer bereavement counseling to assist family and friends to perform their roles as the dying individual's most intimate care providers. Hospice counselors also encourage the caregivers and survivors to express their loss and pain and to engage in their own searches for meaning during the dying process and after the death.

Perhaps the hospice movement's major appeals to gay men and lesbians are its respect for the individuality of the dying person and its attention to that person's choice of lifestyle and social relationships. Unlike most modern health care settings, hospices are committed to tailoring their services to the idiosyncratic needs of their clients. Most institutional settings, explicitly or implicitly, require the patient to conform to the routine and regulations of the institution. Under these conditions, gays and lesbians have traditionally been deprived of visits by lovers, friends, or surrogate family members who may not fit the facility's limited definition of family as people "related by blood, marriage or adoption."(4)

To counter this discrimination, a routine part of hospice care today involves counseling dying individuals to make certain that their wishes are explicitly known to all who may be involved with them during the dying process. This includes advising the dying about, and even sometimes assisting them with, arranging legal affairs and funerary plans through the promulgation of a written, durable power-of-attorney form and a last will and testament. In those states where these documents are legally recognized, dying individuals can name a lover, a friend, a family member, or anyone they choose to act on their behalf. This action will effectively preclude the possibility that a relative, perhaps hostile to the individual and his lifestyle, will claim a right to intervene in that person's care and in the distribution of the estate.(2) (See the Legal Issues section of this book for further discussion of legal health care issues.)

The home-based focus of hospice care represents another source of appeal to gay men and lesbians. It is well recognized that the choice of friends, acquaintances, artwork, literature, and style of environment all reflect a person's sense of identity. Nowhere is this more apparent than in the individual's home, where one maintains substantial control over who visits and when, decides what is on the walls, and in general sets the pace of the household. Particularly for gays and lesbians, the home is that domain in which one can be most like oneself. Home-based hospice care thus offers appeal and advantage to gays and lesbians because it allows them to retain their privacy and maximal control in a setting most familiar to them. The issue of who has control in a caregiver-patient relationship is often taken for granted in hospitals or institutional settings, where the balance is clearly tipped in favor of the professionals. In hospice care, however, the home-based practice intentionally favors the clients, who are encouraged to retain as much control as possible over the events in their lives, homes, and care.

For the caregivers and survivors, the pain of loss and the experiences of fear and loneliness culminate at the point of the terminally ill individual's death. These feelings are not unique or limited to gay men and lesbians. But they are, perhaps, more painfully experienced by them because of their socialization in a homophobic culture which repeatedly gives the message that to be gay or lesbian is to be alone, and by extension, to die alone. These are regarded as deserving consequences for people judged to be social outcasts who lead, presumably, meaningless lives. With the death of such persons, society would just as soon have other gay and lesbian people join them.(3) Not surprisingly, gay men and lesbians have developed few or no grieving rituals of their own, and in the absence of such, often find themselves participating in funeral events where the fact of the deceased's gay identity is never mentioned.

Here, again, the hospice philosophy provides an alternative. A basic tenet of hospice care is to attend to the needs of bereaved survivors, much the same as it addresses the psychosocial needs of the terminally ill individual. Each type of hospice client, the dying person or the bereaved person, confronts the dying process and attempts to draw something from the experience. For a bereaved gay or lesbian, it may be especially important for recognition to be given to the deceased person's sexual orientation and the role it played in that person's social relationships. To do otherwise would only reinforce negative social messages of personal meaninglessness and isolation, all of which might further complicate the survivors' bereavement. Addressing these needs in a structured way, hospice care provides survivors with assistance in planning funerals or memorial services. It offers them the availability of bereavement counselors for individual counseling, and bereavement groups for shared reflection and resocialization. In so doing, hospice acts to honor the complete memory of the deceased individual, while taking care to reduce the survivors' risks of succumbing to psychological and physical illnesses themselves.

EMERGING GAY AND LESBIAN HOSPICE SERVICES

Because hospice serves to counter our society's considerable uneasiness with mortality and death, the movement to develop hospice services typically arises from a small, grassroots group of individuals who share a basic philosophy about how one should die. Basic to this philosophy for gay men and lesbians in the second decade of the Gay Liberation Movement is a strong sense that no one in the gay community should experience death alone; nor should dying and deceased gay people be subjected to discrimination or other degradations at the hands of an historically hostile majority culture.

In San Francisco in 1980, one hundred lesbians and gay men participated in a community meeting convened to raise questions about whether there was a shared sense of need for a specific gay and lesbian hospice. Numerous persons there spoke about the real and perceived injustices they had personally experienced surrounding the deaths of gay persons. By the end of the evening, those assembled charged a core group of men and women — primarily helping professionals (a counselor, a rabbi, a social worker, a priest, a dentist, and several political aides) — to conduct a more thorough needs assessment of mainstream service-provider agencies, as well as of known gay and lesbian professionals, to determine whether there was a significant need and desire for a gay and lesbian hospice. The responses to their survey questionnaires uniformly showed two results: the mainstream providers (including hospitals, physicians, and counseling agencies) rarely acknowledged or recognized that they had gay or lesbian clients; and conversely, gay and lesbian professionals who worked in those traditional settings consistently reported that they recognized gay men and lesbians in agency or private practice caseloads who could benefit from hospice services sensitive to gays and lesbians.

With the needs assessment data analyzed, the core group moved ahead to formalize an organization to implement a gay and lesbian hospice. In 1981, the organization Coming Home was founded as a non-profit, charitable corporation dedicated to providing hospice care to lesbians and gay men. Then, following a path previously traveled by similar organizations, Coming Home struggled for almost two years to determine whether the proposed hospice should be primarily comprised of trained volunteers (under the supervision of a paid executive director), or whether it should follow a more professional model staffed by nurses and social workers, with volunteers and physician consultation available.

At the same time, as the beginning of the AIDS epidemic started to tax the resources of mainstream service providers, an already-existing volunteer counseling service for dying persons and their families stepped in to begin addressing the needs of persons afflicted by the mysterious AIDS illness. The Shanti Project, founded in Berkeley, California as a non-gay organization, eventually emerged as a leading gay-identified service organization when it moved its base of operations to San Francisco to meet the burgeoning needs of the AIDS epidemic. Shanti, which is a Sanskrit word meaning "inner peace," developed a comprehensive volunteer counseling program which provides individual counseling, support groups, residences for able-bodied PWAs, a practical support program (e.g., volunteers to provide help with practical matters such as shopping, laundry, and physicians' appointments), and a unique on-site counseling service for PWAs who are hospitalized on the AIDS-designated ward at San Francisco General Hospital.

With the Shanti Project's volunteer counseling services successfully established, the Coming Home organization then identified the provision of skilled, professional services (i.e., medical, nursing, social work) as the major remaining unmet need for terminally ill lesbians and gay men. Consequently, in 1983, Coming Home approached the mainstream Hospice of San Francisco agency with a proposal to provide that organization with a variety of auxiliary supports in return for a commitment of gay-sensitive service delivery by its professional staff. Under an agreement between the two organizations, Coming Home participated in funds development, in in-service training, in outreach and publicity, in volunteer and employee recruitment, and in representation on the policy-making body of the Hospice of San Francisco. In return, the *non-gay* Hospice of San Francisco has become one of the leading service providers to the lesbian and gay communities in San Francisco.

In 1984, the Hospice developed a specific AIDS Home Care and Hospice team which currently serves a daily caseload of fifty-five. To accommodate this dramatic growth in service capacity, Hospice of San Francisco has necessarily expanded its professional staff and volunteer cadre, in which gay and lesbian professionals and volunteers are well represented. In 1985, Coming Home and Hospice of San Francisco were approached by a Roman Catholic parish located in the Castro Street district of San Francisco to explore the feasibility of converting an abandoned convent to become a residence for terminally ill older persons and those dying with AIDS. The prospect of establishing a hospice facility in San Francisco's noted gay neighborhood, based on cooperation between the lesbian and gay communities, the Roman Catholic

Archdiocese of San Francisco, the Hospice of San Francisco, and public and private monies, gives testament to the powerful appeal the hospice philosophy holds for gay men and lesbians, and the degree to which their needs are being integrated into mainstream service delivery models.

IMPLICATIONS FOR COMMUNITY DEVELOPMENT

The successful introduction of gay-and-lesbian-sensitive hospice services to the human services field bodes well for the evolution of the gay and lesbian communities. For students of organizational theory, the hospice experience in San Francisco has shown that gays and lesbians, as a minority group, not only can create their own viable volunteer service agency, but they can also successfully negotiate with mainstream service providers to respond to specific lesbian and gay needs. The existence of the two types of agencies — one clearly gay-identified and the other non-gay, but having a gay-identified auxiliary to reinforce its accessibility and sensitivity — reflects more accurately (and can respond more appropriately to) the diversity of needs in the lesbian and gay communities. There are now hospice services available for those who clearly wish to receive care from a specifically gay or lesbian provider. And there are services available from a respected mainstream provider, where quality care is the primary issue and gay and lesbian acceptance and sensitivity are assured.

Looking ahead to the turn of the next century, when large numbers of gay and lesbian "baby boomers" begin to have later-life dependency needs for which they will likely come to expect gay-and-lesbian-sensitive services, the organizational experiments of the 1980s hospice pioneers will hopefully have introduced some of the basic infrastructure for the health and social welfare institutions of the gay communities of the twenty-first century.(1) One of the ironies of the AIDS crisis is that it may prove to be, in retrospect, the opportunity that led us to be creative in planning now for the type of human service organizations we hope to have available in the future.

REFERENCES

1. Catalano, D., Velentine, W.E., and Greever, L. (1981). Social services for aging gay men. *Catalyst: Journal of the Institute for Social Service Alternatives, 3*, 47-60.

2. Dlugos, T. (1980). Gay widows: Your lover just died and the family arrives to take everything. *Christopher Street, 4*, 23-24.

3. Rofes, E. (1983). *"I thought people like that killed themselves:" Lesbians, gay men, and suicide.* San Francisco: Grey Fox Press.

4. Stevenson, J.S. (1977). *Issues & Crises during middlescence.* New York: Appleton-Century-Crofts.

Chapter 30

Self-help groups for gays, lesbians, and their loved ones

Michael Eller and Douglas J. King

The self-help group functions for its members. It is organized around addressing a common concern. Individuals' separate agendas are transcended. Continual focusing on the common agenda leads to unity and a power base that is collectively sustaining and useful. The group usually functions without professionals, though some support groups, such as Survivors of Incest or AIDS support groups, may employ a group facilitator to assist the group in exploring its common concerns.

The Boston Women's Health Collective, for example, describes their group experience as one which "may and does include individual action, but it is based on mutual support and shared experiences." They point out that what seems to be a personal problem often can eventually become identified as a political, social, or cultural problem. The group breaks down that sense of personal isolation and singularity caused by an unhealthy condition or habit. It gives persons the strength to change or to cope.(1) Self-help cannot be a closet activity.

We do not mean "self-care" when we discuss non-professional "self-help." "Self-care" means those personal-care activities delegated to us by health care practitioners. Examples of self-care would be giving ourselves injections or monitoring our urine. The goal of self-care, however, is not to put control of care in the hands of the people, or even to encourage them to define their own needs. Self-care can be thought of as cost containment: the procedure and the process remain under professional control.

Self-help, on the other hand, as a defining and growth-enhancing experience, exists in many formats within the gay and lesbian community. There are self-help groups which are directly related to mainstream recovery groups (such as the "anonymous" twelve-step programs of Alcoholics Anonymous, Narcotics Anonymous, Valium Anonymous, etc.), and issues-oriented groups such as those dealing with relationships or recreation. Then there are self-help groups unique to the gay and lesbian experience, such as coming-out groups and support groups for the heterosexual loved ones of gays and lesbians.

COMING-OUT GROUPS

Staying closeted is all too inviting in a homophobic society. By hiding, the individual experiences a sense of isolation, self-pity, anxiety, and resentment which thrives in the darkness of closets. For persons who can no longer live with these darkly-lit monsters, the coming-out group provides opportunities that no other service can offer. Gays or lesbians seeking help will probably meet people in the group who are happier and more comfortable with themselves than they are. The group members will be able to share feelings and fears along every step of coming out, and they can offer a sense of acceptance which, in turn, melts isolation, the sense of differentness, and low self-esteem.

MIXED-ORIENTATION GROUPS

Sometimes gays and lesbians enter into male-female, or mixed-orientation, marriages while passing as straight. Later, when they find that they want to become involved in the gay and lesbian community and come out, they find that they and their loved ones need the expertise of those who have been in a similar life situation. The heterosexual marriage partner, for example, will need much support, the opportunity to grieve, and opportunities to work through any bitterness or feelings of inadequacy. An example of a group specific to heterosexuals is Straight Partners and Parents and Friends of Lesbians and Gays (P-FLAG). Examples of those groups specific to gays and lesbians are Bi-Ways, Gay and Lesbian Parents, and the Gay Married Men's Association (GAMMA).

SINGLE-GENDER GROUPS

Lesbian and heterosexual women's groups may serve some of the same purposes as coming-out groups by relieving the sense of aloneness or isolation. Women together can struggle to define their own health care needs and social and support issues. Women-only groups provide a sense of personal control over their own health and welfare. Likewise, gay men's groups, like other men's groups, provide an atmosphere where men can be free to discuss their unique problems and needs.

COPING WITH AIDS

AIDS and ARC support groups, support groups for the "worried well" (those who test positive for the AIDS antibodies, but who are symptomless for AIDS and ARC), and survivor groups are invaluable for the task of grieving and getting over the loss of health or life. Many gay men report that, although health care providers attempt to reassure them, their fears of dying and fears of living in poor or diminished health will not go away. Here, mutual experience and sharing provide the inducements for opening up about and discussing the fears of death and the subsequent at-hand struggle to live richly. Sometimes, another patient can do more toward relieving another's nagging fear than a host of health professionals. AIDS and ARC support groups are especially helpful for the ARC patient. Typically, the patient with ARC experiences great distress, since he is unsure if he is living or dying. Such individuals often need the ongoing support and confrontation that a group of peers will offer. The "worried well" and loved ones surviving the deaths of persons with AIDS can also benefit from self-help groups.

SURVIVOR GROUPS

Often men and women are survivors of traumatic experiences and harbor deep-seated feelings. Members of incest-survivor groups, for example, find a deeply needed opportunity to share their pain, their sense of rage, and the feelings of being "unlovable" which grow from their long-held secrets.

TWELVE-STEP PROGRAMS

Compulsive or addictive persons and their loved ones often find solace and a rekindled hope in twelve-step programs which are based upon the twelve suggestions for attitude and behavior changes developed by Alcoholics Anonymous in the 1930s. In the groups, the persons share their experiences, strengths, and hopes with each other. They tell what their lives used to be like before coming to the group, what prompted them to join the group, and what their lives are like now. One of the most powerful aspects of these groups is the "can do" mentality, rather than the attitude of "Thou shalt not." Rather than being taught to repress negative behaviors, one is encouraged and supported to develop positive concepts, perspectives, and behaviors. Whether the newcomers join involuntarily, or are drawn to a twelve-step program out of a sense of hope, they are all looking for proof that the program can work for them. Thus, role models (persons who have been helped by the group) are critical. Their sharing of self, their enthusiasm, and their encouraging the newcomer to talk all make the programs work.

Twelve-step programs have blossomed in the past few decades both in the types of programs and in the numbers of members. Some of the twelve-step groups for the addicted or compulsive person are Alcoholics Anonymous, Alcoholics Together, Narcotics Anonymous, Valium Anonymous, Cocaine Anonymous, Sex Addicts Anonymous and Sexaholics Anonymous, Gamblers Anonymous, Overeaters Anonymous, Smokers Anonymous, and Parents Anonymous (for parents prone to abuse their children).

For the co-dependent person, persons who suffer greatly as a result of their closeness to the addicted or compulsive loved one, group experience is equally vital. But denial is common in co-dependent persons. They feel their lovers or other loved ones who suffer from addiction or compulsion are the ones with the problem and that the problem is not shared. Often this denial is broken down only slowly, and the co-dependent client may need repeated trips to a co-dependency twelve-step group before he realizes the group's value. Examples of groups for co-dependent persons include Al-Anon, Alatot, Co-Sexaholics Anonymous, and the like.

There is a rich variety of self-help groups available, and all offer strength, hope, power, and acceptance to their participants.

THE ROLE OF THE HELPING PROFESSIONAL

Helping professionals, those who provide direct, trained, social intervention and service, either upon request or by provocation (such as within the criminal justice system), can and do provide a valuable service to self-help groups, in particular to gay and lesbian self-help groups. In fact, sometimes self-help groups form, in large part, because of the prodding of a helping professional who recognizes a need not being met with existing resources.

The helping professional can assist the members of a newly forming group to overcome some of their fears and doubts and increase their feelings of strength. This can be done by encouraging the group's success and by expressing the need for such a group to be formed. The professional can bring to the attention of the group such items as literature, research articles, individuals with expertise, and information on similar groups.

The helping professional can also refer clients to the group. Many times it is to the professional that the client first turns with a problem, a problem which may be effectively treated with the aid of a self-help group. The helping professional can also let colleagues in the area know about the existence of the group. Because self-help groups, especially the twelve-step ones, are anonymous, they are often difficult to locate. This clandestine nature of some groups, especially gay and lesbian ones, often prevents persons who need them from obtaining their services because the clients cannot find the locations of the meetings. The helping professional is advised to know the location of these self-help groups, or to assist their gay clients in locating them.

Finally, helping professionals should be familiar with the types of groups to which they are referring their clients so that the clients are not disappointed by going to a group inappropriate for them. For example, a teenage gay alcoholic may be erroneously referred to Alateen, when he should actually be referred to Alcoholics Anonymous. The former organization is for teenage children of alcoholics, while the latter is for alcoholics themselves. Similarly, some self-help groups are just for gay men, some are just for lesbians, and yet others are open to all gay people. Knowing the particular natures of the self-help groups to which referrals are made is an imperative for helping professionals. Also, since some groups have "open" meetings, which anyone may attend, it is advisable that helping professionals go to these meetings for first-hand experience.

THE ROLE OF THE SELF-HELP GROUP

The healthy relationship between self-help groups and helping professionals depends on both parties recognizing their inherent limitations in helping. The group and the professional do not function exclusively from one another, but rather complement and augment each other for the client's growth or recovery. For example, the client may spend a few hours a week discovering self-knowledge and awareness in professional therapy, but the members in the client's self-help group may provide the inspiration to put this self-awareness into action. Likewise, professionals can provide specialized services because of their training, which members of a self-help group perhaps cannot — services such as psychotherapy, career counseling, or sex therapy.

The self-help group can assist helping professionals by providing "in-house" dialogues for them regarding gay and lesbian concerns which might be new to local service providers. The self-help group could further assist professionals by referring potential clients to them for problems that the self-help group does not address. Referrals made in this manner are encouraging and reassuring for potential clients, who often have apprehensions about approaching counselors on their own.

PITFALLS

Newcomers to self-help groups are usually fearful of others discovering their problems and are full of shame. They often fear that if they begin doing something about their difficulties, worse things will happen to them. Self-help groups can counteract some of these feelings by offering a group of people who share, or who have shared, the same predicament as the newcomer. These people have not only learned to live with their problems, but have gained strength in the process. Newcomers may make many excuses as to why such groups are not for them. They may say that they do not need helping groups for problem resolution because they can do it on their own. Or they may say that they do not like the people, the environment, or the topics; or that they do not have time, or that the meetings are too far away, or that someone might recognize them. Virtually anything can become an excuse, and it often does. Also, newcomers usually believe that they are alone in experiencing their problems. But with continued participation in the group, this feeling of separateness soon wears off. The group has much to offer, and newcomers must allow the newness to dissipate in order to avail themselves of the sense of belonging that heals. This initial reluctance to participate is part of the grieving process, grieving for something lost, for things such as alcohol, over-eating, narcotics, gambling, or promiscuous sex. This griev-ing process often manifests itself by denial, anger, ration-alization, and depression. Of course, a resolution of problems and an attainment of self-acceptance are the desired and anticipated outcomes of the grieving process.

Some people are shy. The task of reaching out to people who are afraid is an important task of self-help groups. Research indicates that loneliness is often a product of poor communication skills development. Alcoholic clients, for ex-ample, will think that they are unable to interact without being intoxicated. They may be overwhelmed with so much anxiety or shame that they cannot open themselves up for peer support. Newcomers should always be encouraged to return, even if they say, "I can't talk to these people." Some clients may not like the people they meet, but they should be reminded to place their health or life goals before individual idiosyncrasies. After all, the group members are collectively achieving those things which the client has yet to achieve, things such as gay or lesbian self-esteem, sobriety, freedom from gambling or overeating, and the like. Further, first impressions are usually not very accurate or lasting. The client should, therefore, be asked to "give it time."

Sometimes, newcomers come to gay or lesbian self-help groups from general groups. Because twelve-step programs encourage one to meet oneself, a change of sexual self-image may be necessary for some. A few gays and lesbians entering twelve-step programs believe that by fixing their addictive or compulsive behaviors, their same-sex sexual orientation will somehow disappear. This is not the case. Rather, as persons begin dealing with the problems which brought them to the twelve-step group in the first place — be it alcoholism or any other addiction — they find they still must deal with accepting their sexual orientations. It becomes important, then, for gays and lesbians to accept their sexual orientations as a positive aspect of self, just as it is critical for all compulsive or addictive persons to increase their self-esteem. Recovery itself is contingent upon acquiring a healthy sense of self-regard.

Gay and lesbian addicts may need a place to feel okay about discussing their homosexuality. Feeling a double stigma from both their addiction or compulsion problem and their sexual orientation may make them feel twice damaged or unacceptable. Finding affirmation regarding both areas is essential. (See Kus's discussion in the Alcoholism chapter in this book.)

Newcomers are an invaluable asset to the old-timers of the group. They remind them of their common and primary purpose: the sustaining of the group (the "belonging" milieu) through the power of sharing, of walking with one another. In time, deeper issues are explored among the group as trust and understanding develop, and as the group experience becomes less a necessity and more a desired way of life.

STARTING AND MAINTAINING SELF-HELP GROUPS

Much of our discussion has presumed the existence of self-help groups to which referrals can be made. In many places, especially in rural areas, self-help groups (other than A.A., perhaps) do not exist. So the charge of the helping professional and the client could be to start one. The initiation of a self-help group does not have to be elaborate. The only necessary ingredients for establishing a self-help group are: a place to meet, two or more people who share a common problem and who have the desire to work on it, and a format, or program, of recovery.

The search for a meeting place can begin with churches, hospitals, civic halls, or mental health centers, since these facilities often provide meeting space for self-help groups for free or for a nominal donation. In particular, gays and lesbians might look into the Metropolitan Community Churches (M.C.C.), Unitarian-Universalist Societies, or United Churches of Christ. These denominations have a national reputation of receptivity to gay and lesbian activities and events. This search may require the contact person to "come out," that is, to be open about her or his sexual orientation. We strongly suggest the group be honest from the very beginning as to its nature to avoid later problems. If the client is reluctant to come out, the professional may intervene in finding a meeting place.

The next necessity is a program. This might require some inquiry into established programs. The creation of rap groups or coming-out groups could be facilitated by contacting existing groups in major cities around the country to find out their formats. Some established organizations, such as A.A., have literature on how to start a new group. The prospective group might do well to study the Twelve Traditions of Alcoholics Anonymous and to adapt certain aspects of them for use by the group. Our following suggestions are taken from these Twelve Traditions, which developed through fifty years of trial and error.

Groups which want to sustain themselves beyond an immediate need or fad are encouraged to foster a sense of collective unity — a feeling that the group is "ours," our responsibility, and dynamically suited to us and our common goals.

Groups need to keep their primary purpose in focus, which helps sustain the group's autonomy and sufficiency. Money and property can be problematic responsibilities for groups. Both should be acquired and handled cautiously so that money or property does not transcend the group's purpose. Usually, money should be under collective group control.

It takes two or more persons to get a group going. Often,

a person might wish to begin a self-help group, but does not know of others who would be likely candidates. This is where helping professionals can be of assistance. One professional, knowing that his or her client wants to start such a group, may put the word out to colleagues to be on the lookout for other like clients. Or the professional may already know clients who would be good for this type of group and recommend them with their permission.

The wish to form a group can be advertised in the newspaper. Many states and cities have magazines or newsletters that are geared toward the gay and lesbian communities. Bear in mind that national news magazines, such as *The Advocate,* will many times reach gays and lesbians in rural areas. Also, there are publications specific to rural gay persons, such as *RFD,* a national gay men's country journal. Putting signs up in gay and lesbian bars, in bookstores, in church bulletins, or on college campuses may also attract interested individuals.

Groups will often grow slowly; this should not deter the fledgling members. Our experience has shown in a multitude of self-help settings that, although the growth is slow, the group will generally materialize with persistence and patience.

In closing, we would like to stress that self-help groups for gays and lesbians and their loved ones are not a replacement for professional counseling or medical treatment. Although oftentimes self-help groups are all the client needs, sometimes they are not. Thus, self-help groups may encourage individual members to seek professional treatment for some things, while professionals, in turn, may refer clients to self-help groups for exploring new and beneficial ways of living.

REFERENCES

1. Schaps, M. and Young, R. (1985). Interview with Norma Swensen and Esther Rome of the Boston Women's Health Book Collective. *Health and Medicine, 3,* 2-3.

Chapter 31
Accessing gay and lesbian health resources

Caitlin C. Ryan

Before the Stonewall Rebellion of 1969, visible gay and lesbian communities were virtually nonexistent. Few, if any, services were available then to meet the special needs of lesbian and gay clients. Those services which were available evolved mostly out of the women's health movement, which organized self-help clinics and referral networks of practitioners sensitive to the needs and concerns of women. Many women who were involved with organizing these women's services later contributed to the development of either the gay liberation movement or the lesbian feminist movement in the early and mid-seventies.

Since most lesbians and gay men were afraid to live openly in the 1950s and 1960s, an awareness of their specialized health care needs was non-existent beyond a sense of their deviance on the part of many health care workers. The perception of homosexuality as mental and social deviance had evolved over time into an official medical classification of deviance which influenced the treatment that these clients and patients would receive. Changes in the *Diagnostic and Statistical Manual* of the American Psychiatric Association reflect social and political changes in attitudes toward homosexuality, occurring largely as a result of the emergence of increasingly vocal and organized lesbian and gay communities. In 1952, the *Diagnostic and Statistical Manual* categorized "homosexuals" with individuals who committed antisocial or destructive crimes. In 1968, homosexuality was listed as a "sexual deviation" and was classified with child molesting, voyeurism, and exhibitionism. As a result of extensive lobbying on the part of many lesbian and gay rights groups and practitioners, in 1973 the American Psychiatric

Association removed homosexuality from the list of mental disorders and reclassified it as a sexual orientation disturbance only if the individuals were severely in conflict with their sexual orientation and wished to change it.

This sense of deviance, however, has continued to affect the services that many gays and lesbians have received. Patients identified as lesbian or gay have been known to receive inferior and painful treatment, as well as needlessly delayed medication and services. Those patients seeking help for a chemical dependency problem, or for clearly articulated emotional concerns, may find their sexual orientation made the issue for treatment rather than their addiction or emotional problems. Gays and lesbians who are reluctant to disclose their sexual orientation, for fear of reprisal or rejection, may be improperly screened or misdiagnosed through the practitioner's assumption of heterosexuality. For example, there could be a problem in misdiagnosing sexually-transmitted diseases (STDs) among gay men or in making inaccurate assumptions of reproductive concerns among lesbians presenting other complaints. The lack of validation for same-sex relationships and same-sex family structures has often prevented access to critically-ill patients of all but the patient's biological family, and denied lovers' rights in decision-making, a right routinely afforded heterosexual spouses. A lack of awareness of lesbian and gay health needs and concerns has prevented the development of outreach methods and the development of health maintenance programs appropriate to these special needs. Nowhere is this more evident than in the slow start of education and risk-reduction strategies offered in response to the AIDS epidemic. The lack of appropriate AIDS resources and materials becomes even more critical as one realizes that the possibility of a vaccine is still uncertain, while the number of cases of AIDS continues to rise dramatically.

In responding to an insensitive and uninformed health care system, lesbian and gay practitioners began organizing to identify the special health care needs of lesbians and gay men and to educate their colleagues. In the early 1970s, the Gay Nurses Alliance was founded as the first gay and lesbian professional health-related organization to provide support to lesbian and gay practitioners, and to forcefully impress upon local and national nursing associations the need for appropriate education and services. By 1980, almost all of the major professional health organizations had adopted public policy statements on gay and lesbian concerns and had established standing, or ad hoc, committees on such issues. Through annual national lesbian and gay health conferences and smaller local and regional events, the National Gay Health Coalition and the National Lesbian and Gay Health Foundation have shaped a national network of lesbian and gay health care workers and activists who can respond in a variety of ways. They have worked to develop appropriate curricula within the professional schools, carried on research to identify lesbian and gay health concerns, presented educational events through local organizations and institutions, and encouraged agencies to hire openly gay and lesbian practitioners and to provide outreach programs and services to lesbian and gay patients and clients. Some founded lesbian and gay health clinics and counseling centers staffed with gay and lesbian practitioners.

At present, many of these specialized services are only available in larger cities or in areas serving large lesbian and gay populations. In other areas, and even in institutions within large cities, gays and lesbians continue to encounter practitioners who are unaware of their needs. Nevertheless, with the recent proliferation of written materials and research data, and with the availability of workshops and seminars at conferences and professional meetings on lesbian and gay issues, it becomes more difficult for practitioners to remain uninformed of the health concerns of this population. An awareness of the risk factors, sexual practices, and relationship issues unique to gay and lesbian clients will help practitioners respond more accurately and sensitively to the health care needs of these clients. Also, by being aware that lesbian and gay clients often fail to divulge their sexual orientation to helping professionals for fear of homophobic reactions, professionals can try harder at establishing trusting relationships with this population and at never assuming that clients are heterosexual in orientation or in behavior.

Typical lesbian and gay health services provide STD

screening programs for gay men, lesbian health clinics, alcoholism education and aftercare programs, counseling and referral services, and AIDS-related services, including public education and direct services to people with AIDS, their families, and their friends. Most of these agencies serve lesbian and gay client populations exclusively, though the AIDS service organizations deliver services to all individuals affected by AIDS and to the general public. These agencies and clinics are usually funded through private donations and grants and with some public funding through city, county, or federal sources. Many of these agencies attempt to broaden their visibility within the larger community by developing relationships with mainstream agencies, clinics, and hospitals. Often they present in-service workshops and seminars to their staffs. For the community-based AIDS organizations, founded by concerned gay, lesbian, and heterosexual persons, extensive outreach is provided through professional training to mainstream agencies on the health care needs of people with AIDS, three-quarters of whom are gay men.

Referrals are easily made by contacting the lesbian and gay health facility to find out about available services and referral procedures. Often specialized support groups are available, in addition to basic services. Fees are usually nominal or on a sliding scale. Sample support groups would include those for lesbian mothers, gay fathers, lesbian or gay couples, gay and lesbian adolescents, individuals just coming out or acknowledging their gay or lesbian identity, and gay, lesbian, or gay-lesbian AA meetings. Likewise, there are groups for gay or lesbian batterers as well as for the victims of domestic violence, groups for lesbian or gay incest survivors, for parents of gays, for people with AIDS and with AIDS-Related Complex (ARC), groups for friends, lovers, and family members of people with AIDS, and for the survivors of those who have died from AIDS. Lesbian and gay health clinics can provide basic STD screening and health maintenance services. Referrals can be made through the clinics to sensitive specialists or to lesbian and gay practitioners for physical or mental health concerns. Most importantly, all services are provided in a way that affirms the dignity of gay and lesbian clients or patients while protecting their confidentiality.

For practitioners in rural areas, information on services may not be readily accessible. However, referral sources can be gained in a number of ways even in the most rural of areas. First, write or call your national professional organization. It will have a gay and lesbian committee or task force which will provide addresses of area representatives who can help locate local referral sources. Second, the National Gay Yellow Pages, a national annual listing of gay and lesbian businesses, organizations, and service providers, contains state-by-state listings of health practitioners and clinics that are sensitive to lesbian and gay concerns. If no health service is listed in your state, a third way to get information is to call your local college or university. Most have gay and lesbian student organizations that keep themselves up to date as to what services and resources are available in their area. The persons representing these organizations are fountains of knowledge and can lead you to lesbian or gay physicians, clergy, nurses, counselors, lawyers, and the like. Fourth, even in the most rural of states there are congregations of the Metropolitan Community Churches which are gay-and-lesbian-identified. These churches are usually listed in the Yellow Pages under "F" for Fellowship of M.C.C., under "C" for Community, or under "N" for Nondenominational. Fifth, you may contact gay or lesbian bars. In rural America, such bars serve not only as places for recreation, but also as referral and news sources. Sixth, you may use publications of the National Lesbian and Gay Health Foundation: the *National Gay Health Directory* and the *Sourcebook on Lesbian/Gay Health Care.* These include a national listing of gay and lesbian organizations, services, and practitioners. Through an annual national conference, NLGHF interacts with thousands of lesbian and gay service providers and organizations, offering a broad network extending from urban to rural areas. Seventh, community-based AIDS service organizations can often provide access to gay health networks and additional services.

Many AIDS service organizations are currently operating in major cities nationwide. A bimonthly newsletter, edited through the National Coalition of Gay Sexually Transmitted Disease Services, offers recent news on lesbian and gay health conferences, research, and related items, and is available by subscription. Inquiries for specialized service needs can be routed through the editor to practitioners and services across the country.

Since the lesbian and gay health network is extremely well developed, making a contact in one part of the country can often yield a referral source in other locations through the assistance of several individuals or organizations.

Contributors

Jan Bearwoman, B.A., is a maverick Wiccan priestess-counselor. For over ten years, Ms. Bearwoman has been doing Tarot readings and workshops on the paranormal, and for over seven years she's been teaching feminist Wicca and spiritual healing courses. At present, Jan teaches courses in meditation, relaxation, and psychic phenomena in the Iowa City area. She's been featured in several newspaper articles and television news clips, and she's currently beginning work on a book about Tarot. Jan makes her home in Coralville, Iowa, with her cat Francine.

Raymond M. Berger, M.S.W., Ph.D., is professor of social work at California State University, Long Beach. Dr. Berger is author of *Gay and Gray: The Older Homosexual Man* (University of Illinois Press, 1982 and reprinted by Alyson Publications, 1984). A nationally recognized expert in gay and lesbian aging, Dr. Berger was granted the Humanitarian of the Year Award by the Dade County Coalition for Human Rights in 1979, and the Evelyn Hooker Research Award by the Gay Academic Union in 1982. He recently co-authored a two-volume research textbook, *Planning for Research and Implementing the Research Plan,* (SAGE Publications, 1988). Dr. Berger is growing old gracefully.

Ethan Bickelhaupt, M.D., is both a family-practice physician and a psychiatrist. Dr. Bickelhaupt received his M.D. degree from the University of Washington School of Medicine in Seattle in 1978. He then did a one-year medical internship and a three-year psychiatric residency at the Menninger Foundation in Topeka, Kansas. In 1982 he realized his dream of combining the practices of both family medicine and psychiatry, specializing in the treatment of AIDS, borderline personality disorders, and administrative-forensic psychiatry. For fun, Ethan is currently writing a novel.

Frederick W. Bozett, R.N., D.N.S., a family health care nurse, received his doctor of nursing science degree from the University of California at San Francisco. Currently he's a professor in the graduate program in the College of Nursing at the University of Oklahoma Health Sciences Center in Oklahoma City. Dr. Bozett's primary interests are in fathering and homosexuality in the family, and he has written widely on gay fathers. He has edited *Gay and Lesbian Parents* (Praeger, 1987), and with Dr. Shirley Hanson he co-edited *Dimensions of Fatherhood* (Sage, 1985). He has recently reported his research on the children of gay fathers. Fred is currently working on three research projects: one on gay grandfathers; another comparing gay and nongay fathers and their children's perceptions of the fathers' parenting style and behaviors; and a longitudinal study of gay-father families.

Dana L. Broadway is a senior psychology major at the University of South Florida. She's preparing for graduate school where she hopes to work on her doctoral degree in clinical psychology. Ms. Broadway also works as a teaching assistant in a classroom with severely and profoundly handicapped children in the six-month to five-year age range. She lives in St. Petersburg, Florida, with her life partner Tammy, their dog Sappho, and their cats Butch, Smoke, and Ferron. Dana and Tammy spend their free time biking, canoeing, and enjoying the Florida sun.

Donald J. Catalano, M.S.W., M.P.H., a psychiatric social worker and gerontologist, is currently a geropsychiatric social worker at Pacific Presbyterian Medical Center in San Francisco and is president of Coming Home, a gay and lesbian auxiliary of the Hospice of San Francisco. Committed to the field of aging in both research and practice, Mr. Catalano has been a research associate with the University of California San Francisco Medical Center Anthropology Program studying family supports to older persons, and currently he's president of the National Association for Lesbian and Gay Gerontology. Besides community development and fundraising for gay and lesbian institutions and causes, Don loves to cook Italian food for his lover of ten years, watch films, sunbathe, and enjoy other pursuits befitting a California native.

Montana Christmas is the pen name of an author whose real name appears elsewhere in this book. Christmas is a behavioral scientist who is interested in gay men's spirituality. Although he uses Roman Catholicism and Alcoholics Anonymous as his spiritual base, he loves to explore how various religions deal with the issues of same-sex sexual orientation and sexual behavior. Montana makes his home in the heartland of America.

Michael Eller is currently a social psychology researcher at the Howard Brown Memorial Clinic in Chicago working through a sub-grant with the University of Michigan in Ann Arbor. Mr. Eller is supportive to addiction recovery services and has assisted local gay service agencies and political organizations.

He is also a freelance artist and writer for projects and publications in his community. Mike and his shepherd dog, Clyde, live on Chicago's North Side.

William S. Etnyre, M.S.W., A.C.S.W. is a Board Certified Diplomate in Clinical Social Work doing private practice in psychotherapy, consultation, and training. Having lived with an ileostomy since 1973, Mr. Etnyre served on the National Board of Directors of the United Ostomy Association (UOA) from 1983 to 1987 and was chairperson of its Gay and Lesbian Concerns Committee for four years. Bill was group facilitator of an AIDS support group in Seattle, and in his private practice, he currently works with individuals who have HIV illnesses. He has lectured on psychosocial issues concerning AIDS clients in Washington, Montana, British Columbia, and Alberta. A psychotherapist since 1975, he's worked with many gay clients. With Arleen Nelson, he co-authored "Counseling married gay men, married lesbians, and their spouses" in *Advances in Clinical Social Work* (1985). Other articles related to gays and lesbians who have had ostomy surgery have appeared in *The Link* (journal of the Canadian Association for Enterostomal Therapy and *The Journal of Enterostomal Therapy* (journal of the International Association of Enterostomal Therapy). Bill's other interests include backpacking, skiing, working out, running, music including piano playing, and spending time with friends.

Dana G. Finnegan, Ph.D., C.A.C., an alcoholism counselor, is Co-Director of Discovery Counseling Center in Millburn, N.J. and New York City. Dr. Finnegan is the co-founder and past co-coordinator of the National Association of Lesbian and Gay Alcoholism Professionals (NALGAP), an organization which in 1985 held its first national conference in Chicago. Currently she is a member of the Board of Directors of that organization. With her lover, Emily McNally, Dr. Finnegan co-authored *Dual Identities: Counseling Chemically Dependent Gay Men and Lesbians,* published by Hazelden in 1987. Dana teaches courses at the Rutgers Summer School of Alcohol Studies on supervision, group dynamics, change, and sexual identity. She also lectures and conducts training seminars on sexual identity issues in recovery. She and Emily live in New York City.

Bernice Goodman, M.S., A.C.S.W., C.S.W., a lesbian-feminist psychotherapist, is in private practice in New York City. Ms. Goodman is the founding chair of the National Task Force on Lesbian/Gay Issues of the National Association of Social

Workers. In addition, Ms. Goodman is president of the Board of Directors of the National Lesbian/Gay Health Foundation. Bernice has been the author of several books and articles on lesbian mothers and other lesbian and gay issues in the past. She makes her home in New York with her lover Deanna, a lesbian mother who lost her child through the law and homophobia.

Joanne Hall, R.N., M.A., is a Ph.D. candidate in nursing at the University of California, San Francisco. She is currently conducting her dissertation research about alcoholism recovery in lesbians and is funded by a fellowship from the National Center for Nursing Research within the National Institutes of Health. She has been in recovery from alcoholism throughout her fifteen years as a professional nurse. Joanne has published several articles about lesbian health and recovery from alcoholism, as well as mental health aspects of AIDS. She has presented workshops about lesbian and gay health to a variety of local and national audiences. With her lover, Pat, she enjoys running, walking, music, and movies. They live in San Francisco.

Betty Havey, M.A. is a marriage, family, and child counselor living and working in Santa Cruz, California. In addition to being a transpersonal feminist therapist for nine years, Ms. Havey is a member of a Protestant woman's community and has had fourteen years of ministry experience. Betty's special therapeutic interests include lesbian relationships, coming out issues, chemical dependency, and the special needs of adult children of parents addicted to alcohol or other chemical substances. Betty enjoys photography, outdoor activities, sunset and moonrise walks, and simple, intimate time with friends.

Cheryl Hetherington, Ph.D., is a counseling psychologist in private practice and has been a faculty member at several universities. Dr. Hetherington has worked with many individuals and couples who are dealing with addiction and co-dependency. She provides workshops across the country on nurturing healthy relationships, personality type, and gender roles. Her research interests include women's concerns, gay and lesbian issues, and health and wellness. Cheryl lives happily in Iowa City with her partner, and spends her free time gardening, making stained-glass windows, and weaving.

Mary E. Hunt, Ph.D., is a Roman Catholic theologian in the Washington, D.C. area. As the director of the Women's Alliance for Theology, Ethics and Ritual (WATER), Dr. Hunt works on a wide range of theologically-related issues. In addition, she enjoys working with women in Argentina and Chile as part of WATER's "Women Crossing Worlds" project. Dr. Hunt is on the Boards of Directors of Catholics for a Free Choice and New Ways Ministry, and on the Editorial Board of the *Journal of Feminist Studies in Religion*. Mary's hobbies include gourmet vegetarian cooking, swimming, jogging, and tennis, and currently she's writing a book titled, *Fierce Tenderness: Toward a Feminist Theology of Friendship*.

Andrew C. Irish, R.N., M.N., was practicing as an oncology nurse in Seattle while working on his master's degree at the University of Washington at the time he wrote his chapter. Mr. Irish held various national leadership positions in the Gay Nurses' Alliance between 1977 and 1987 and has been visibly active in professional nursing associations in both New York and Washington states. He has addressed audiences and classes about the interface between nursing and homosexuality from both consumers' and providers' points of view. Andrew has since completed his Master of Nursing degree and works in hospice care with the Visiting Nurses' Association of Los Angeles. Among his writings are: "Straight talk about gay patients," *(American Journal of Nursing*, August 1983); "Student of nursing ... student of life," *(Imprint*, November 1984); and his unpublished master's thesis, "Adaptation to AIDS: Changes in social network and social support as reported by gay men," (University of Washington, 1987).

Douglas J. King, A.I.A., M. Arch., is an architect with an internationally based design and engineering company. Mr. King has co-founded numerous support groups in Iowa, Michigan, and Illinois. He is involved with self-help groups in Chicago, where he also conducts and organizes workshops and seminars concerning addictions for the benefit of the gay community. In 1986, Doug was a research assistant for a study on gay men's sobriety being conducted at The University of Iowa. Also that year, he presented a paper "Starting and maintaining self-help groups for gays and lesbians" at the annual International Institute on the Prevention and Treatment of Alcoholism in Budapest, Hungary. Currently, Doug is writing a monthly column on recovery for a gay newspaper. Along with his lover Bob, a fellow architect, Doug is enjoying his new home in Chicago.

Charna Klein, as president of Consultant Services Northwest, does training and consulting in microcomputers and ethno-

that organization. With her lover Dana Finnegan, Dr. McNally co-authored *Dual Identities: Counseling Chemically Dependent Gay Men and Lesbians* for Hazelden Publications in 1987. Emily and Dana have published numerous articles on sexual identity and chemical dependency and, together with Steven Berg, they co-edited the *NALGAP Bibliography*. In her 1989 doctoral dissertation at New York University, Emily developed a stage model of identity transformation of lesbian recovering alcoholics in Alcoholics Anonymous. Emily teaches Alcoholism & Sexual Identity and Women & Alcoholism in the Rutgers Summer School of Alcohol Studies. Emily makes her home with Dana in New York City.

A. Elfin Moses, D.S.W., is currently an associate professor in the Graduate School of Social Work at the University of Tennessee, Knoxville. In addition to her teaching and writing, Ellie conducts workshops for clinicians on intervention with lesbian and gay clients and has done clinical treatment with lesbians. Dr. Moses is co-author with Robert O. Hawkins, Jr. of *Counseling Lesbian Women and Gay Men: A Life Issues Approach* (Merrill, 1982) and author of *Identity Management in Lesbian Women* (Praeger, 1978). Ellie is on the editorial board of the new *Journal of Gay and Lesbian Psychotherapy* and a member of the Lesbian and Gay Task Force of the National Association of Social Workers. She also served as special editor for lesbian and gay issues for the third edition of Kozier & Erb's book, *Fundamentals of Nursing: Concepts and Problems*. Ellie lives in Knoxville with her partner Janet and an assortment of cats and dogs.

Paul A. Paroski, Jr., M.D., a pediatrician, is currently the director of the Department of Ambulatory Care, Woodhull Medical and Mental Health Center in Brooklyn, New York. He holds an appointment as Clinical Assistant Professor, Department of Epidemiology and Social Medicine at the Albert Einstein College of Medicine in the Bronx. Dr. Paroski received his M.D. degree from the State University of New York at Buffalo and completed his residency in pediatrics at Montefiore Medical Center. Dr. Paroski has much experience in the area of health care delivery to lesbian and gay individuals. He was actively practicing at the St. Mark's Clinic, a New York gay and lesbian health facility, when he gathered the data for his chapter. In addition, Dr. Paroski is the founder and past president of the National Lesbian and Gay Health Foundation, Inc.; the founder of Lesbians and Gay People in Medicine; a former board member of the American Association of Physicians for Human Rights; a founding member of the National Gay Health Coalition; a former board member of the Institute for the Protection of Lesbian & Gay Youth, Inc.; a former board member of the New York Physicians for Human Rights; and former president of Gay and Lesbian Alcoholism Services, Inc.

Eric E. Rofes, author, community organizer, and social service administrator, recently served as executive director of the Los Angeles Gay & Lesbian Community Services Center. He is the author of several works including: *"I Thought People Like That Killed Themselves:" Lesbians, Gay Men & Suicide* (Grey Fox, 1983); *Socrates, Plato & Guys Like Me: Confessions of a Gay Schoolteacher* (Alyson, 1985); *The Kids' Book of Divorce* (Random House/Vintage, 1982); *The Kids' Book About Parents* (Houghton Mifflin, 1984); and *The Kids' Book About Death & Dying* (Little, Brown, 1985). He has recently been honored for his community work by the Human Rights Campaign Fund, Gay & Lesbian Latinos Unidos, and Temple Beth Chayim Chadashim in Los Angeles.

Duane L. Rohovit, J.D., an attorney in private practice, is also an adjunct assistant professor in the College of Nursing at The University of Iowa. In addition to the usual array of cases dealt with by attorneys, Mr. Rohovit has a broad range of experience handling gay civil rights law, and has long been active in the gay, women's and lesbian communities. Recently Duane was involved in lecturing on civil rights issues concerning persons with AIDS and is currently serving as president of the Hawkeye Chapter of the Iowa Civil Liberties Union. Duane resides in Iowa City.

Karl G. Rubesh, J.D., is a Chicago attorney in private practice. As past president of the Rodde Center, Chicago's gay and lesbian community center, Mr. Rubesh orchestrated the purchase of the community center building. In addition to his work for the community center, Karl serves the gay community in Chicago by volunteering for many agencies such as Horizons (a gay/lesbian social service agency), the Gerber-Hart Library (which contains the gay/lesbian archives), Professionals Over Thirty, Asians and Friends, and Toddlin' Town Performing Arts. Mr. Rubesh's law partner, Nancy Carper, is also active in the gay and lesbian communities, serving on the Board of Chicago House and Social Service Agency, Inc.

Caitlin Ryan, A.C.S.W., is a clinical social worker in the Washington, D.C. area. Ms. Ryan brings to her private psychotherapy practice a wealth of clinical and community service experience. Among her past and present involvements include being president of the National Lesbian and Gay Health Foundation, the project coordinator of the National Lesbian Health Care Survey, and a commissioner on the Commission on Lesbian/Gay Issues of the Council on Social Work Education. Caitlin is also an AIDS consultant.

Ron Sable, M.D., is an attending physician at the Cook County Hospital and Cook County Jail. At the hospital, Dr. Sable's work involves caring for people with AIDS, and at Cook County Jail, one of his central concerns has been the prevention and treatment of sexual assaults. Ron has been involved with a gay and lesbian prisoner support project of the Illinois Gay/Lesbian Task Force, and he's done workshops on gays in prison at two National Gay Health Conferences. He was a candidate for the Chicago City Council in 1987.

Judith M. Saunders, R.N., D.N.Sc., F.A.A.N., a nurse-thanatologist, is currently an assistant research scientist at the Department of Nursing Research and Education, City of Hope National Medical Center in Duarte, California. She is project director of a nursing research study, Improving the Cancer Patients' Hospital-Home Transition (NRO1493). In addition to her research and writing in the broad areas of bereavement, suicide, and coping with terminal illness, she has published on lesbian violence and AIDS-related suicide. Dr. Saunders has worked to improve services to the gay and lesbian communities through many speaking engagements and through volunteer activities with organizations such as Shanti and Southern California Women for Understanding.

Charles Silverstein, Ph.D., is a psychologist in New York City. Dr. Silverstein is the author of *Man to Man: Gay Couples in America* (William Morrow & Co., 1981), *A Family Matter: A Parents' Guide to Homosexuality* (McGraw-Hill, 1977), and, with Edmund White, *The Joy of Gay Sex* (Crown, 1977). He was the founding director of Identity House and the Institute for Human Identity, both in New York City, and the founding editor of the *Journal of Homosexuality.*

Jerry Solomon, Ph.D., is a clinical psychologist in Santa Cruz, California. In addition to an active private practice, Dr. Solomon teaches on the undergraduate and graduate levels. He is a founder and former president of the Santa Cruz AIDS Project. Dr. Solomon lives in Monterey County with Alan, his lover of nine years. Besides being an avid science fiction reader, Dr. Solomon unwinds by playing the piano and gardening.

Pat Stevens, R.N., M.A., a nurse for 13 years, is a Ph.D. candidate in nursing at the University of California, San Francisco. Her dissertation research about lesbian health is funded by a fellowship from the National Center for Nursing Research within the National Institutes of Health. She has published about lesbian health, lesbians' experiences with health care providers, feminist research methods, and the mental health aspects of AIDS. With her lover and colleague, Joanne, she has presented a number of workshops on lesbian health for diverse local and national audiences. A current interest is lesbian and gay history. She and Joanne live in San Francisco.

INDEX

Acceptance, 37–38; and alcoholism, 69; and gay and lesbian teens, 164; and gay fathers, 115; and lesbian mothers, 120–121; and the single gay or lesbian, 195–196

Acquired Immune Deficiency Syndrome (AIDS), 15, 17; and bars, 202; and a body-image case study, 54–55; and caregivers, 82–89; and death, 86–88; emotional ventilation of, 88–89; and the gay or lesbian prisoner, 187–188; health resources for, 341, 343; homophobia, 83, 84–85; and the hospice movement, 322, 326–327, 328; and religious homophobia, 275; and self-help groups, 332; and spirituality, 87; and suicide, 102–103; and support networks, 87; and widowhood, 224, 235, 241

Adult Children of Alcoholics, 158

Aging Services Network, 179, 180

AIDS-Related Complex (ARC), 82, 343

Al-Anon, 157–158

Alateen, 157

Alcoholics Anonymous (AA), 157, 333

Alcoholism in gay and lesbian communities, 15–16, 66–81; case histories of, 76–79; and the coming out process, 34–35; incidence and etiology, 68–70; and internalized homophobia, 94; the nature of, 66–68; problem areas in staff and treatment centers, 70–73; and the professional, 73–76

American Civil Liberties Union (A.C.L.U.), 190, 195, 299

American Lawyers' Guild, 195, 299

American Library Association, 195

American Medical Association, 195

American Nurses' Association, 195

American Teachers Union, 195

Androgyny, 59

Bars, gay and lesbian, 201–202

Bearwoman, Jan, 287–295, 346

Bereavement in gays and lesbians. See Widowhood, gay and lesbian

Berger, Raymond M., 170–181, 346

Bickelhaupt, Ethan, 12–18, 346

Bisexual lifestyles, 126

Body image and gay men, 45–58; the average gay man, 56–58; case histories, 51–55; definition of, 46; development of, 46–47; disruption of, 47–48; gay men's body image, 48–49; and the helping professional, 55–56; and problems, 49–55

Body image in lesbians, 59–65; and the athletic or "jock" type, 63; and body language, 62–63; and body size, 63–64; dress, 60–62; effects as a result of rape, 64

Bozett, Frederick W., 106–118, 346–347

Broadway, Dana L., 59–65, 347

Catalano, Donald J., 321–329, 347

Catholics, gay and lesbian. See

Other books of interest from
ALYSON PUBLICATIONS

LAVENDER COUCH, by Marny Hall, $8.00. A lesbian psycho-therapist gives valuable guidelines to gay men and lesbians interested in therapy.

THE ALYSON ALMANAC, $9.00. Almanacs have long been popular sources of information, and here at last is an almanac specifically for gay men and lesbians.

ONE TEENAGER IN TEN, edited by Ann Heron, $4.00. One teenager in ten is gay. Here, twenty-six young people from around the country discuss their coming-out experiences. Their words will provide encouragement for other teenagers facing similar experiences.

REFLECTIONS OF A ROCK LOBSTER, by Aaron Fricke, $7.00. Aaron Fricke made national news when he sued his school for the right to take a male date to the prom. Here is his story of growing up gay in America.

GAY AND GRAY, by Raymond M. Berger, $8.00. In this fascinating study of older gay men, Raymond Berger looks at the special circumstances of this group, and dispels many myths in the process.

THE GAY BOOK OF LISTS, by Leigh Rutledge, $8.00. A fascinating and informative collection of lists, ranging from history (6 gay popes) to politics (9 perfectly disgusting reactions to AIDS) to useless (9 Victorian "cures" for masturbation).

LESBIAN LISTS, by Dell Richards, $9.00. Fun facts like banned lesbian books, lesbians who've passed as men, black lesbian entertainers, and switch-hitters are sure to amuse and make *Lesbian Lists* a great gift.

KAIROS, by Zalmon O. Sherwood, $7.00. The words "gay" and "priest" are rarely spoken together in public. Here, Zal Sherwood shares the ordeal he faced as a gay man who refused to hide behind his clerical collar.

TESTIMONIES, edited by Sarah Holmes, $8.00. In this new collection of coming-out stories, twenty-two women of widely varying backgrounds and ages give accounts of their journeys toward self-discovery.

REVELATIONS, edited by Wayne Curtis, $8.00. For most gay men, coming out is a continuous process, but often there is one early moment which stands out as a special and crucial time. In *Revelations,* twenty-two men tell their stories.

THE MEN WITH THE PINK TRIANGLE, by Heinz Heger, $8.00. Thousands of gay people suffered persecution at the hands of the Nazi regime. Of the few who survived the concentration camps, only one ever came forward to tell his story. This is his riveting account of those nightmarish years.

COMING OUT RIGHT, by Wes Muchmore and William Hanson, $8.00. Coming out can be frightening and confusing, but with this recently updated book it's a little easier for you, your family member, or your friend who's taking that first step.

COMING ALONG FINE, by Wes Muchmore and William Hanson, $7.00. A look at subjects ranging from problems with interpersonal relationships to the anxieties caused by AIDS to the how-to's of setting up a gay business.

THE ADVOCATE ADVISER, by Pat Califia, $9.00. Whether she's discussing the etiquette of a holy union ceremony or the ethics of zoophilia, Califia's advice is always useful, often unorthodox, and sometimes quite funny.

LONG TIME PASSING, edited by Marcy Adelman, $8.00. In a series of personal accounts, older lesbians tell of their lives, loves, and of the building of a sense of community.

UNBROKEN TIES, by Carol S. Becker, $8.00. Through a series of personal accounts and interviews, Dr. Carol Becker, a practicing psychotherapist, charts the various stages of lesbian breakups and examines the ways women maintain relationships with their ex-lovers.

OUT OF ALL TIME, by Terry Boughner, $7.00. In this entertaining survey of history's most interesting gay and lesbian figures, Terry Boughner tells the part of history that other books have left out.

IN THE LIFE, edited by Joseph Beam, $9.00. In black slang, the expression "in the life" often means "gay." In this anthology, black gay men from many backgrounds describe their lives and their hopes through essays, short fiction, poetry, and artwork.

BROTHER TO BROTHER, edited by Essex Hemphill, $9.00. Black activist and poet Essex Hemphill has carried on in the footsteps of the late Joseph Beam (*In The Life*) with this new anthology of fiction, essays, and poetry by black gay men.

LIFETIME GUARANTEE, by Alice Bloch, $7.00. A personal chronicle of a woman faced with the impending death of her sister from cancer while she is also dealing with her own lesbian feelings.

DADDY'S ROOMMATE, by Michael Willhoite, $15.00. In this first book for the children of gay men, a young boy, his father, and the father's lover take part in activities familiar to all kinds of families: cleaning the house, shopping, playing games, fighting, and making up. Ages two to five.

HEATHER HAS TWO MOMMIES, by Lesléa Newman, illustrated by Diana Souza, $8.00. As the daughter of a lesbian couple, three-year-old Heather sees nothing unusual in having two mommies. When she joins a playgroup and discovers that other children have "daddies" her confusion is dispelled by an adult instructor and the other children who describe their own different families.

BETTER ANGEL, by Richard Meeker, $7.00. Fifty years ago, *Better Angel* provided one of the few positive images available of gay life. Today, it remains a touching story of a young man's discovery of his sexuality in the years between the World Wars.

WORLDS APART, edited by Camilla Decarnin, Eric Garber, Lyn Paleo, $8.00. The world of science fiction allows writers to freely explore alternative sexualities. These eleven stories take full advantage of that opportunity as they voyage into the futures that could await us.

CHOICES, by Nancy Toder, $8.00. In this straightforward, sensitive novel, Nancy Toder conveys the fear and confusion of a woman coming to terms with her attraction to other women.

SUPPORT YOUR LOCAL BOOKSTORE

Most of the books described above are available at your nearest gay or feminist bookstore, and many of them will be available at other bookstores. If you can't get these books locally, order by mail using this form.

Enclosed is $_____ for the following books. (Add $1.00 postage when ordering just one book. If you order two or more, we'll pay the postage.)

1. _____

2. _____

3. _____

name: _____address: _____

city: _____ state: _____ zip: _____

ALYSON PUBLICATIONS
Dept. B-86, 40 Plympton St., Boston, MA 02118

After December 31, 1992, please write for current catalog.